MUSIC DOWNTOWN EASTSIDE

Music Downtown Eastside

HUMAN RIGHTS AND CAPABILITY DEVELOPMENT
THROUGH MUSIC IN URBAN POVERTY

Klisala Harrison

OXFORD
UNIVERSITY PRESS

OXFORD
UNIVERSITY PRESS

Oxford University Press is a department of the University of Oxford. It furthers
the University's objective of excellence in research, scholarship, and education
by publishing worldwide. Oxford is a registered trade mark of Oxford University
Press in the UK and certain other countries.

Published in the United States of America by Oxford University Press
198 Madison Avenue, New York, NY 10016, United States of America.

Library of Congress Cataloging-in-Publication Data
Names: Harrison, Klisala, author.
Title: Music Downtown Eastside : human rights and capability development through
music in urban poverty / Klisala Harrison.
Description: [1.] | New York : Oxford University Press, 2020. |
Includes bibliographical references and index.
Identifiers: LCCN 2020018932 (print) | LCCN 2020018933 (ebook) |
ISBN 9780197535066 (hardback) | ISBN 9780197535073 (paperback) |
ISBN 9780197535097 (epub) | ISBN 9780197535080 (updf) | ISBN 9780197535103 (online)
Subjects: LCSH: Popular music—Social aspects—British Columbia—Vancouver. |
Poor—British Columbia—Vancouver. | Downtown-Eastside (Vancouver, B.C.)
Classification: LCC ML3917.C376 H37 2020 (print) | LCC ML3917.C376 (ebook) |
DDC 306.4/8420971133—dc23
LC record available at https://lccn.loc.gov/2020018932
LC ebook record available at https://lccn.loc.gov/2020018933

9 8 7 6 5 4 3 2

Paperback printed by Marquis, Canada
Hardback printed by Bridgeport National Bindery, Inc., United States of America

Contents

Acknowledgments

THIS BOOK EMERGES from the popular music scene of Vancouver's Downtown Eastside, and within its community centers, health centers, churches, and performing arts companies where I participated as a violinist as well as a researcher. My involvement in the neighborhood over two decades has resulted in now uncountable interactions and communications as well as deepening friendships. The research collaborators to thank are many. They include musicians, performing artists, administrators, and community-engaged academics as well as urban poor participants in popular music-making, too many of whom have died. Heartfelt thanks to many locals and artists who contributed their musical words and ideas to this book: Shannon Bauman, Dalannah Gail Bowen, Robert Chippeway, Stephen Edwards, Marlene George, Jim Green, Leith Harris, Donna Wong Juliani, May Kossoff, Andy Kostynuik, Frances McAllister, Larry McCully, Susan Musgrave, Mark Oakley, Earle Peach, Mike Richter, Marcus B. Roy, Joanne Shuttleworth Roy, Geetha Subramaniyam, Priscillia Tait, Manon Tremblay, Lori Wilson, Stewart Wilson, Taninli Wright, and Bruce Vincent. I remain incredibly grateful for group interviews with participants in music-making at the Evelyne Saller Centre including, among others, those who asked to be named as Christopher, Connie, and Nancy, and in the Women Rock program, particularly Angela, Anita, Heather, and Theresa. Thank you for inputs over the years from Michael Ames, Grant Chancey, Marie Clements, Rosemary Collins, Patrick Foley, Stan Hall, Jay Hamburger, Miko

Hoffman, Fred John, Caleb Johnston, Sharon Kravitz, Rick Lavallee, Karen Lee-Morlang, Kuei-Ming Lin, Doreen Littlejohn, Robyn Livingstone, Victoria Marie, R. H. Maxwell, Valerie Methot, Wilhemina Munro, Naomi Narvey, Kat Norris, Gerry Oleman, Joey Only, Joelysa Pankanea, David Roy Parsons, Jim Piché, Tom Pickett, Wyckham Porteous, Jim Sands, Jeffrey Smith, Ann Suddaby, James Fagan Tait, Brian Tate, Gena Thompson, jil p. weaving, Brenda Wells, Susan Poshan Wong, Elwin Xie, and Fanna Yee.

Music Downtown Eastside would have been impossible to write without profound support from Laura Barron, executive director of Instruments of Change; music therapists Stephanie Swenson and Carol Wiedemann; musician extraordinaire Peggy Wilson; Ken Tabata, photographer and music facilitator; Savannah Walling and Terry Hunter, artistic director and executive director of Vancouver Moving Theatre; Rika Uto, the arts programmer at the Carnegie Community Centre; and Jeffrey Hatcher, music therapist and clinical counselor. Special thanks to my greatest institutional supports: the Carnegie Community Centre, the Evelyne Saller Centre, First United Church, the Health Contact Centre, Instruments of Change, Vancouver Native Health's Sheway and Positive Outlook programs, the Residential School Healing Centre, Savage God theater company, and Vancouver Moving Theatre.

My writing and analysis benefited incredibly from several extremely bright and sharp minds who offered great peer reviews and comments on this manuscript, especially Samuel Araújo (Universidade Federal do Rio de Janeiro), Aaron Fox (Columbia University), and Pirkko Moisala (University of Helsinki). My editors at Oxford University Press, Suzanne Ryan and Norman Hirschy, gave fantastic supports and inputs. Many thanks also to my academic colleagues who have encouraged the development of this work over the years. I continue to benefit from ever-stimulating intellectual conversations and inputs from Jeff Todd Titon, Svanibor Pettan, and Joel Robbins. So many academic friends have gone out of their way to support my research work on music in urban poverty. Warm appreciation to Anthony Seeger, Michael Frishkopf, Naomi Sunderland, Tara Browner, and Byron Dueck. Many thanks also to academic colleagues who invited me to give talks at their academic institutions on research developed in this book and offered insightful feedback on my work there, especially Susana Sardo, Simon McKerrell, Johannes Brusila, Catherine Grant, Ana María Ochoa Gautier, Brydie Leigh Bartleet, Tina K. Ramnarine, Eva Bojner Horwitz, Walter Osika, Christopher Butterfield, and Joseph Salem. Thank you to other colleagues who have supported my work on music–poverty relationships, and on applications of music toward concrete social change, through invited publications that informed this book, particularly Don Niles, Anna Morcom, Larry Witzleben, Timothy Taylor, and Boyu Zhang.

I started my research in the Downtown Eastside as a PhD student. My doctoral supervisor, Beverley Diamond, contributed much to this work in its early stages, as did my supervisory and defense committee members including Robert Witmer, Louise Wrazen, Adelaida Reyes Schramm, Celia Haig-Brown, and Judith Rudakoff. Thank you also to Dorothy Deval for her encouragement.

Crucial for the continued research was support that I received from 2009 to 2011 while a postdoctoral fellow at the University of British Columbia School of Music, which enabled me to combine my teaching with continuing research involvement in the Downtown Eastside. Enormous thanks to Michael Tenzer, Nathan Hesselink, Richard Kurth, and Gage Averill for essentially starting me on this book project.

I also received contributing feedback on conference papers on this research from members of the Study Group on Applied Ethnomusicology and Study Group on Music and Minorities of the International Council for Traditional Music as well as participants in the Society for Ethnomusicology's Applied Ethnomusicology Section.

My research benefited from funding from the Academy of Finland (decision numbers 294769, 306767 and 328476) and the University of Helsinki most of all as well as, early on, from the Social Sciences and Human Research Council of Canada; the Ontario Ministry of Training, Colleges and Universities; and the University of British Columbia Learning Exchange. A fellowship at the Helsinki Collegium for Advanced Studies from 2012 to 2015 facilitated the development of my thinking considerably.

As always, many thanks to my family and close ones for their enduring love and support. You are the peace in which my thoughts dwell.

INTRODUCTION

DRAWING ON TWO decades of research in one of Canada's poorest urban neighborhoods, Vancouver's Downtown Eastside, this book examines a type of context infamous for its human rights deficits: poverty (Pogge, 2002). It insists that people who experience poverty should enjoy human rights all of the time, even at the time of music-making. One should be careful to avoid rights violations, including in situations with good intentions. Also a critical ethnography of human rights in artistic practice, this book furthermore considers what musicking (Small, 1998), or the social processes of engaging music, does and does not do for urban poor from the perspective of capability development. Developing capabilities is a key element of struggling toward human rights (Nussbaum, 1997–1998, 2011; Sen, 1985, 1987, 1999, 2009), but these capabilities may not be human rights in themselves.

In the Downtown Eastside, musicking becomes a way in which urban poor, together with arts workers at aid organizations and at performing arts companies, exercise and attempt to strengthen their human rights. Some of their music-making also raises questions about conflicts between different human rights and about human rights violations.

Music Downtown Eastside. Klisala Harrison, Oxford University Press (2020). © Oxford University Press.
DOI: 10.1093/oso/9780197535066.001.0001.

I discuss music jams and music therapy sessions, both of which use popular songs, as well as performances of popular music theater. Facilitators of these events do their best to promote different capabilities and human rights of urban poor. They use musical approaches motivated by human rights discourses, such as undertaking—via music—harm reduction, a means of addiction management.

The work of these facilitators and music therapists should be celebrated. They operate in difficult conditions and do their best. The struggles of urban poor who make popular music should also be celebrated. They face systemic oppressions that negatively impact their health and well-being, and often adversely affect women more than men. They struggle with issues of self-determination and sometimes with addiction. Gaining capabilities—for instance, those of living in good health, thriving without gender discrimination, and exercising human rights like self-determination—means striving for change.

I came to do long-term research in the Downtown Eastside as a violinist. I was invited to volunteer in the Downtown Eastside community play *In the Heart of a City* because I had expressed an interest in studying Indigenous women's music-making. Jay Hamburger, an acting coach for that production, knew that there was in the Downtown Eastside an active local scene of Indigenous women's music. When playing violin in the community play, I heard much about music activities going on in the neighborhood. No academic was interested in them, nor writing about them. Music involving urban poor became my PhD dissertation topic. Then the project evolved into 20 years of periodic fieldwork.

Thus, I started to engage with urban poor in the Downtown Eastside as a musician in a performance event involving about 500 people, and not as a researcher at first. Many people knew me through my musician role. People experiencing poverty called me "the Downtown Eastside's violinist." That provided lovely musical access on the level of a musician on the scene, in comparison to being a complete outsider and researcher coming only to ask questions. Still, I have a middle-class background and don't struggle with similar kinds of life situations as people who experience poverty. After making music and speaking with homeless people, for instance, I could sleep at home, not on the street. Despite socioeconomic differences, what kept me coming back was one of the strongest values that I experienced in the Downtown Eastside throughout these years: inclusiveness. This means that every human being is first and foremost met as a human being, and that every human being is welcomed to be a part of the musical activities.

I played violin in the popular music jams and music therapy sessions. In addition to being a researcher, I engaged in the local popular music scene in arts organizer roles, such as when attempting to start a grassroots theater company with urban poor. Their idea was for the poor to run their own theater company and make the key decisions about it, yet for professional artists to train and mentor them. Our attempt proved unsuccessful due to no infrastructure or fundraising expertise, and limited theater experience in the group. Similar ideas were success-fully implemented later on by arts administrators and theater professionals who interviewed local urban poor, then retained administrative control and benefit, while including the poor as key advisors, collaborators and participants. Our idea was not the original one, but through public meetings, gave air to the capability levels and artistic ambitions of the poor, including a desire to enjoy higher profile roles in artistic decision-making. I also taught courses at the University of British Columbia, during which I organized for my students to offer coaching sessions in musical performance, give music performance and composition workshops, take part in local music theater performances, document local music theater, and make a television documentary on music in the neighborhood. The performance activi-ties enriched my understanding of the local musical scene from the points of view of organizing and hosting musical events.

Yet this research has been difficult to share with the public. Although I conducted research in the Downtown Eastside for my PhD dissertation until 2005 (Harrison, 2008), the permission form for use of interviews for publication, developed through the guidelines and mandatory approval processes of York University and its employees, stated that the information gathered could only be used in the dis-sertation. When many of my consultants died due to poverty issues, I could not use their interviews. Over the next 14 years, in and among other projects, I did a new ethnographic study to reflect current conditions, conducted additional ethno-graphic work, and wrote this entirely new monograph.

Although I am an ethnomusicologist by training, this book does not empha-size ethnic backgrounds, customary in conventional ethnomusicology. I interpret "ethno-" as in its origins with the ancient Greek *éthnos* or ἔθνος, which may be defined as a group of people and a class, among other things, but not, remarkably, an ethnicity specifically. This is a conscious choice that I have made in the same spirit that people often are met in Downtown Eastside musical contexts, as human beings with equal rights. Therefore, the topic of this book does not emphasize ethnic differences. However, local ethnic-specific musical events do exist in the Downtown Eastside, and some, like Indigenous drumming circles, I have written about separately (Harrison, 2009, 2019). I could not access some other ethic-based events due to life situation or language—for example, drum groups for Indigenous battered women, or Chinese musical activities in Mandarin or Cantonese. Various music events, such as Ukrainian dancing, a Japanese festival, and certain choirs, did not fundamentally seek to include urban poor.

In writing this text, I engaged in extensive dialogues with people of the Downtown Eastside by sending them parts of my manuscript. This went far beyond the ethnographic interviews and participant observations that formed the basic research data. The music facilitators, music therapists, and organizations I detail had the opportunity to offer feedback on the text about themselves, in most cases multiple times. Also, some organizations have their own research ethics review processes, in which I took part. This generally involved a committee or an institution's representative going through and critiquing my text concerning that organization.

This research process presented particular challenges. Some community ethics reviews, I felt, challenged my academic freedom and right to self-determination. Certain representatives tried to censor the text. Often organizations had strong views on what I could and couldn't write about them. To get around these kinds of problems, I fictionalized and anonymized sensitive human rights violations that I nonetheless observed.

When I interviewed music facilitators, many of them told of how people have benefited from their work. It is understandable that they wanted to share success stories that give meaning to their work and give them energy to keep doing it. They need to be as positive as they can to work in harsh circumstances and avoid becoming cynical. Therefore, it is understandable that they may not have told about stories that did not end so well. In my dialogues with urban poor, I noticed that some of them wanted to keep their identities and life stories to themselves by changing their names or changing their stories. Deviating from the truth in interviews is also about exercising power and keeping a distance. Sometimes the interview was successful and it felt like an atmosphere of trust was created, but at other times it wasn't.

This is an academic book. Academic analysis including of arts and culture is indispensable for understanding dynamics of human rights and capability development that inform musicking in urban poverty. In a community ethics review at a Downtown Eastside organization, however, two reviewers critiqued my language because it is academic and therefore middle, or upper, class. They valued the language, and people, of lower educational classes more, in line with their interests and identities. I have included voices of community members as much as possible, yet academic language is always implicated in maintaining socioeconomic, including educational, differences and even conflicts. One of the main points of this book is that differences between who gets to experience human rights like education to the greatest degree, and who doesn't, should be evened out. The kinds of human rights deprivations observed in the Downtown Eastside, and occasionally entrenched through musicking, must be avoided. Yet also, in the ideal case, music can offer ways of working through rights violations and inequities. It is my intention that this book advocates for and therefore supports musical work done in the Downtown Eastside, and elsewhere in the world, in order to promote the human rights and capability development of the poor.

1

MUSIC IN URBAN POVERTY

Why rights? Why capabilities?

THE FOLLOWING COMES from a fieldnote made on a popular music jam on October 9, 2004:

> As usual, the room is jammed full of thirteen men, gaggling, gabbing, shouting, getting excited over the songs that will be played. They, sweaty, kind of smelly, one man making sure that one of three women there doesn't fall over. This hunched over lady with a cane who wears a lot of turquoise eyeliner and is on a trip, tips her head closer and closer to the ground. I also help her: "Sweetie, can you sit up?" "Oh, sorry." She tilts over again. On a flit of alertness, says, "Where is my cane?" "On the chair beside you." She cannot locate the chair.
>
> Leo[1] is there, high on crystal meth, excessively negative and more violent than I have ever seen him. He is skinny, his skin is really red and chapped, and he has cut off the cloth toes of his somewhat expensive running shoes. He comes in and starts yelling at Rick. Rick is a fairly experienced guitarist who semi-commands the room. Rick knows almost every chord, is not high, seems responsible, yet he wears memories of hardship: a marked lack of teeth in an otherwise healthy middle-aged face.

---

[1] This is a pseudonym. First names, full names, and pseudonyms are used throughout this book, as requested by research participants.

Music Downtown Eastside. Klisala Harrison, Oxford University Press (2020). © Oxford University Press.
DOI: 10.1093/oso/9780197535066.001.0001.

Leo screams, "I don't like your face!!" Rick sits back, doesn't say much. "Fuck you!!!" Leo screams. Later to Bryan,[2] "You just about knocked me over. FUCKING IDIOT!" Bryan laughs, "Yes, the fucking idiot is going to leave the room now. I'm glad that I'm a fucking idiot."

People in the room seem to know how to defuse this sort of confrontation. Peggy Wilson, as music jam facilitator, steps in and tells the men to calm down. She leaves when Leo spits in her eyes. Others step in her place, encouraging peacefulness with words and then by starting to play music again, loudly, drowning out the talk.

Andy produces his new CD. I am welcomed into this room of many men like I am one of them, but is this a joke? I must be shown the CD. I receive direction in triplicate or quadruplicate: "Look on the back!!!" On the front is Andy walking naked through a forest. There is a censorship sticker on his penis. But on the back is his ass! Same view, but Andy buck-naked from behind. I wanted to see the playlist. I curl up in a fit of embarrassment as twenty-six eyes watch amusedly. "She's as red as your shirt."

Amidst the gaggling and squabbling, Peggy encourages us to play music again. We play Joan Baez's "Candle in the Wind" and then "Memphis Tennessee." Rick picks "Eleanor Rigby" because I play a violin adaptation of the string part on the Beatles' recording and this really thrills the guys. They sing ultra-loud when I play the descending pedals over an E minor chord. Andy, Rick and Luke play a song of Andy's that the three are rehearsing for a radio show. Rick seemingly hasn't rehearsed a lick that Andy had taught him, and keeps playing it in the wrong place. Andy keeps yelling, "No! No!!!" One of the guys has been waiting for an hour to ask me to play "Annie's Song" while he sings. He seems delighted about there being a violin—he points his cell phone receiver at me, so that I can serenade a call recipient. Anyway, "you know, Annie's Song, that cheesy one," as he describes it, is my last performance before leaving. The high woman continues to tip towards the floor, at angles dramatized by her earrings: vintage, ornate gold-colored hearts that dangle with frosted, elegant green beads.

In urban contexts internationally, vast effort is put into facilitating music and other arts initiatives to alleviate "poverty" (see Harrison, 2008, 2013c; Loughran, 2008). Community members, artists, arts administrators, employees of local non-profit organizations, healthcare workers, and academics host music, dance, visual arts, and theater initiatives. These events include popular music jams like the one described previously at a community and health center—the Health Contact

---

[2] This is a pseudonym.

Centre in Vancouver, British Columbia (BC), Canada—as well as performing arts initiatives that aim to develop or present professional shows. Nonprofit, often community-based organizations (Marwell, 2009: 4) administrate the events, for example, community and health centers, churches, and performing arts institutions with funding variously from governments, corporations and other businesses, private foundations, churches, donations, and, for certain performances, concert tickets. In addition to live music-making, the main focus of this book, there exist recorded media efforts of studios, radio, television, and film.

In nonwelfare states and welfare states[3] unable to meet the social and health needs of their poorest citizens, some of the community-based organizations offer services and resources that fundamentally support the daily survival or needs of the poor, for example, free or cheap food, clothing, and showers. They target the "indigent," citizens who have no viable means of financial support and for whom providing basic needs and possibly mental health or substance misuse treatment may be essential prior to considering employment (Photos 1.1 through 1.3). In this context, organizers and participants often understand music- and art-making as interventions as well as opportunities for recreation and capability creation. These musical events embrace amateur and emerging musicians—almost anyone can join in their participatory music-making. According to Tom Turino, "the primary goal [of participatory music-making] is to involve the maximum number of people in some performance role" without any "artist-audience distinctions" (Turino, 2008: 26). Performing arts companies and arts-training academies also work with locals who experience poverty. In addition to the indigent, the varied locals may fit the interrelated academic and policy categories of the working poor, persistently unemployed, and dependent poor who rely on income support if and as available (Torjman, 1998: 22–23). The performing arts companies I've worked with emphasize skill development of the poor toward employment, especially in the creative industries. They aim at public performances, called presentational performances by Tom Turino. These refer to "situations where one group of people, the artists, prepare and provide music for another group, the audience, who do not participate in making the music," (Turino, 2008: 26). Policies, international agreements, national laws, and political discourses motivate these different kinds of artistic work, which are sometimes robustly budgeted by diverse funders (with government often as one supporter in Canada).

---

[3] After economist Nicholas Barr, the phrase "welfare state" is used here as shorthand for "the state's activities in four broad areas: cash benefits; health care; education; and food, housing, and other welfare services" (Barr, 2012: 8).

PHOTOS 1.1 THROUGH 1.3. Street and alley scenes showing the homeless, to whom nonprofit organizations offer music-making in the Downtown Eastside. I took the photos outside the nonprofits of the Health Contact Centre, Carnegie Community Centre, and First United Church. The first photo shows a person in black pants wearing an aluminum survival blanket, trying to get warm on a winter day. The person covers his or her head and torso in the shiny blanket, and bends over his or her belongings on the sidewalk. Another person's foot and leg peek out from under the umbrella at the bottom of the photograph. Belongings of a group of homeless people huddling at the side of a building include umbrellas, clothing, two bicycles and other valued things stored in two shopping carts. The second photo also shows what it means to live on the street. The final photo shows clusters of people in an alley, which can mean drug use, drug dealing, or visiting.

Photos by author, 2019.

POVERTY AND MUSIC

In this book, I offer an ethnography and critical analysis of musical and artistic practices in a neighborhood context of urban poverty, the Downtown Eastside of Vancouver, BC, Canada. This is a longitudinal study for which I conducted the ethnographic fieldwork over two decades, since 2000. I use the tools of ethnomusicology, particularly ethnography and cultural analysis, to build understanding of the sorts of musical and artistic practices through which practitioners make—and administrators support—interventions on poverty issues. I focus on interventions related with human rights discourses and capability development toward job creation.

I put ethnomusicology to use (Harrison, 2016) in an approach often called applied ethnomusicology research. Applied ethnomusicology research uses the intellectual toolkit of ethnomusicology to broaden and deepen knowledge and understanding toward solving concrete social problems. It does so in ways that centrally involve applications of music that not only have relevance within the academy but also address social issues beyond it (Harrison, Mackinlay and Pettan, 2010; Pettan and Titon, 2015; Titon, 1992). When focusing on social "problems," an applied ethnomusicology researcher is guided by values. Throughout this book, I value (Harrison, 2015) the quality of life and well-being of the poorest of the poor who experience "misery verging on death" and "whose greatest task is to try to survive" (Immanuel Wallerstein in Farmer, 2005: 6). In my research analysis, I'm particularly interested in what happens at points where music is thought of, by music project facilitators and participants, as improving the welfare of the poorest citizens that neither a nation-state nor any other over-arching sociopolitical system adequately provides. This is music for and of the disenfranchised (Schwartz, 2012; Seeger, 2010).

My analysis of the sometimes torturous and sometimes uplifting engagements with music in a Canadian urban poverty context complements a body of academic work on music and poverty in the global South, interpreted here as a postnationalist concept of spaces of subjugated people living under contemporary global capitalism, including poor people living on the margins of wealthy nation-states (Comaroff and Comaroff, 2012). Through investigating formal music initiatives offered via organizations in the Downtown Eastside of Vancouver, including popular music and music theater, I contribute to the increasing English-language publications on music and poverty.[4] Prior research has explored, for example, musical representations and engagements of poverty (Ellison, 1985; Hepburn, 2000), music technology use and lack thereof in poverty (Schön, Sanyal, and Mitchell, 1999), and the poor's engagements with the music industry (Bishop, 2004) or particular musics. It has undertaken and studied a variety of human development works through music and performing arts involving but not limited to music therapy and music for health projects (Dingle et al., 2013; Kim, 2017; Nagel and Silverman, 2017), music education (Baker, 2016; Kallio and Westerlund, 2016; Wald, 2017), and music eco-tourism and sustainable development (e.g., Impey, 2002). It has created and theorized ways of working musically with urban poor that resist systematic oppression, including violence (Araújo, 2006a, 2010; Cambria, 2012), for example, in *favelas* of Brazil and poor city neighborhoods of Portugal (see Araújo, 2006b, 2008; Miguel, 2016; Oenning da Silva, 2006; Sardo, 2018). It has forged global South relationships across national, linguistic, racial, and ethnic lines, and amongst different musical peoples living in poverty (Harrison, 2013a). It has documented and analyzed musical initiatives funded by nation-states (Ochoa Gautier, 2003), for instance, the El Sistema orchestra education system targeting impoverished youths and originating in Venezuela, but now globally adopted and adapted (Baker, 2017). Additionally, it has dealt with music vis-à-vis some of the multiple determinants of poverty although sometimes without using the term itself, such as political struggles, sociohistorical and environmental events (Silvers,

---

[4] In the twentieth century, certain classic fields of ethnographical study—for instance, Indigenous American music, African American music, and Roma music in Europe—were located in contexts of colonialism, civil rights deficits, and industrialization that resulted in ethnic poverty. A trend of mentioning the term "poverty" in academic music publications emerged only in the 1970s and became much more intense starting about 1995.

2018), ethnic/racial discrimination, marginalizing health and welfare policies, and educational approaches that promote precarity (Moore, 2017), among others.

This book offers new and detailed insights on music–poverty relationships, particularly on how musical practices in poverty settings engage ways in which poverty is understood. When focusing on music of and for people deprived of certain rights, privileges, and influence in society (the disenfranchised), I explore if music can enhance their human rights and capabilities, two terms important within definitions of poverty.

Key ways in which poverty has come to be understood are starting to be explored by music and arts academics (see Harrison, 2013a). Since the 1970s, international bodies like the International Labour Organization (ILO) and United Nations (UN) gradually broadened definitions of poverty to encompass a wider set of basic needs compared to the financial needs that characterized poverty definitions earlier.[5] Today, "poverty"—in addition to considering income—includes lack of health, education, and basic social services. It also includes deprivations of security as well as the capabilities and human rights that this book focuses, on and that interrelate with the aforementioned deprivations (see Sen, 1985, 1987, 1999, 2009). Table 1.1 lists types of social deprivation included in contemporary subcategories and conceptualizations of poverty. I define social deprivation as individuals, families, and groups experiencing a lack of resources, of participation in activities, and of living conditions "customary, or at least widely encouraged and approved" in society (after Townsend, 1979: 31).

CAPABILITY DEVELOPMENT AND HUMAN RIGHTS

In the pages that follow, I particularly consider how via musical expressions, people may strengthen and weaken human rights as well as enhance human capabilities threatened by poverty and its involved social deprivations. I investigate how musical engagements with poverty in the Downtown Eastside localize international trends in human rights promotion and capability development.

Table 1.1 lists capability development as one example of human development and human rights as a kind of entitlement. Scholars have defined poverty, for example, as including capability deprivation—a type of social deprivation of human development. This refers to the idea that poverty of income emerges from people

---

[5] Financial need characterized 1800s and early 1900s definitions of poverty. Examples include Charles Booth's (1892) pauperism and B. Seebohm Rowntree's notion that poverty results from insufficient "total earnings . . . to obtain the minimum necessaries for the maintenance of merely physical efficiency" (Rowntree, 1901: 117).

TABLE 1.1

Subcategories of poverty, poverty risk descriptors, and types of social deprivation involved in poverty

Absolute poverty	Subsistence is below a minimum socially acceptable living condition.
Relative poverty	Exclusion from a standard of living that is widely considered in society to be reasonable and acceptable
Primary poverty	Income too low to provide basic necessities
Secondary poverty	Income at the margin of primary poverty (will be considered poor if budgeted unwisely)
Vulnerability to poverty	Due to abnormal life circumstances (e.g., seasonal stress, shocks such as war, drought, or illness)
Income-based poverty	Disposable income serves as the benchmark for calculating measures of this (e.g., Canada's low-income cut-off).
Consumption-based poverty	Food consumption is the indicator of poverty (the current international standard is 2,200 calories per day).
Relative deprivation	Evaluated in comparison with a reference group in society (poverty includes deprivation in terms of what poor people do not have as well as what they perceive they should have)
Social exclusion	Exclusion from participation in "mainstream" economic, political, and cultural life; indicators of social exclusion are unemployment, low income, poor housing, poor health, high crime, and low education level
Livelihood sustainability	How sustainable is a person's livelihood vis-à-vis avoiding poverty
Basic needs	Poverty is defined as physiological deprivation of so-called basic human needs: food, shelter, schooling, health services, potable water and sanitation, employment opportunities, and opportunities for community participation.
Well-being	Poverty's relationship to human well-being, which refers to health and mortality, or to a lack of poverty circumstances

Continued

TABLE 1.1 *Continued*

Entitlements	Entitlements are widely understood as rights. Some are supported by legislation (e.g., human rights legislation).
Human development	The removal of obstacles to what a person can do in life, thereby expanding a person's choices. Capability development constitutes one example of a human development approach.
Cultural poverty	Deprivation of the means to express culture, which has strong and dynamic interrelationships with absolute poverty, relative poverty, primary poverty, secondary poverty, income-based poverty, and consumption-based poverty (Fiol, 2008, 2013)
Musical poverty	Musical poverty may be understood as a subcategory of cultural poverty, in other words, a lack of means to express music in culture. It also may refer to a lack of (a particular kind of) music or musical expression (Fiol, 2008, 2013; see Kartomi, 2012).

Elaborated from Mabughi and Selim (2006: 201); for an additional discussion of the contents, see Harrison (2013c).

not having certain capabilities. A missing capability could be the skill of musical performance, or it could be the capability to be free from harm, preventable disease, violence, and so on.

Economist and Nobel laureate Amartya Sen, a main theorist of capability development, defines capabilities in the specific way described in the previous paragraph as well as in a broad way, as the opportunities of people to choose and achieve the kinds of lives that they want to lead (Sen, 1999: 63). His studies show that certain factors strongly affect the relationship between income and capability, including a person's gender, age, social roles, handicaps or lack thereof, and location including its insecurity or violence. Sen gives particular attention to the capability to live to a mature age without succumbing to early death. This capability is at issue for the poor and for women (also discussed in Sen, 1999: 96–107) in the Downtown Eastside, where music organizers try to use music to address it. Notably, though, people who happen to be poor may well have strong personal and social skills— just not those skills that allow them to thrive in a late capitalist or neoliberal environment today. As arts education scholar Vincent C. Bates summarizes, studies find that "compared to the wealthy, the poor tend to be more ethical (Piff et al.,

2012), compassionate (Stellar et al., 2012), and altruistic (Miller et al., 2015); are no more likely to abuse alcohol or drugs; and are just as hard-working and communicative (Gorski, 2013)" (Bates, 2016: 3).

Many of the music initiatives the Downtown Eastside work to develop human capabilities as an incidental benefit or a central aim. While studying musical practices in the Downtown Eastside from the point of view of human rights, I will examine related capabilities that they enhance. I include those capabilities that connect directly with income, but fundamentally I address capabilities that allow for a person to flourish enough to generate income, and for the exercise and promotion of human rights.

Sen's award-winning contribution to economics includes the idea that to alleviate poverty, one must develop human capabilities in ways that allow one to no longer live in poverty (Sen, 1999: 90). He argues that enhancing human capabilities tends to accompany the expansion of productivity and earning power. Sen writes of an indirect link "through which capability development helps both directly and indirectly in enriching human lives and in making human deprivations more rare and less acute" (Sen, 1999: 92).

Economic philosopher Martha Nussbaum points out that people may or may not have the capability to exercise human rights (Nussbaum, 1997–1998, 2011). Capability development can also refer to strengthening the ability to exercise human rights. Capability deprivations, human rights deprivations, and poverty all intertwine.

Human development[6] expands human capabilities and quality of life. Sen understands human rights as strong ethical pronouncements about what should be done (Sen, 2009: 257). The pronouncements can invite the initiation of fresh legislation (Sen, 2009: 359). Anthropologist Ellen Messer elaborates that a human right "as a philosophical concept refers to the reasonable demands for personal security and basic well-being that all individuals can make on the rest of humanity by virtue of their being members of the species *Homo sapiens*" (Messer, 1993: 222). Capabilities are also choices about whether to exercise a human right or not—but the key thing is that one has the choice to do or not do so (Sen, 2009: 235–238). Human development also includes enhancing people's productive abilities and economic opportunities (see Sen, 1999: 144).

---

[6] Human development has been associated historically with the Human Development Report Office of the United Nations Development Programme (UNDP). Sen has had a major role in intellectually framing the program's annual report results; however, they do not incorporate all elements of Sen's practical and result-oriented theory.

However, developing capability is more difficult with and for people who face disadvantages, which may be multiple (Sen, 2009: 234, 255–256). For this reason, developing the capabilities of people living in poverty, involving its overlapping disadvantages such as illness and violence, are worthy of concentrated local efforts. Yet when occurring within a late capitalist or neoliberal context like the Downtown Eastside, local efforts meet contradictions and social-structural challenges in actually succeeding to overcome inequity.

Human rights that I will discuss include the rights to health and security of the person, women's rights, educational rights, economic rights, and civil and political rights. In this way, I contribute to an opening for new research, forged by scholars such as Samuel Araújo, Ana María Ochoa Gautier, Silvia Ramos, and Pirkko Moisala on the importance of scrutinizing human rights aspects of music projects involving poverty (Araújo, 2006b: 208–209; Araújo, 2009; Ochoa Gautier, 2003; Moisala, 2013; Ramos and Ochoa, 2009; see also Weintraub and Yung, 2009). Through a localized case study of Canada's "poorest postal code" (Smith, 2007: 103), the Downtown Eastside of Vancouver, I will make observations relevant for a range of music initiatives in poverty that are global in scope, extending from socioeconomically depressed areas of cities in Rio de Janeiro, Brazil; to Penang, Malaysia; to Durban, South Africa; to Stirling, Scotland (Araújo and Cambria, 2013; Borchert, 2012; Silva, 2011; Tan, 2008; Whittaker, 2014); to Vancouver; to many cities beyond and rural settlements too.

Through my ethnography of urban poor making music in organized settings, I ask: Which kinds of capabilities are developed via music initiatives in the Downtown Eastside, and, particularly, what is their relationship with human rights? My aim in asking this question is not to go deeply into the philosophical capabilities approach, which categorizes types of and processes of realizing capabilities (Nussbaum, 2011: 33-34) that are not but could be interpreted in terms of specific human rights (Nussbaum, 2011: 62-68). My point, rather, is to observe, in artistic and cultural practice, capabilities' concrete usefulness to the promotion of particular human rights. Both Sen and Nussbaum point to but do not elucidate the practical usefulness of capabilities to human rights (Nussbaum, 2011; Sen 1999, 2009). I also consider which kinds of capabilities are blocked; on whose terms capabilities of the poor are developed or not developed; and who benefits the most economically. I address the dynamics of artistic capability development during gentrification, a controversial urban redevelopment process.

I query related human rights: Are specific human rights promoted, strengthened, threatened, violated, and respected in music-making by urban poor in the Downtown Eastside? I discuss what one can conclude about how human rights operate in musical moments based on the research data, including, in chapter 9, vis-à-vis both capabilities, and structures of inequality that are key in generating and perpetuating poverty circumstances. After all, poverty is fundamentally a problem of social inequality, especially economic (wealth and income) inequality (Bates, 2016: 3; see Baker, 2016; Seery and Arendar, 2014). I consider what people working to promote human rights through music and culture can bear in mind. Whether and how one intends to implement human rights through culture matters. As well, musical and cultural formats and genres sometimes themselves influence rights outcomes.

Thus, I investigate human rights and capability development together in relation to music and poverty. When doing so, I reveal approaches, ideas and policies that can inform the facilitation of music-making in urban poverty toward promoting human rights and capabilities.

THE DOWNTOWN EASTSIDE POPULAR MUSIC SCENE

In the Downtown Eastside, the institutionally organized music programs directed at people experiencing poverty use an array of formats including music therapy; music jams; addiction treatment through music, including for Indigenous people and mothers of young children; popular music theater; and training programs culminating in public performances, among many others such as choirs, dance productions, and band performances. Popular songs used in jams and music therapy sessions, which are predominantly for adults (in one case with babies and toddlers), feature dated Billboard Top 40 radio hits as well as other songs commonly known through other means. Popular songs created locally draw inspiration from mass-mediated popular musics; some have Indigenous Canadian elements. Popular music theater consists mostly of newly written popular songs by local English speakers.

The neighborhood setting encompasses a population of about 64% speaking English as a home language, 28% speaking Chinese, and 8% speaking another mother tongue, a percentage that has been much higher in the past (e.g., 19% in 2001; City of Vancouver, 2013: 8, 10). Despite the large Chinese population, musical events in Chinese language and for the poor are few and far between. Ten percent of the population is Indigenous. Additional gatherings of local, traditional Indigenous music go beyond the frame of this book, but form the focus of Harrison 2009 and 2019. Here, I discuss points at which Indigenous ritual and historically based traditions briefly engage the popular music scene. I also study popular music initiatives of Indigenous organizations.

Popular music is the only music type extending across all of the organizations. Therefore, my ethnography—which crosscuts different institutions and music initiatives across the neighborhood—necessarily focuses on popular music.

I consider perspectives of event organizers and facilitators alongside those of urban poor as well as the aims and operating procedures of local organizations. What I describe here, then, is a popular music scene (Bennett and Peterson, 2004; Shanks, 1988; Straw, 1991) in the Downtown Eastside—a local music scene that breathes in and breathes out diverse influences while changing over time. This book is not, however, an all-encompassing ethnography of music of the poor in Vancouver or the Downtown Eastside in general—I follow people experiencing poverty outside of local nonprofit organizations like churches or health and community centers only if that ties to an institutionalized music initiative. At the same time, music initiatives of Eastside organizations almost have a monopoly on music-making of the poor in the downtown Vancouver area. Since 2004, stringent laws against panhandling in BC (under the province's Safe Streets Act) have effectively prevented combining music-making with so-called aggressive solicitation (begging); musicians living in poverty generally cannot afford to busk in Vancouver because most locations require paid-for permits. Due to lack of security in single-resident occupancy hotel rooms where many urban poor live (if not on the street or in limited social housing), it is unsafe to keep or use the musical instruments one would need for busking, and it is unfeasible to rehearse in most of their cramped hallways.

The variety of local poverty-related circumstances that music initiatives attempt to address is as diverse as it is troubling. The Downtown Eastside neighborhood of over 18,400 people (according to the most recent count: City of Vancouver, 2013) is an intensive meeting point for the homeless. I will focus on indigent and homeless people in this book as well as organizers of musical initiatives undertaken for and with them. According to official numbers, the homeless count has hovered around, and recently exceeded, 2,000 people in Vancouver. In the Downtown Eastside, about 1 out of every 18 people was homeless in 2017 (Swanson, Mugabo, and Chan, 2017). I give these numbers with the acknowledgment that homeless counts are only ever partial, and that what is defined as homeless may be skewed for political reasons. Yet as anthropologist Catherine Kingfisher writes, "various phenomena associated with economic restructuring" that affect Vancouver and its Downtown Eastside—"unemployment, gentrification, decreases in affordable housing, cuts in social programs, deinstitutionalization of the mentally ill, and the privatization of public space—serve to both increase the numbers of homeless and render them more visible to a public eye" (Kingfisher, 2007: 92). Although homelessness has long been viewed as a male problem, Canadian women experience homelessness more frequently than men because many come from backgrounds of violence. They may feel safer on the streets than in a shelter or hostel. Some live on the streets to escape domestic violence in their families. The homeless more often tend to be racial minorities and have more issues with mental health and substance misuse (Novac, Brown, and Bourbonnais, 1996). Other local health issues include epidemic HIV/AIDS (Taylor, 2003: 193), tuberculosis, hepatitis A–E, and physical and mental disabilities. A thriving, local survival sex industry and needles shared for drug use transmit HIV and hepatitis whereas tuberculosis is more easily communicated in crowded housing. People with mental illness have lived on Vancouver's streets more often since the 1990s, when BC started defunding and closing live-in mental health institutions. The 1996 closure of the Woodlands psychiatric hospital in Greater Vancouver particularly increased people suffering from mental illness in the Downtown Eastside. In this context, human rights problems affect the most vulnerable. For example, high incidences of assault and sexual assault impact the right to safety of the poor. Epidemic murders of female sex workers, disproportionately of Indigenous heritage, extinguish their right to life.

Economically, people living on the street suffer primary poverty in which any income received is too little to provide basic necessities (e.g., buying underwear or supplies for a woman's period is often considered too expensive; Hancock, 2000: 20). The poor also suffer from income-based poverty and consumption-based poverty, or being unable to consume enough food. The indigent particularly suffer the deprivation of the requirements for meeting basic human needs such as food, shelter, schooling, health services, sanitation, and employment opportunities. Many other people—like the unemployed, persistently unemployed, and dependent poor—live in relative poverty (historically called absolute poverty or subsistence poverty), which refers to their exclusion from a standard of living thought widely in society to be reasonable and acceptable. Emerging performing artists suffer vulnerability to poverty due to often sporadic or low-paid work. They therefore confront issues with livelihood sustainability, or how sustainable a person's livelihood is in terms of avoiding poverty, although that is usually better than having no work at all (Harrison, 2013c: 4–7). Among residents of the three economically poorest subareas of the Downtown Eastside (total population: approximately 6,500), 84% to 89% lived below Canada's low-income cut-off dollar amounts[7] in 2001, within my first year of research (City of Vancouver, 2006: 13, 75).[8] As the 2000s and 2010s progressed,

---

[7] The low-income cut-off is an income threshold below which the Canadian government characterizes people as spending more than average on food, shelter, and clothing. The government calculates this measure of income-based poverty (see Figure 1.1) for each year based on disposable income statistics.

[8] The 2001 low-income cut-off was $15,748 CAD for one person and $23,867 CAD for a family of four persons (Statistics Canada, 2019). Although Canada does not use any official definition of poverty or a poverty line,

though, shifting neighborhood demographics (e.g., to 70% to 79% of people living below the low-income cut-off by 2013; see City of Vancouver, 2013: 11) reflected a displacement of urban poor due to the intensification of economic restructuring in the form of city redevelopment and particularly gentrification. Gentrification refers to the redevelopment of a socioeconomically depressed urban neighborhood, which eventually displaces urban poor as developers reconstruct the area for use by middle and upper economic classes.

Today, the Downtown Eastside displays one of the starkest contrasts between rich and poor in Canada, a member of the G7 and one of the richest countries in the world. Renovated art deco hotels, condominiums, yuppie shops, new boutiques, and food outlets selling fashionable foods exist alongside tent cities and street people thronging on the sidewalks, sometimes with shopping carts—visiting, selling used goods, or maybe doing drugs, visibly suffering from poverty, with no money and no permanent home. Nearby, social service organizations—visibly grimy, some with barred windows (even smashed or with metal sheets installed in their place) and others with vigilant security guards (Photos 1.4 and 1.5)—offer or have offered music initiatives, as have the performing arts and Indigenous organizations. I will address gentrification as a force that informs reshapings of music in a gentrifying neighborhood as well as the kinds of human rights and capabilities that music does or does not enable.

In keeping with the by now widespread recognition that poverty is a site of human rights deficits (Pogge, 2002), Downtown Eastside organizations featuring music initiatives inscribe in their organizational missions, models, mandates, purposes, or philosophies terms or phrases whose broader discourses engage human rights, or that facilitators and organizers of music associate with human rights–related approaches and ideas. This echoes human rights arguments being a longtime battle cry against marginalization of the poor in the neighborhood, including by the poor themselves, as evident in local speaking events or publications like the *Carnegie Newsletter*, which has printed short essays, poems, news stories, song lyrics, and line drawings of urban poor since 1986,

---

Statistics Canada identifies a modest, basic standard of living called the Market Basket Measure ($24,955 CAD for a family of two adults and two children in Vancouver in 2001; Statistics Canada, 2015) whose annually changing thresholds accommodate geographical variations in costs of goods and services. From 84% to 89% of Downtown Eastsiders also did not meet the Market Basket Measure that year. One can interpret anything below thresholds like the income cut-off dollar amount and Market Basket Measure as relative poverty, or living in relative deprivation, a concept that connects closely with the idea of social exclusion from "mainstream" economic, political, and cultural life in Canada—although, to be sure, it is far above the $1 or $2 per day extreme "poverty line" of the UNDP or World Bank.

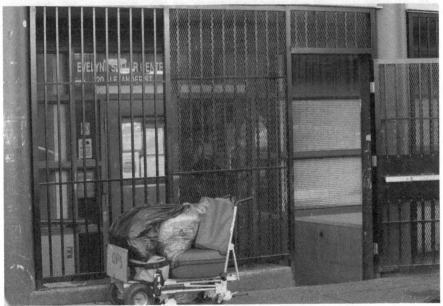

PHOTOS 1.4 AND 1.5. Entrances to nonprofit centers that have hosted popular music-making, First United Church and the Evelyne Saller Centre.
Photos by author, 2019.

twice monthly (Taylor, 2003). In a tent city in the neighborhood's Oppenheimer Park in 2019 (Photos 1.6 and 1.7), graffiti proclaimed "HUMAN RIGHTS ARE GOD GIVEN NOT MAN MADE." Other graffiti, which read "Unceded Territories," referred to Indigenous rights to land, including those enumerated in the UN Declaration on

PHOTOS 1.6 AND 1.7. A tent city in the Downtown Eastside's Oppenheimer Park.
Photos by author, 2019.

the Rights of Indigenous Peoples (United Nations, n.d.-a), which Canada adopted in 2016. Vancouver sits on unceded traditional lands of the Musqueam (xʷməθkʷəy̓əm), Squamish (Skwxwú7mesh Úxwumixw), and Tsleil-Waututh Indigenous peoples. Signs (Photo 1.8) taped in the park building's window referenced the Universal

Declaration of Human Rights when asserting "Humane housing, not handcuffs!" and "Housing is a <u>human right</u> *UNHDR*." Another sign indexed part of Canada's constitution, the Canadian Charter of Rights and Freedoms, especially legal rights enshrined therein by quoting from article 7: "Everyone has the right to life, liberty and security of the person and the right not to be deprived thereof except in accordance with the principles of fundamental justice" (Government of Canada, 2019).

This book explores the social qualities of the popular music scene of the Downtown Eastside as they engage poverty, and particularly its embedded deprivations of human rights and capability development. I focus on people—what people do with music, what music does to them, and what happens in musical events. Within the popular music scene of the Downtown Eastside, which by and large is a scene of popular songs, lyrics are very important. I consider behavior in relation to music (I focus on human rights and capabilities), music itself (I focus on song lyrics and repertoire), and conceptualizations of music. In the Downtown Eastside, I investigate how ideas about how to use music emerge from a human rights–inspired approach to addiction management called harm reduction, and a social work method called noninterference. I will also investigate local musical ideas and approaches associated with the health equity movement, which takes support from human rights. Political philosopher Thomas Pogge writes that the negative impacts on health of rights deficits are so severe that they dramatically increase death rates: "Despite a high and growing global average income, billions of human beings are still condemned to . . . severe poverty, with all its attendant evils of low life expectancy, social exclusion, ill health, illiteracy (and) dependency. . . . The annual death toll from poverty-related causes is around 18 million, or one-third of all human deaths, which adds up to approximately 270 million deaths since the end of the Cold War" by 2005 (Pogge, 2005: 1). Additionally, I discuss the roles of urban poor in popular music theater performances occurring during gentrification, especially its displacement of the poor. I explain how resisting gentrification through music can take support from the "right to the city," a concept that opposes gentrification when it promotes human rights of the displaced. According to its key proponents such as Henri Lefebvre and David Harvey, the right to the city refers to the vision that each of us—including workers and the dispossessed—has "the right to remake ourselves by creating a qualitatively different kind of urban sociality" (Harvey, 2003: 939; see Lefebvre, 1996 [1967]). Rather than any human right enshrined in law, the right to the city makes space for realizing human rights, plural, in urban spaces in liberatory ways.

PHOTO 1.8. Human rights graffiti and signs in the tent city in Oppenheimer Park. Note the two small signs, taped onto the window, that reference specific rights.

Photo by author, 2019.

HUMAN RIGHTS AND MUSIC

Some of the human rights explored and engaged through the musical approaches and relevant policies investigated here are legally enforceable, whereas others are not. I list examples of legally binding UN covenants and conventions in Table 1.2. Canada has ratified or accessioned the six listed treaties, which in principle obligate a nation to uphold them within national laws. To put this in a North American context, Mexico has done the same, and the United States has signed and ratified or accessioned three (the Convention on the Elimination of All Forms of Discrimination against Women, International Covenant on Civil and Political Rights, and Convention on the Elimination of All Forms of Racial Discrimination). Out of a possible 18 human rights treaties of the UN, Mexico has ratified or accessioned 16; Canada, 13; and the United States, 5. By contrast, international human rights declarations serve as guidelines and express shared values, but are not legally enforceable by national governments. One example adopted by Canada, the United States and Mexico is the UN's Universal Declaration of Human Rights (UDHR) from 1948.

In addition to many efforts to improve people's lives via music in the Downtown Eastside, I witnessed deprivations of disturbing kinds during my research. These motivated me to write this as a critical book for the human rights of the poor.

TABLE 1.2

Examples of United Nations' human rights covenants and conventions that are legally binding including in Canada

- International Covenant on Economic, Social and Cultural Rights, or ICESCR (effective 1976; ratified by 164 nation-states)
- International Covenant on Civil and Political Rights, or ICCPR (effective 1976; with 169 state parties)
- Convention on the Elimination of All Forms of Discrimination Against Women, or CEDAW (effective 1981; ratified or acceded to by 189 states)
- Convention on the Rights of the Child, or CRC (effective 1990; with 196 state parties)
- Convention on the Rights of Persons with Disabilities (effective 2008, 173 state parties)
- Convention on the Elimination of All Forms of Racial Discrimination (effective 1969, 179 state parties)

One day early on in the research, I went into a single-room occupancy (SRO) hotel called the Jubilee Rooms within a "home visits" part of a music therapy program. A woman was saying that she would kill herself. She was telling me why. I didn't do anything because I was naïve and scared. I thought, incorrectly, that the music facilitator whom I accompanied had the power and responsibility to intervene, not me. Human rights and safety are everyone's responsibility, even though rights violation situations may be scary. The music therapist, who regularly offered counseling and came from a health center that routinely dealt with every kind of health issue, did not offer suicide prevention assistance either. The therapist directed attention to a music therapy participant only instead of the woman, who did not take part in music therapy yet was in the same space as the outreach program—the SRO building hallways.

In the Jubilee Rooms hotel, I realized that within situations of immense suffering and threats to human rights, professionals running music initiatives make choices about whether to promote or violate what I will call a human right and, at other times, which human right to promote and to what extent. Such a choice, in urban poverty, can just as easily have a deathly and unnecessarily traumatic result as an uplifting one perhaps expected of activist intentions. When actions have a result that only ingrains poverty or associated issues, they also often deny people an opportunity to enhance their capabilities.

I am fully aware that the concepts and wording of human rights are general policies made for political purposes, and that they are not academic analytical concepts. However, I find it important to examine activities on the grassroots level in relation to these general terms of policy, which in most cases discussed here are supposed to inform national laws. The purpose of policy is for it to be put into practice. Drawing on the academic literature of human rights studies, music, anthropology, and other social sciences, among other disciplines, I examine social hierarchies surrounding human rights attribution and negation in the Downtown Eastside. Middle-class facilitators of music initiatives and urban poor participants take very different roles; there exist relationships of social manipulation and imbalances of opportunity between and among these different actors, including those relationships that resist and allow human rights violations. I also consider where the money for music projects comes from, to whom it goes—urban poor or facilitators—and which forces, institutions, and actors have the most power in setting human rights and capability development agendas.

Since human rights are a key framework informing policy, music-making, and activism in the Downtown Eastside, I investigate musical expressions in terms of human rights and related inequities affecting urban poor. Too many scholars, in my view, have resisted taking the analytical step to strongly advocate for human rights, including for and with people vulnerable to violations (see Cowan, Dembour, and Wilson, 2001; Cowan, 2006; Goodale, 2009). Not being critical about human rights–related oppressions and hiding human rights violations led medical anthropologist and physician Paul Farmer to write that "hiding this suffering, or denying its real origins serves the interests of the powerful. The degree to which literate experts, from anthropologists to international health specialists, choose to collude with such chicanery should be the focus of brisk and public debate" (Farmer, 2005: 17). Ethnomusicologist Andrew Weintraub, in his introduction to the landmark volume *Music and Cultural Rights*, added his support to this perspective when writing that "the considerable problems in circumscribing and implementing frameworks of mutually agreed-upon rights for all human beings in every human society does not condone basic human rights violations" (Weintraub, 2009: 2–3). For these reasons, I take additional inspiration from the rare scholars who write about how people engage and struggle with human rights and related power imbalances via culture in everyday life, for instance, Paul Farmer (2005), Sally Merry (2006), and Shannon Speed (2006). I build on a small literature on music and poverty (Dirksen, 2013; Fiol, 2013; Harrison, 2013a, 2013c; Moisala, 2013; Titon, 2013) by further developing the literature on music and human rights (see Peddie, 2011a, 2011b), including when attempting to reduce inequity, via music, by developing capabilities of and with the poor.

I urge music and arts practitioners as well as culture scholars to start thinking more about how the contexts in which they work engage human rights. We live on the cusp of a time when human rights of culture are guided increasingly by policy and enforced by law within nation-states. As well, human rights are emphatically under new levels and forms of threat. In legally binding and international human rights covenants and declarations, human rights already should be legally justiciable within nation-state parties by definition. In 2012, the Committee to the International Covenant on Economic, Social, and Cultural Rights (ICESCR), through an Optional Protocol, became able to receive and consider communications from individuals and social groups (see Yupsanis, 2010: 261) when inquiring into potential cultural rights violations—violations of human rights that explicitly mention culture. This Optional Protocol entered into force in May 2013 after intensive debates about it since the 1960s (Dennis and Stewart, 2004). As well, indicators for human rights implementation, including of and via culture, are in the process of being developed at the UN for measuring implementation success.[9]

---

[9] These indicators to a great extent are quantitative. Leaving out qualitative research inputs very likely leads to major oversights and errors when it comes to culture and arts.

Because culture is fundamental to the engagement, promotion and weakening of human rights, social-scientific understandings of culture and particularly the complexity of cultural moments are increasingly being recognized in international policy and law (summarized at Wiesand et al., 2016: 281), after decades of excluding culture scholars from treaty development processes for international human rights (Merry, 2011). Contemporary anthropological understandings of culture as fluid and ever-changing have much to contribute to human rights policy and law, especially the copious work on culture as "unbounded, contested and connected to relations of power" (Merry, 2003). This makes ethnomusicology—with its close ties to the anthropological study of culture—well suited to the analysis and understanding human rights in musico-cultural expressions. Ethnomusicologists, when we borrow from anthropologist Clifford Geertz, analyze music with the understanding that it forms and is part of culture, which is historically constructed, socially maintained, and individually adapted and experienced (Geertz, 1973: 363–364; see also Rice, 1987). We understand culture, for example, in terms of habits of collective thinking and action, as well as cultural and biological processes like enculturation and neurological pathways that music engages (Murdock, 1960, in Moisala, 1991). We also have long worked with at least several analytic levels of music in culture: conceptualizations of music, behaviors in relation to music (informed by the conceptualizations), and musical sound itself. The fluidity and changeability of musical processes form a continued and intensifying focus of the theorization of culture in ethnomusicology (e.g., Moisala et al., 2014).

The legally binding national laws and international treaties that feature human rights point to a persuasive argument—legality—for taking seriously cultural activities with human rights entanglements and their outcomes. When nation-states have not agreed to (legally enforce) human rights, or human rights are threatened, I am among those who advocate for them, particularly in the case of gross rights violations like those seen in poverty.

Even so, the notion of human rights can be critiqued, but, as I will observe later, so can human actions at least partly undertaken in their name, which may have altogether different and less liberatory goals or outcomes. To focus on the first here, certain scholars have condemned concepts of human rights as politically ideological and unsupportable in terms of political theory (Mendus, 1995; Reinbold, 2011; Stammers, 1993). Others have dismissed human rights as utopian political myths and symbolically charged narratives (Reinbold, 2011: 149). Of course, the implementation of international human rights treaties seemingly contradicts, or turns a blind eye to, these claims.

Still other academics have somewhat misunderstood human rights as being Western. I will pause on this for a moment, to offer a clarification, which also provides a very brief history of human rights. The phrase "human rights" is indeed Western in origin. The concept of human rights arose out of natural law philosophy of the European enlightenment (Shafir and Brysk, 2006: 276). Hugo Grotius's natural rights formed "a contractual basis for social life that is not rooted in religious law," affirmed during the French and American Revolutions (Shafir and Brysk, 2006: 276). However, human rights practice within UN covenants, conventions, and declarations are less Western than some people might believe. So-called Western and non-Western nation-states, together, first developed notions of human rights within the context of international human rights treaties that followed from the Nuremberg War Crimes Tribunal and the establishment of the UN after World War II. However, human rights (including of culture) have been overwhelmingly exploited in non-Western, regional human rights systems like the inter-American human rights system of the Organization of American States, in which Canada and the United States are not fully participating members. Other examples include the African Charter on Human and Peoples' Rights, the American Convention on Human Rights, and the ASEAN Declaration on Human Rights (Donders and Vleugel, 2014: 658). Indigenous peoples have made the swiftest and widest-reaching use of human rights concepts of any organized group (e.g., Merry, 1997; Sandler, 2009). The nation most heavily resisting human rights has been the United States, ostensibly for economic reasons (Dennis and Stewart, 2004).

By focusing in the coming chapters on urban people struggling with poverty-related issues and developing capabilities, I will extend a tendency of music scholarship on human rights to concentrate on cultural groups while at the same time acknowledging the importance of individuals within groups. Case studies in the edited volume *Music and Cultural Rights* (Weintraub and Yung, 2009) emphasized the question of group rights, which "arises when a group's access [to] or ownership of culture has been threatened, limited, or appropriated by other people, groups, or institutions through conquest, occupation, settlement, or other means" (Weintraub, 2009: 4). Although international legal instruments privileged individual rights historically, today the international human rights system is not blind to communities and groups,[10] like the urban poor of Downtown Eastside Vancouver.

---

[10] For example, the African Charter on Human and Peoples' Rights, American Convention on Human Rights, and ASEAN Declaration on Human Rights incorporate both individual and collective rights (Donders and Vleugel, 2014: 658).

I

Popular music for Vancouver's poor

After I park on Columbia Street, I meet Jay Hamburger, a community theatre director, walking off the Carnegie Community Centre's steps. I mention that I am on my way to First United Church; he will come along to say hello to Ann Suddaby, a church volunteer. Jay gives me a lift the necessary two blocks in his white, rusty pickup truck; we park underneath the church. Once inside, we find the gym door locked, but a hand-printed sign on the door reads "Full House." "You can usually get in through the back," Jay says. We unsuccessfully try the gym's locked back door. "The kitchen": Jay swings open the kitchen door, and I bump in behind him, my violin case over my shoulder.

Inside, about fifty people—mostly street-involved people and homeless—eat free Easter dinners. It is the Wednesday before Easter. Ann immediately asks whether I might play music with Leo and continue the music jam originally of the Residential School Healing Society. Leo has his guitar slung around his shoulder and gulps down three plates of turkey, stuffing and coleslaw. The seams of Leo's guitar are plastered with packing tape, the sound hole thickly circled with brown glue—an extension of his habit to tape up his body parts and shoes. A fellow supper eater tells Leo that he might get Hepatitis A or B from eating people's leftover dinners, which he is doing.

Ann brings us a couple of chairs and I get out my violin. I start with "Amazing Grace," playing the song twice, richly, beginning on the open G string. I stop and a beat-up, thin Indigenous

Canadian girl eating carrot cake urges, "Play it again." I do. A pig-tailed woman wearing blue eyeliner and vermillion lipstick requests "Happy Birthday."

Leo joins us as soon as Ann brings books of song lyrics and chords. Leo begins the Beatles' "Yellow Submarine" and a couple of other songs, but stops us in the middle of each. "Yellow . . . " has too many chord changes, he complains flatly. Leo talks a lot about how he loves crystal meth, and how he hasn't had a fix in four days.

Then Leo "catches fire." I lead the American fiddle tune "Boil Them Cabbage Down" and Leo picks up the chords quickly. At the request of the lady with the eyeliner, we play Hank Williams's "Your Cheatin' Heart" and "Old Time Rock and Roll" (inspired by Bob Seeger's cover recording). Leo's guitar playing changes from a scrubby timbre with many hesitations to a consistent tempo with motivating rhythm. I play *spiccatto*, chords, walking basslines (transposed up an octave), melodic counterpoints. People start to dance. A man washing dishes and the woman with the eyeliner are jigging behind Leo. I close my eyes and enjoy the moment. Leo smiles and seems happy: no more complaining about not taking his "medication" today, or about his missing Canadian General Sales Tax cheque. (fieldnote, April 7, 2004)

The above fieldnote conveys one of my experiences of a popular music jam in the Downtown Eastside. Part I, which follows, documents music-making practices in popular music jams and music therapy sessions for adults as they unfold at community and health centers as well as churches in Vancouver's Downtown Eastside (Photos 2.1 and 2.2). The popular music jams and sessions form a basis of the popular music scene throughout the neighborhood. The music scene includes, for example, protests, music theater, and special popular music programs that address any gaps in the jams and music therapy practices. I compare the frameworks (aims, missions, and mandates) of organizations hosting these participatory musical events with those of some key organizations hosting presentational music-making—the performing arts companies and music academies. I also compare how the participatory and presentational music events are financed, observing a susceptibility of participatory music initiatives to low payments of their music facilitators and to closure.

PHOTOS 2.1 AND 2.2. Music therapy participants at the Evelyne Saller Centre, with a close-up of Robert Chippeway featuring Connie (surname anonymous) in the background.

Photos by author, 2016.

2

JAMS AND MUSIC THERAPY SESSIONS

AS ONE ENTERS a popular music jam or therapy session, which both use the same participatory format in the Downtown Eastside, one is included affably if one is a man, and even more cordially if one is a reproductive-aged, healthy woman, by the far more numerous males in the jam. This gender balance exaggerates the neighborhood's 60% male/40% female split of residents surveyed by Statistics Canada (City of Vancouver, 2013: 6). Over 45% of the Downtown Eastside's residents are also over age 45 according to the most recent statistics (from 2006; City of Vancouver, 2013: 6). When I arrive to a jam at First United Church on a welfare check day, a lot of people, a worker says, are "off buying dope and getting loaded and/or getting their belongings out of a pawn shop" (fieldnote, March 24, 2004). While wondering if the worker's statement carries stigma, observation, or both, I watch and hear the music therapy session gradually grow over 90 minutes to 20 participants, including five youth church volunteers wearing name tags. The local men, as in other jams and music therapy sessions, say hello or acknowledge me with a nod of the head. They call me by name or ask my name. The participants may ask where any visitor (new person) lives or other questions to find out his or her socioeconomic position. They make space in the circle in which they sit, normally together with the facilitator, while directing me to a chair or seating

Music Downtown Eastside. Klisala Harrison, Oxford University Press (2020). © Oxford University Press.
DOI: 10.1093/oso/9780197535066.001.0001.

place in that circle. Female participants greet or question me too but appear more withdrawn—men tend to play instruments more often and dominate chit-chat. Everyone entering the jam is included in this way. The music therapist running this session added, "I rarely met a woman who said they played an instrument. If they did play a guitar or piano or whatever, they never said so" (interview with Jeffrey Hatcher, March 24, 2004).

Jams and music therapy are called by different names according to whether a music therapist is present or if an organization decides to call music therapy a "jam." The music facilitator may say hello to the visitor but generally takes a low profile in the social dynamic. Everyone looks the newcomer in the eyes. Everyone takes part in the singing, and one is expected to join in as soon as one enters the room. I sing and play my violin too. We cycle through a Gene Autry–like rendition of "Blue Canadian Rockies," "Four Strong Winds" after the Canadian folk duo Ian and Sylvia, "Take Me Home, Country Roads" recorded and popularized by John Denver, the Beatles' "Help!" plus "Looking Out My Back Door," and "The Midnight Special" recorded by Credence Clearwater Revival, as well as a couple of country rock– and bluegrass-influenced songs that participants render with particular gusto, Hank Williams's "Your Cheatin' Heart," and Bill Munroe and his Bluegrass Boys' "Blue Moon of Kentucky." In the room, people are usually careful not to put anything on the floor due to bed bug and lice infestations. I've been in jams where the facilitator warns a newcomer not to do so with a shriek and strong-voiced command. No one physically touches anyone else in the jams usually. Today is a bit different—a blind young woman named Kelly offers to give me a shoulder massage when I get a break.

Today, singers, other participants who play guitars while singing, and onlookers express keenness about music—an older man named Les laughs at musical sounds, so excited that he cannot sit down when one church volunteer, Ann, offers him a chair. At my violin, he grins and grins. "You can really make that thing dance if you want to." Many people stand around a core group of music-makers watching only, or singing quietly then loudly—often progressively making more sound. One of the participants calls First United Church the "church of what is happening now," and as if on cue, a Latin American man parades into the church hall, singing Stevie Wonder's "I Just Called to Say I Love You" at the top of his lungs. Les asks for the group to perform the African American spiritual "He's Got the Whole World in His Hands," starting to sing that song as loud as he can too, while the music therapist laughs. At other times, musicians express their keenness with what is called jam-hopping. Today I have agreed with another participant, Bob,[1] after sharing lunch at the Carnegie Community Centre to attend together another music session, at the Evelyne Saller

---

[1] This is a pseudonym.

Centre. At the Carnegie, music program facilitator Ken Tabata comments that making music is often central to the lives of participants in the popular music sessions:

> Usually most people don't have a good job, or they might be down on their luck in one way or another. They might have some sort of disability. So music is a huge part of their life, just like [for] a music student or a professional musician. (interview, June 7, 2005)

I frequently heard participants say that music was one constant in their lives that they valued; they felt they would never lose music.

Musicians playing instruments are much appreciated. If I take an instrument out of its case, the participants will express excitement that it is great to "have" the instrument that day. If someone plays a more unusual instrument, many people will want to shake that musician's hand or ask him or her to teach them even though no practice instrument may be available. I've received fan letters in appreciation for playing violin. Yet guitar is the most typical and popular instrument. First United Church always has a demand for guitars—street people ask first thing in the morning when the church opens its doors if they can borrow or play a guitar. Most of the urban poor taking part in the jams and music therapy sessions, though, cannot afford to own an instrument, or if they have owned one, it has been pawned or stolen. Many live in single-resident occupancy (SRO) hotels, which have cramped rooms with space only for a bed but no kitchen, and a shared bathroom for whole floors. SROs are often insecure (the locks don't work/the rooms are broken into) and have sanitation and fire hazard problems, but they may be the only type of accommodation people receiving welfare can afford in downtown Vancouver.

Bob and I had invited Kelly to join us for lunch and the Evelyne Saller Centre session, but she replied that no, she couldn't make it because there was a woman in her building who was "wigging" (on drugs) and had threatened physical violence against her. Kelly turned her body fully away from us in one motion, telling over her shoulder that she feels scared. She has a home! Other musicians sleep on the streets or in homeless shelters; the lucky ones, in social housing. If someone owns an instrument, this marks him or her as not the poorest of the poor or indigent. It may be that one is borrowing an instrument from a local community center, but still that means that one's living situation is stable enough to keep an instrument.

If one doesn't own an instrument, one will be welcomed by the facilitator or participants to choose one from the music program's instrument collection, if it has one. Common guitars are steel string acoustic, electric guitar, acoustic bass, and electric bass, whereas other typical instruments include piano, synthesizer, and percussion (e.g., drum kit, bongos, cajón, and conga). A music facilitator practically sets up the room for a session, which includes taking out and distributing the instruments as well as setting up chairs and then later breaking down, often with participant help. When Bob and I arrive at the Evelyne Saller Centre, locally known as "The 44," music therapist Stephanie Swenson, with participant help, takes out of a cupboard that center's instruments, kept under lock and key. Sometime after this music session, First United Church shuts its music-making down because all of its instruments have been stolen; music re-emerges years later following the donation of new instruments.

After sitting on one of the chairs before starting to participate, one orients oneself further in the room, visually and aurally. Rooms for jams or music therapy tend to have nothing that one could steal in them. The room used at The 44 has stackable chairs, music stands, and the padlocked cupboards for instruments and music stands. In some of the centers, furniture helps people feel more at home, for example, an old couch or, at an organization for Indigenous mothers, a used-looking rocking chair for holding their babies. The wall may have a distinctive paint color, like bright apple green. Here at The 44, the room has gone unpainted for years, graying over time and betraying starved funds for building upkeep. In most cases, like here, the music is part of low-threshold support, which means support for people in active addiction that puts no or minimal demands on addictive behavior.

Each participant selects a song for the group to play, going around the circle in which you sit, in counterclockwise order. Choices today include John Denver's cover of the Beatles' "Let It Be," the Rolling Stones' "Wild Horses," Pink Floyd's "Comfortably Numb," and R.E.M.'s "Everybody Hurts," among others. One of the participants gives me a running commentary between songs, mostly about death and illness. He leaves the impression that he knows how many songwriters died: John Denver, for instance, in a small plane; various other popular musicians, in automobile accidents. "Paul Simon is manic depressive; did you know that? He has been in observation for 30 years. That is why he could write songs like 'Bridge Over Troubled Water.'" The somewhat dubious pop music trivia continues. "John Kennedy also died in a small plane crash." "What? No he didn't," someone interjects. "John Kennedy, the son" (John F. Kennedy Jr.). "Small planes are bad. More dangerous than buses." The choice of Lynyrd Skynyrd's "Free Bird" brings up the memory for my narrator of several members of the band dying also in a plane crash, and he then lists ways in which buses are dangerous.

Such song circles have a history in the Downtown Eastside going back at least to the early 1980s. At the Carnegie Community Centre at that time, popular music jams had been compared to a "club" in which people could participate (interview with Ken Tabata, June 7, 2005). Peggy Wilson, who facilitated a popular music jam called the Song Circle at the Carnegie Community Centre, which started in 1996, remembers that the format originated with one participant, Joanne

Hamen (Wilson and Hamen, text messages, June 22, 2017). Hamen observed that the jams were good, but it would be really nice to just be able to sit around in a circle and take turns playing songs (interview with Ken Tabata, June 7, 2005). Counterclockwise is the sacred direction of Pacific Northwest Coast Indigenous people—the Musqueam (xʷməθkʷəy̓əm), Squamish (Skwxwú7mesh Úxwumixw), and Tsleil-Waututh—on whose traditional lands Vancouver is built. In some jams and music therapy sessions, a song selector may also sing the song solo, into a microphone. Sometimes the song circle evolves into an open mic format, a public performance in which musicians—singer-songwriters with a band, or singers, if there is a house band—have a set time slot during which they perform.

Since the 1980s, participants have chosen songs from one or more songbooks. Songbooks may be published volumes but more usually are a binder filled with photocopied lyrics and song charts. Depending on resources, everyone may share one songbook, or each participant may have a songbook in the session, like at The 44. I select my song: "Hotel California!" I call out, and the participants flip through binders to find its lyrics and chart.

The repertoire played in song circles like those at The 44 or Carnegie unfolds according to a typically unspoken rule that a chosen song should be one that most people present know. What that means in terms of repertoire and genre has varied over the years because most participants have consistently been middle-aged but grew up progressively later. In the mid-2000s, most songs chosen charted on the Billboard Top 40 in the 1950s to 1970s and, to a lesser extent, the 1940s (i.e., the songs were frequently heard on the radio in the United States, as well as in Canada for which no comparable rating system exists for those periods). In a series of surveys I conducted in 2004 at local organizations offering jams or music therapy using popular music, out of 120 songs surveyed, 82, or 68.3%, charted among *Billboard* magazine Pop Singles, Country Singles, or R&B/Hip-Hop Singles.[2] Out of 145 total performances, 106, or 73.1%, were of Billboard hit singles. At another local low-threshold organization called the Health Contact Centre, 30 out of 48 performed songs had charted (62.5%). At The 44, 59 out of 71 performed songs had charted (83.1%). At the Residential School Healing Centre jam at First United Church, 17 out of 26 performed songs had charted (65.4%).[3]

---

[2] For complete survey results, see Harrison (2008: 256–262).

[3] I based these numbers and percentages on Joel Whitburn's classifications of American chart positions published in cooperation with *Billboard* magazine (see Whitburn, 1994, 2003, 2004, 2005). Whitburn's categories are delimited by music genre, but are composites of multiple charts published by *Billboard*. The Billboard charts are American, and of course Vancouver is a Canadian context. A comprehensive compilation of analogous Canadian information does not exist for the relevant years. While the US chart information can only be taken as a rough estimation of Canadian popularity, it signals that musical familiarity was important in music repertoire selection.

In a music jam at First United Church in 2016, participants selected and played songs by well-known artists popular starting about a decade later—for example, David Bowie, who was most popular in North America in the 1980s; the Rolling Stones (popular in the 1960s to 1980s); Willie Nelson (1960s to 1980s); and Neil Young (mostly 1970s to 1980s). At the 2016 jam, songs by the Beatles were still performed ("Yesterday," recorded in 1965; "Get Back," 1969; "Real Love," 1988) as well as songs by Johnny Cash ("Sunday Mornin' Comin' Down," 1969, written by Kris Kristofferson) and the Eagles ("Hotel California," 1977). More recent hits began to be performed too, for example, by Blind Melon ("No Rain," 1993) and Coldplay ("Yellow," 2000).

Genres most popular within these song choices have been classic rock and pop as well as country music. Music facilitators and organizers often say that country music is the stereotypical music of the Downtown Eastside (interview with Jim Green, December 8, 2004). Homeless and street-involved people frequently choose country songs. Many people in the neighborhood have migrated from small towns where they heard country music on the radio as youths. In the early and mid-2000s, music participants often chose songs by the following country artists (popular in the periods in parentheses): The Bluegrass Boys (1940s), Bob Wills and His Texas Playboys (1940s), and Mitch Miller (1950s). Hank Williams's music (from the late 1940s to early 1950s) was the most popular across all music jams and music therapy sessions. Street-involved and homeless participants chose to play Williams's "Your Cheatin' Heart" and "Jambalaya (On the Bayou)" more frequently than the other country songs. Outlaw country artists such as Willie Nelson and Johnny Cash enjoyed local popularity. Jimmie Rodgers's (1920s) songs also were performed sometimes. Musical tastes started to shift further from country in the 2010s. In this period, the urban redevelopment and class shifts of gentrification pushed more and more indigent and other urban poor out of the Downtown Eastside. Developers built more and more high-end living spaces and stores, meanwhile various music programs for urban poor shut down. By 2016, classic rock enjoyed greater popularity than earlier, but urban poor accessing the jams and music therapy that still existed showed minor continuing interest in country music, as illustrated in Table 2.1. Some facilitators say that rock and pop have always been a bit more popular than country in the music sessions (interview with Ken Tabata, June 7, 2005), but the former genres proliferated.

Most participants choose to perform songs from their youth and hold that music repertoire in common. Recalling the music of one's youth is well documented in the music literature as evoking memories, reflecting a tight relationship between music and memory (see Barz and Cooley, 2008) that gets tighter for adults as they age (Schulkind, Hennis, and Rubin, 1999).

TABLE 2.1

Song choices at two 2016 jams at The 44/Evelyne Saller Centre, in order of choice, showing local popularity of classic rock and, to a lesser extent, country

Jam 1. "Jonnie B. Goode" (Chuck Berry, 1958), "As Tears Go By" (Rolling Stones version, 1965), "Indian Reservation" (Paul Revere & the Raiders version, 1971), Hotel California (Eagles, 1976–1977), "Your Cheatin' Heart" (Hank Williams, 1952–1953), "Goin' to Heaven" (by Bruce, a local participant), "I Washed My Hands in Muddy Water" (Stonewall Jackson, 1965), "Comes a Time" (Neil Young, 1978), "Cold Cold Heart" (Hank Williams, 1951), "Mrs. Robinson" (Simon & Garfunkel, 1968), "Before You Accuse Me" (Eric Clapton version, 1989), "California Dreaming" (The Mamas & the Papas version, 1965), "Please" (by Bruce, a participant), "Give Me One Reason" (Tracy Chapman, 1995–1996)

Jam 2. "Sweet Caroline" (Neil Diamond, 1969), "Cold Cold Heart" (Hank Williams, 1951), "Suzanne" (Leonard Cohen version, 1967—the only commercially recorded song here that did not chart), "Hotel California" (Eagles, 1976–1977), "Vincent" (Don McLean, 1971), "As Tears Go By" (Rolling Stones version, 1965), "In the Wine" (by the participant Bruce), "The Thrill Is Gone" (B. B. King version, 1969), "Comes a Time" (Neil Young, 1978), "Lyin' Eyes" (Eagles, 1975)

As suggested, the majority of jam and music therapy participants are in their 30s and older. A music program facilitator at the Carnegie Community Centre, Ken Tabata, commented, "It is usually an older crowd, right? So the music is usually like 20 years after it has first come out" (interview with Ken Tabata, June 7, 2005). Some senior citizens take part, but young adults rarely. Death is never far away. In 2004–2005 jams, I played violin with 70-year-old Pete, a guitarist and singer. As Pete grew up in the 1940s and 1950s, he played the guitar and yodeled. In one session, he chose to play Jimmie Rogers's "Waiting on a Train" (1928) because many jammers knew it and there was yodeling in it. After singing the song, Pete pointed out that he had done a single yodel in it. He could also perform a double yodel, in which the highest note is leapt up to twice, quickly. Pete skillfully demonstrated a double yodel. His song choice allowed expression of musical skill and pride. He died soon after this jam.

In the early 2000s, when participants could be of an earlier generation, they didn't only play mass-mediated hits. Participants also chose songs that they learned as children in the 1950s and 1960s through school or family sing-alongs. Music therapist Jeffrey Hatcher commented on popular song choices of Indigenous

Canadians in his music therapy practice at the Residential School Healing Centre (hosted by First United Church):

Other songs chosen by participants were not widely known through commercial channels, but were "hits" in their own right, and popularized by other means. Clients at this and other similar facilities were in their youth during the 1950s and 1960s when, by various means, they had learned songs like "Goodnight Irene," "Midnight Special," "You Are My Sunshine," etc. Such songs were as popular to the mainstream listener as the charted hits of the day though they seldom found their way to the Top 40 charts. Nonetheless, these songs were loved, learned and sung by millions. Usually [the songs were] learned through singing at home or at school—both activities were much more common then than now. The important point is that the songs chosen were well known to participants and they could reasonably expect others to know them, too. (interview with Jeffrey Hatcher, March 24, 2004)

According to Hatcher, participants in the jams and music therapy sessions chose songs held in common, on purpose.

If participants who grew up in North America knew the songs from sing-alongs and mass media, new Canadians from Hong Kong tended to know and select songs from the mass media of their youth only. An influx of people arrived from Hong Kong before 1997, when the rule of Hong Kong reverted from the United Kingdom to China. Music participants who grew up in UK-ruled Hong Kong had heard popular-song hits from the UK, on Hong Kong radio stations, during their youth. A participant, Connie, told me:

I came from a poor family, a neighborhood that is so poor in Hong Kong. Also, I came from a turbulent family. I was very young when I got hourly work with all these neighborhood kids. We had child labor. I worked in a factory at age 11 and there they had the radio on. Working, working, doing this on the doll-line: you put the arm, leg, head in the doll. At that time in the factory, they put on the radio. We all sang these songs to the radio. That's why I know the old songs more than the newer songs. (interview with Connie, October 19, 2016)

Asians together with Anglo-North Americans and Indigenous Canadians are the most frequent participants in music jams. These repertoires of the music sessions do not reflect the African ethnic backgrounds of some people living in the Downtown

Eastside, whereas Latin Americans occasionally request and get participants to play Latin American hits, especially those known by most participants.

I asked the musicians why they chose and valued the particular songs and genres they did. They typically answered that popular songs that everybody knew allowed the greatest number of participants easy access to performing the music, at the least by singing along, because they already knew the songs. Thus, the participants focused on their own and peers' inclusion in the music groups and music-making. Many participants first started to perform music in the jams and music therapy in the Downtown Eastside after a long hiatus in music-making. For one example, a drummer and singer at The 44 and many other music therapy and jam sessions, Christopher, told me that he hadn't had a close relationship with music for many years, but still he could easily take part when he first encountered a neighborhood jam:

> I used to listen to the radio a lot, when I was in my 20s. Then after that my whole world changed and the music stopped. When I came to [the] Carnegie [Community Centre] and I was looking for something, this girl took me down to the music room. I saw this hand drum and she played a little bit and I said, "Gee, I can do that." That's how I really got into that and that was 18–20 years ago. (interview with Christopher, October 19, 2016)

Even though adults frequenting the community centers where the music sessions happen may have not have made music for decades, they easily can join in making musical sound by singing along with songs from their youth—sometimes even if, as adults, they had an accident or developed a disability or illness that changed their lives irrevocably.

In addition, other participants begin to learn as adults instrumental performance, typically through self-teaching and peer learning outside the sessions. Then they find it easier to join in sessions that feature familiar songs versus unfamiliar songs (interview with Nancy, October 19, 2016). Many participants in music therapy at the Positive Outlook program for Indigenous people with HIV/AIDS first started to play instruments when serving prison sentences, then continued playing in the Downtown Eastside. Learning to perform music as an adult strongly relates to capability poverty, especially not being capable of performing music earlier in one's life due to coming from a poor family not having money for musical instruments or music lessons, for example. A minority of participants, from more affluent families, enjoyed private music lessons as children, stopped playing, and then, while living in poverty as adults, took up performing music again (interview with Mike Richter, November 4, 2016). Responding to such desires to learn, music therapist Stephanie

PHOTO 2.3. Music therapist Stephanie Swenson.
Photo by author, 2016.

Swenson (Photo 2.3) set aside slots for private instrumental lessons as part of her practice at The 44, one example of the limited formal music education in popular music jams or music therapy practices locally. Swenson also nurtured songwriting techniques and made recordings of new songs by jam participants. To further develop musical skill, participant musicians engage in (additional) peer learning and teaching of reading music and playing instruments, often with utmost seriousness, within the sessions or their host organizations. For indigent poor who had the means for music lessons during their youth, taking up music performance again after a hiatus meant recalling life before the current level of poverty.

Inclusivity isn't the only reason for selecting repertoire—its fan base may motivate it. There are participants who advocate for the classic rock, pop, and country repertoire because it is their listening or playing passion. For example, after The 44's music therapy group played Bob Marley and the Wailers' "No Woman No Cry," an Indigenous Canadian participant, Joanne, said that she likes to listen to Marley's "One Love" on a local radio station, Rock 101, which plays that song often. The Vancouver-based commercial radio station airs classic rock and greatest hits from the 1970s, 1980s, and 1990s (Rock 101, 2019). Other participants added comments of agreement, that Rock 101 is a shared, favorite radio station.

Music program participants, in addition to knowing the popular music hits from their youths, also in one way or another already have access to them for free, without any financial cost, before going into a music session. Besides being able to freely recall songs from memory, Joanne, Bob, and other participants spoke of often listening to the radio and, in particular, songs aired from their youth. Radios are the cheapest to buy, and most participants are too poor to own a more expensive stereo, iPod, or mobile phone,[4] let alone buy CDs or recordings online. An exception was Bruce Vincent, who owned a mobile phone. He said that he doesn't listen to the radio anymore, but to MP3s downloaded for free to his phone, for example, through peer-to-peer sharing:

> The only time I ever listen to radio is in my vehicle and now I don't have a vehicle. But I always have MP3s on my phone but it's more or less what I can get people to download for me so it's not necessarily what I want to listen to— it's just whatever I can get on there for free. (interview with Bruce Vincent, October 26, 2016)

Vincent is an example of someone who goes along with hits chosen by others in the sessions, and then when it is his turn to choose a song, sometimes he selects a popular song he has composed. Even though participants usually choose popular hit songs from a session's songbook(s), their freedom is respected to select any song they wish, which, if they consider themselves singer-songwriters, includes their own compositions. I discuss in chapter 7 how group responses to choosing original compositions have historically been nonaccepting.

Besides in jams and music therapy or alone, participants practice performing by playing popular songs along with the radio, in the rare case that they have an instrument. Robert Chippeway told me about being able to have instruments at home nowadays due to an improved financial situation. He explained, "I've been a guitar player since I was a teenager, [but] I could never hold anything [because] I was a drug addict and an alcoholic for [30] years" (interview with Robert Chippeway, October 26, 2016). Being able to keep instruments became a source of pride, he added:

> I could never do it before. I would keep getting a really good instrument and I'd keep on pawning and then getting it out, pawning it, and end up losing it.

---

[4] Homeless and street-involved people generally communicate with people outside the Downtown Eastside, if at all, via handwritten or telephoned messages left at community centers or SROs. The messages may or may not reach their intended recipients. Some of the centers also offer free use of a landline at specific hours.

I've lost so much things over the years. Now, in two years six months, I have instruments. I'm on a payment plan, with the local music store and I've got an account there. (interview with Robert Chippeway, October 26, 2016)

Chippeway practices guitar and singing to the same songs that he performs in jams and music therapy, at home to the radio:

Rock 101 and any radio station: I put the radio station on and I play along with it, for hours on end. That's how I learned to play, like 20 years ago, I put the radio on and I played every song. Still today, once in a while, oh yes. Today, yeah. I have the radio on, play along with it. (interview with Robert Chippeway, October 26, 2016)

Another participant told me in a jam that he routinely played guitar to Rock 101 all through the night, aided by amphetamines.

Jam and music therapy participants (again—if they had an instrument or knew someone who did) also might try to practice on the streets or in other public spaces outside of jams and music therapy. They succeeded with this mostly before 2004, at which point British Columbia (BC) criminalized so-called aggressive solicitation (pan-handling) with its Safe Streets Act. For busking in Vancouver, most locations require paid-for permits that urban poor can ill afford. Thus, nowadays urban poor playing music on the street is rarely heard and seen except at six street locations, parks, and SkyTrain (rapid transit by automated train) stations, where the city does not require busking permits. Music therapist Jeffrey Hatcher recalled, in the early 2000s, hanging out with locals performing popular music in spaces shared with the general public:

There is a real rebel spirit. They'll take the guitar and sit on the front, side-walk, and sing. They'd get on the bus and take out a guitar and sing, a lot of those guys. Like, there's a real exuberance and buoyancy to the spirits there. And some of the musics up there, just fucking great. Some of those groups that I've been part of or witnessed, incredible, like 12 and 14 people just bashing away. And the fact that they're comfortable enough to want their voice to be heard and to really belt it out, that's kind of a rebel stance too because you're supposed to be at the bottom, you're expected to be and stay at the bottom of the social ladder. When you're First Nations [Indigenous] and HIV and drug use and prison history and [have a] psychiatric [back-ground] . . . one thing after another. You have all the zeros thrown at you. So your self-esteem is supposed to be nice and low, and for a lot of them it is. But I see a real exuberance in the music-making there and a lot less tentativeness, which I see other places. It's a barrier to get through. There's a real feeling of "oh what the fuck," "whatever," you know, and then the guitar comes out and they start bashing around and singing. (interview with Jeffrey Hatcher, March 24, 2004)

Hatcher noted, and he does not consider it a contradiction, that many participants have a narrow view of cultural acceptability:

One of the things that I see these people long for is acceptance by the mainstream [by which I mean] really, really mainstream, like most of them describe themselves as Christians in the most traditional sense, not fundamentalists, but what they think of as ordinary church-going Christians, even if they don't go to church. Most would describe themselves as believing in God and being Christian, at least having Christian beliefs, which is the dominant umbrella that we are all living under, regardless of what we individually believe. So spiritually that's the mainstream and that's what they want to be. Culturally, that's what they want to be, too. Socially, that's what they'd like to be too. They'd like people to not look at them as if they are funny. They'd like to blend into the crowd. They'd like to not stand out, for the most part. They want what they think we all have, which is people [not] point[ing] at us and star[ing] at us in the street. Or kick[ing] us out of their stores, which is true. People don't tell you and me, "Move on. You can't sit here. Get the hell out of here." Because we don't have the ragged look. We don't have that "kick me I'm down" kind of look that a lot of people look for. So, like I say, you see this pushing to the margins kind of thing and on the other hand, their desire for the mainstream. It's not really on the other hand, it's really one leading to the other, isn't it. You've been kicked way out and all it's brought you is misery. You'd love to be brought back into the fold, even though the same stupid society and their policies are responsible for you being out there. . . . It's like the dog being kicked and wanting to come back. (interview with Jeffrey Hatcher, March 24, 2004)

Allowing choices of commonly known songs organically to unfold, according to Hatcher, responds to a deep need, among music therapy clients he encountered in the Downtown Eastside, to feel part of a social group, but not excluded or marginalized due to poverty factors. This informed his valuing inclusivity in his music therapy practice.

Whereas participant musicians may have had a narrow view of cultural accept-ability and were drawn to mainstream song choices, facilitators have the possi-bility to broaden common repertoire a bit when creating a homemade songbook, a project sometimes undertaken together with participants in the music jams and therapy. Hatcher found that musical simplicity also could motivate whether to in-clude a song or not: "it is not [always] familiarity that is necessarily the goal—though most people know some or many of these titles—but the simplicity and (musical) timelessness. Chord changes are minimal, easy to remember, and even people who have never played can 'bash' along with these" (email from Jeffrey Hatcher, December 29, 2016).

Through these processes, participants in and facilitators of popular music jams and music therapy create shared ways of thinking and acting on songs. In so doing, they generate a music culture that includes an underlying value of inclusivity, a key repertoire of music from middle-aged people's youths, and the dominant genres of classic rock, pop, and country music—the latter being especially popular with indigent poor, such as street-involved and homeless musicians.

3

ORGANIZATIONS HOSTING MUSIC-MAKING FOR URBAN POOR

BEFORE CONTINUING TO analyze the music culture of the Downtown Eastside and how it engages human rights and capability development, a brief description of the aims, philosophies, funding, and (in)stability of organizations hosting participatory and presentational music for urban poor is in order. These basic details appear in three tables (Tables 3.1, 3.2, and 3.3)—one on aims, one on funding, and one on the continuity of organizations and music initiatives—on which I will comment, supplementing with my ethnographic research, in order to build an understanding of the organizations' operating procedures and historical trends.

Table 3.1 lists the aims, missions, mandates, or purposes of selected organizations that have located in the Downtown Eastside or geographically nearby while working with its homeless and street-involved populations. Some organizations—such as health centers, community centers, and churches—offer to the poor aid and services including participatory music-making. Other organizations focus on presentational music. Most of these organizations are Canadian not-for-profit corporations. I will use Table 3.1 to probe whether organizations, through their aims, hierarchically direct music facilitators to use approaches related to human rights and capability development.

Music Downtown Eastside. Klisala Harrison, Oxford University Press (2020). © Oxford University Press.
DOI: 10.1093/oso/9780197535066.001.0001.

TABLE 3.1

Aims, missions, mandates, purposes, and philosophies of selected Downtown Eastside–affiliated organizations that have offered participatory and presentational music-making

Organization	Participatory and/or presentational music?	Aim, mission, mandate, or purpose
Carnegie Community Centre	Participatory and presentational	The "mission is to nurture mind, body, and spirit in a safe and welcoming environment. Through the leadership and participation of our volunteers, we provide social, educational, cultural, and recreational activities for the benefit of the people of the Downtown Eastside" (City of Vancouver, 2019a).
Downtown Eastside Women's Centre	Participatory	The mission is "to provide for basic needs and to work toward positive change for women and children in the Downtown Eastside of Vancouver." The center's formal purpose is: "To provide a comfortable, safe drop-in centre. To provide recreation and self-help programs. To act as a source of information by assisting women with referrals concerning their needs. To provide a social space and facilitate the opportunity for women of diverse backgrounds to interact and build community. To educate the public and all levels of government about issues concerning women in the area" (Downtown Eastside Women's Centre, 2014–2015: 19).

TABLE 3.1 *Continued*

Organization	Participatory and/or presentational music?	Aim, mission, mandate, or purpose
The 44/Evelyne Saller Centre	Participatory	"Operates for the prime purpose of providing a variety of life support services to people with low incomes and special needs. We focus on supporting the physical, mental and social well-being of others in order to help stabilize people's activities of daily living (provisions for food, hygiene care and social supports) and enhance their quality of life.
		The Centre recognizes the importance of developing relationships between staff and people who come to the Centre thereby helping to provide a safe, secure, healthy, supportive and caring place to be, thus meeting a variety of needs.
		The Centre recognizes that all individuals who need our services have a right to them, providing they respect the conditions & guidelines for proper behaviour expected of those who gather in the Centre" (City of Vancouver, 2012).
		"Provides a variety of services to low income and at risk adults living in the Downtown Eastside. The centre supports the physical, mental, and social well-being of community members to enhance their quality of life" (City of Vancouver, 2019b).

Continued

TABLE 3.1 *Continued*

Organization	Participatory and/or presentational music?	Aim, mission, mandate, or purpose
First United Church	Participatory	"First United is a place of welcome for people who experience homelessness, poverty, and mental health and addictions issues in Vancouver's Downtown Eastside. Our programs include: legal advocacy; emergency shelter and social housing; meals; the Community Help Desk (health and hygiene supplies, community referrals, taxes, foot-care, and phone and mail); and spirit programs. We support and celebrate the inherent strengths of all people, of all walks of life" (First United, 2017).
Gathering Place	Participatory	"Operated by the City of Vancouver since 1995 in partnership with BC Housing and the Vancouver School Board, the Gathering Place is a safe, social place for everyone in the community including seniors, people with disabilities, people on low income, youth and people who are homeless. The Centre is a place to build community and create positive change. It provides accessible services and enables people to participate in programs that support their health and well being" (Vancouver Heritage Foundation Places That Matter Community History Resource, 2016–2019).

TABLE 3.1 *Continued*

Organization	Participatory and/or presentational music?	Aim, mission, mandate, or purpose
Health Contact Centre	Participatory	The Health Contact Centre promoted itself as a place where health and social services professionals first met people with substance misuse problems in the Downtown Eastside. Some did not have medical insurance. Thus, in addition to referrals to and assessment and education on drug and alcohol addiction recovery services, a nurse and healthcare workers offered basic healthcare. The Health Contact Centre hosted workshops and basic life skills training, which presumably included its popular music jams. The center's workers also provided health information. It made referrals to other healthcare services, and offered education and employment training (Vancouver Coastal Health, 2012).
Instruments of Change	Participatory and presentational	"Instruments of Change uses the arts as an educational tool to empower people to become instruments of transformative change in their own lives. By expanding community access to cultural activities, we allow diverse populations the opportunity to make and experience music and art. Through our arts-based community development projects, which serve schools, hospices, shelters, community centres and prisons, we create synergetic experiences that give both our facilitating artists and our participants a means of expression to find their authentic voice using a variety of artistic modes" (Instruments of Change, 2012b).

Continued

TABLE 3.1 *Continued*

Organization	Participatory and/or presentational music?	Aim, mission, mandate, or purpose
The Kettle Society	Participatory and presentational	"The Kettle Society is a charitable organization and society located in Vancouver, British Columbia.

We work with people living with mental illness, poverty, homelessness, and substance use. We serve 5,000 individuals each year, manage over 400 units of supportive housing, and operate a Mental Health Drop-In Centre that provides meals every day of the year. We also provide Advocacy services, an ID Bank, Homeless Outreach, a women's transition house, Health Clinic, volunteer program, and supported employment.

Every program and service we offer is guided by the following values:

– We value a client-centred approach— we use a self-empowerment model, recognizing that people are the experts in their own lives. We help our clients to develop new skills and confidence.

– We value a non-judgmental, respectful and compassionate approach—we treat our clients with respect and dignity.

– We value every person's right to the dignity of having a home—we believe that everyone has the right to a safe place to live.

– We value professional integrity and consistency—we demonstrate integrity in our work.

– We value safety—clients in our programs experience a sense of safety that they may not have experienced in the community" (The Kettle Society, 2019).

TABLE 3.1 *Continued*

Organization	Participatory and/or presentational music?	Aim, mission, mandate, or purpose
PHS Community Services Society	Participatory	Its mission is "to develop, maintain and promote affordable housing"; "to provide housing, service and advocacy to all in need"; and to "foster a sense of community within the PHS and society at large," including self-determination of any therapeutic treatment (PHS, 2019).
Positive Outlook	Participatory	"The Positive Outlook Program is a community-based, grassroots HIV/AIDS model that emphasizes multidisciplinary care to link clients with primary and specialized health care at health services in the neighborhood. A core component of the program is informed by Aboriginal [Indigenous] philosophies of health and well being, emphasizing holistic health by combining spiritual, traditional, mental, and emotional needs with physical. It accounts for the specific socio-cultural context that shape participants' lives in the Downtown Eastside, working to meet their needs for innovative interventions. Positive Outlook Program Philosophy • Each of us has our own dignity, deserves the respect & autonomy to direct our care • Links HIV+ persons into a network of health related social, cultural, emotional, and proactive support • Offers respect and understanding of First Nations Cultural history and tradition Provides a harm reduction approach Services are provided in a flexible, non-judgmental, nurturing, accepting manner" (Vancouver Native Health Society, 2006).

Continued

TABLE 3.1 *Continued*

Organization	Participatory and/or presentational music?	Aim, mission, mandate, or purpose
Saint James Music Academy	Presentational	"Inspiring Vancouver's inner city youth to bring social transformation through the power and joy of music" (SJMA, n.d.).
Sarah McLachlan School of Music	Presentational	"SOM provides high quality music education at no cost. Our programs have limited space available with a commitment to enrolling applicants whose lives will be most impacted by attending SOM" (Sarah McLachlan School of Music, n.d.).
Sheway	Participatory	"Provides health and social service supports to pregnant women and women with infants under eighteen months who are dealing with drug and alcohol issues. The focus of the program is to help the women have healthy pregnancies and positive early parenting experiences" (Sheway, 2019b). "Service Philosophy • Provides services in a flexible, non-judgmental, nurturing and accepting way • Uses a women centered approach that supports women's self-determination, choices and empowerment • Offers respect and understanding of First Nations culture, history, and tradition • Uses a harm reduction approach • Offers a safe, accessible, and welcome drop-in environment • Links women and their families to a network of health-related, social, emotional, cultural, and practical supports" (Sheway, 2019a).

TABLE 3.1 *Continued*

Organization	Participatory and/or presentational music?	Aim, mission, mandate, or purpose
Residential School Healing Centre	Participatory	"The AHF [Aboriginal Healing Foundation; the funder] supports culturally-appropriate, community-based healing programs which address the needs of members of the Aboriginal community. The Foundation also supports healing programs that are designed to meet the needs of special groups, including women, Elders, youth, the incarcerated, two-spirited people, disabled people and those whose bodies, minds, hearts and spirits have been affected by the legacy of sexual and physical abuse in residential schools, including intergenerational impacts. While Healing Centre Programs will differ according to community needs and community-based initiatives, the well-being of Aboriginal communities requires that all Healing Centre Programs meet similar standards of safe operation and sound management. The AHF has developed a Model of Healing Centre Programs. . . . The Model has been structured to preserve the safety of participants, ensure accountability to survivors and those impacted intergenerationally, and promote and incorporate effective, holistic healing approaches that directly address the legacy" (Aboriginal Healing Foundation, 2000: 15).

Continued

TABLE 3.1 *Continued*

Organization	Participatory and/or presentational music?	Aim, mission, mandate, or purpose
Vancouver Moving Theatre	Presentational	"Vancouver Moving Theatre (VMT) creates art that celebrates the power of the human spirit; builds shared experiences that bridge cultural traditions, social groups and artistic disciplines; and gives voice to residents of the Downtown Eastside and beyond. VMT creates original theatrical, concert and interdisciplinary repertoire; produces the Downtown Heart of the City Festival, multi-disciplinary events, and special projects for diverse audiences; provides cultural services, information, educational and legacy resources; and delivers professional services with an attitude of cooperation and respect for community needs" (Vancouver Moving Theatre, 2019).

Although one cannot tell everything about an organization from its aim, mission, mandate, or purpose, the above table gives some indication of the main objectives specified ahead of any music-making. Music programs themselves have not, within any service organization acting as their umbrella, had their own formal objectives.

Although many local music facilitators engage human rights and related capability development, just 1 of 15 organizations listed, the Evelyne Saller Centre, or The 44, mentions in its purpose that individuals have a "right" to their services. An indirect connection to human rights exists in the mention of harm reduction in the philosophy of Positive Outlook. As described in chapter 5, harm reduction discourse strongly connects with human rights. Harm reduction is also central to the operating procedures of Sheway, administered by the Vancouver Native Health Society. The aims of the service organizations offering participatory music-making use terms important in discourses of particular human rights (in parentheses), such as safety (the human right to safety), security (the human right to security of the person), health (the human right to health), and self-determination (the human right of self-determination). Three of the listed terms can be linked to human rights but don't need to be (safety, security, and health). Self-determination, as I explain in chapter 7, strongly associates with human rights. Although some service organizations share priorities of human rights and capability development, their organizational aims are vague on these points. This suggests that music facilitators have considerable freedom to understand and approach music-making how they wish.

Indeed, I found that a lack of institutional oversight of aims and outcomes pervades the music initiatives. Within nonprofits specifically for indigent people, employees usually do not need to report in detail, formally and publicly, on the success or failure of a particular music program as it relates with an overall aim of the organization. Lead administrators, sometimes advised by a board, have the power to make the choice to approve music initiatives or not, or to continue or discontinue doing so. So far it seems enough to justify the benefits of music based on blind faith, as recreation, or through connecting music to the word health in an organization's aims by hiring a music therapist. Administrative reasons given for closing music programs can be none at all—for example, in the case of the Health Contact Centre—and inept. In one case, an administrator fired a music therapist because of a high salary required by a union based on education level, certification, and years of experience working at the same organization. Music facilitators are vulnerable within the organizational structures. Yet nonprofit organizations often take credit for key roles in disseminating human rights ideas internationally (Merry, 2003).

Although music facilitators essentially decide themselves how they think about and act on music within the service organizations, they could hardly be said to approach human rights intellectually independently, given the broader human rights context in the Downtown Eastside. One hears human rights discourse informally in Downtown Eastside service institutions at everything from poetry readings to protest organization meetings. "Human rights" is a buzzword among local activists for poverty reduction, including among the urban poor who write it in graffiti (Photo 1.8).

In Table 3.1, just under half of the aims, missions, mandates, and purposes of the organizations listed mention education (four aims) or arguably related concepts (transformation/transformative and understanding appear in three aims). Education develops capability in whatever skill or knowledge one receives education in. If this reduces any of the social deprivations of poverty, it works toward poverty reduction (as per Table 1.1). It likewise exercises the human right to education. The organizations Instruments of Change, Saint James Music Academy, and Sarah McLachlan School of Music focus specifically on music education, whereas some of Vancouver Moving Theatre's projects include education in performing arts.

Whereas the organizations focusing on presentational music are arts schools or performing arts companies geared toward professionalizing or professional performance, those providing participatory music do so together with goods and services that meet the basic needs of urban poor necessary for their day-to-day survival. I would like to underscore the comprehensiveness of these offerings by the aid-focused organizations to urban poor. Besides offering music-making, they provide free or cheap food programs; free clothing initiatives; programs offering other free items necessary for day-to-day living; temporary shelter initiatives; free or low-cost medical services including counseling and support for specific populations with HIV/AIDS or mental illness, for instance; free showers; laundry and delousing; free legal and advocacy resources; employment-finding assistance; nonmusical recreation activities (e.g., sports); support to ethnic populations such as immigrants and Indigenous people; and free or low-cost computer services. Aid organizations offer other kinds of arts activities in addition to music, for example, visual arts and crafts, dance, theater, and creative writing—usually arts that do not require expensive technology. Even as the Downtown Eastside gentrifies, services and resources for the poor continue to concentrate there, although at reducing levels. In addition to Downtown Eastside urban poor, poor musicians living elsewhere in Vancouver benefit from traveling to the neighborhood and participating in the popular music jams and music therapy sessions that still continue. The latter musicians (not indigent poor) aren't so poor as to suffer from transit poverty, which prevents travel to important destinations, resulting in accessibility poverty that affects the poor who are increasingly displaced into Canadian suburbs by the gentrification of center cities (Allen and Farber, 2019).

In addition to general aims, organizations focused on developing professional performance will have specific aims and operating procedures for each project, for instance, a music theater performance or making a recording (not listed in Table 3.1). Such organizations locally include theater companies like Vancouver Moving Theatre, Savage God, and Theatre in the Raw; dance companies like Karen Jamieson Dance; opera companies like Opera Breve and Vancouver Opera; and community-based organizations like Instruments of Change and the Kettle and Carnegie community centers. In performance projects for which administrators have obtained grant money, the organizations will study, or commission consultants to study, whether aims of a particular project have been achieved and how—common practice in the performing arts. Participants give their consent to participate in a formalized study, for example, when completing a survey or being interviewed. For one example, in 2004, when the music therapy program at the Positive Outlook branch of the Vancouver Native Health Society received a grant from Health Canada to produce a CD titled *Circle of Song*, I supported the music therapist by conducting interviews geared toward a final project report to the funder as well as the CD's liner notes. For another example, in 2003, Vancouver Moving Theatre commissioned a formal study of the impacts of *In the Heart of a City*, the Downtown Eastside community play, which was one of a series of popular music theater performances engaging urban poverty in the neighborhood.

When new service organizations start up, it is a rare occasion for their administrations to gather stories of previous and current music program failures and successes when formulating new project aims and projecting results. Organizations and projects geared toward professional performance will solicit stories among Downtown Eastside community members about why a new program or project could be needed and why, based on gaps in previous initiatives. Occasionally arts workers solicit this information in an informal way among Downtown Eastsiders who may not know they are being interviewed, and afterward they widely express resentment and uncomfortableness because they feel exploited. Arts administrators listen to public discussions on programs' successes and failures or arrange their own forums for information gathering, then put the ideas generated to use. The creation of new artistic expressions is an outcome of listening to stories, but so is economic gain. Although working for registered nonprofit organizations and charities, lead employees have their own salaries to benefit from, which, depending on the financing secured, can get quite large. The director of the nonprofit Downtown Eastside Centre for the Arts, Dalannah Gail Bowen, commented critically:

> I was around when nonprofits were started. [They were] started to be an alternative to the lack of social policy in Canada. The lack of government policy regarding homelessness, poverty and all that stuff. So, now it's a business. There are so many people. There was never a consideration of a $100,000 salary for a nonprofit executive director. Now we're part of the problem. And it should be same as AIDS in the early days, nobody owns a community—this isn't a business. This is community service work. Keyword: service work. It was not a thing where you get into [the] nonprofit sector to get rich. Right? So, that's the climate. (interview with Dalannah Gail Bowen, October 21, 2016)

An inequity exists between where ideas for community music projects come from (often the very poor) and who benefits financially from organizing them (administrators). A salary of a local leader of a nonprofit arts organization can indeed be over $100,000 CAD.

Administrators are much better rewarded than professional musicians. The facilitators of the popular music jams are paid by the hour for short periods of time, which amounts to very little when one considers that each facilitator has considerable musical skill as well as professional performance ability, although typically in progress, limited or no college or university music education. At the Health Contact Centre in the 2000s, the music leader received about $18 CAD per hour, and $1 per hour more if he or she also supervised the two-room center. Supervision meant that the worker needed to facilitate a popular music jam plus deal with any incidents in the main room of the two-room center, possibly violence and harassment in the rough neighborhood. At the Carnegie Community Centre, the starting wage for music facilitators was around $16 per hour. Other workers facilitated popular music jams through the Carnegie's outreach program for $12 to $15 per hour (name withheld, personal communication, August 12, 2019). The positions at Carnegie, starting at over $20 per hour today, are unionized, which means employee benefits like dental services and extended healthcare plans (CUPE Local 15, n.d.).

At the service organizations, non-music therapists have been compensated only for time spent supervising music-making and for getting out (from cupboards) music, musical instruments, and music stands as well as putting them away. A main issue with being paid by the hour, the Health Contact Centre employee said, was that workers would be compensated only for the music program timeslot:

> There were no hours allotted for program prep, unlike with music therapists and other types of teachers, so we needed to change strings, organize song books, etc., during jam hours. So it could have been much more effective with also paying for time to get the equipment up and running better, to process recordings of clients, maybe some one-on-one lesson time, and so on—all suggestions I'd made back at the time to my direct supervisor. (name withheld, personal communication, June 20, 2019)

In dollars, this meant that the employees would be compensated only for four hours per week in case a jam happened twice weekly for two hours—for example, a maximum of $76 per week (before taxes) at the Health Contact Centre.

While some employees felt grateful for any money if they had been homeless, for example (interview with Stephen Edwards, October 25, 2016), from another perspective, their labor and skill are exploited for small sums of money—even if they take over duties that otherwise would belong to an organization's supervisor or a social or health worker. Pay does not compensate for essential preparation time that must happen outside of program timeslots. Program preparation includes, for examples, obtaining sheet music, and instrument maintenance (necessary and sometimes time-consuming). Compared to the fees cited, other music facilitators received less compensation—honorariums for less money, or free food tickets usable at an organization's eatery. In such cases, organizations do not recognize hosting music as "work," but rather as a person, with no professional qualification, "just" playing music with a group. By contrast, music therapists with training and certification are paid much more. One music therapist received $25,000 CAD annually as music therapy director and part-time music therapist for Vancouver Native Health Society from 2001 to 2005. This was a 0.25 contract; one day of work per week.

Inequity regarding payment of the music facilitators who are not music therapists is a concern in view of the salary amounts of lead employees at the same organizations.[1] Table 3.2 enumerates salaries of administrators and other people in leading roles.

A lack of funds given to participatory music-making, despite a frequency of jams and music therapy using popular music as well as Indigenous traditional drumming circles (Harrison, 2009, 2019), contrasts the large budgets (including for charity) of the host organizations. In 2016 and 2017, one church had an annual budget for charitable activities of around $3 million CAD. Proportionally, most of these funds were spent on employee salaries and few on program costs for the needy. The church's 2014 annual report for instance lists almost $3 million in salaries yet only $187,480 for community service and support programs (First United, 2014). The community centers, health centers, and churches—service organizations that target the extremely poor—can be described as being in the business of providing domestic aid.

By contrast, the three organizations in Table 3.2 that declared the lowest salaries for lead staff focused on presentational music—public performance either as a short- or long-term end goal. These were the Instruments of Change Society, Saint James Music Academy, and Vancouver Moving Theatre, with the first and last posting the lowest salaries respectively of $24,000 and up to $39,999. This book highlights the presentational music work that Instruments of Change and Vancouver Moving Theatre do. Salaries were higher at the Saint James Music

---

[1] It is possible to gain financial information about not-for-profit corporations operating in Canada, for instance, via the Internet on the Government of Canada's webpages and procedures described at https://www.canada.ca/en/revenue-agency/services/charities-giving/charities/information-about-a-charity.html (Government of Canada, 2019b). A not-for-profit corporation operates for nonprofit purposes but, under Canada's Income Tax Act, may either be a registered charity (providing relief of poverty, advancement of education, advancement of religion, or benefiting a community in another way) or a nonprofit organization (examples are social, recreational, or hobby groups; certain festivals; and amateur sports organizations) (Government of Canada, 2016).

TABLE 3.2

Annual revenues, budgets for charitable programs or expenses (marked with *), and salary ranges of selected not-for-profit corporations working with vulnerable populations of the Downtown Eastside, as disclosed to the Government of Canada, in Canadian dollars. A dagger symbol (†) designates any salary disclosed, alternatively, by the City of Vancouver. The amounts for annual revenues and charitable programs or expenses are from the earliest and latest years available over a five-year period. I provide salaries or salary ranges for the most recent year available at the time of writing.

Organization	Year registered with the Government of Canada	Annual revenue	Charitable program (or expenses*) annual budget over five-year period	Salaries/salary ranges and other compensation
Carnegie Community Centre Association	2002	$351,931 in 2013; $446,016 in 2017	$237,717 in 2013; $381,859 in 2017	$78,936† for manager and $109,182† for director in 2018; $74,891 for part-time positions
First United Church Community Ministry Society	1967	$3,158,613 in 2013; $4,289,663 in 2017	$2,394,721 in 2013; $3,458,018 in 2017	Nine full-time positions at $40,000 to $79,999 and one full-time position at $80,000 to $119,999 in 2017; total compensation for all positions, $3,061,520 in 2017: 57 full-time and 67 part-time jobs
Instruments of Change Society	2012	$90,400 in 2013; $81,063 in 2017	$14,093 in 2013; $49,236 in 2017	$24,000 in salary for all positions; $41,184 in professional and consulting fees in 2017

PHS Community Services Society (operator of the Drug Users Resource Centre)	2002	$27,540,465 in 2014; $38,632,828 in 2018	$24,304,121 in 2014; $34,831,244 in 2018	Seven full-time positions at $80,000 to $119,999, two positions at $120,000 to $159,999, one position at $160,000 to $199,999; $22,075,538 spent on 360 full-time and 187 part-time jobs; $1,671,019 spent on professional and consulting fees in 2018
Saint James Music Academy	2010	$600,880 in 2014; $904,113 in 2018	$565,443 in 2014; $697,089 in 2018	One full-time position at $40,000 to $79,999; $605,048 spent on 45 part-time positions and the one full-time position; $13,710 spent on professional and consulting fees in 2018
Sarah McLachlan School of Music Society	2011	$1,219,109 in 2014; $1,751,456 in 2018	$828,671 in 2014; $1,280,667 in 2018	One full-time position at $1 to $39,999, four positions at $40,000 to $79,999, one position at $80,000 to $119,999; $1,199,512 total compensation for the six full-time employees and an additional 36 part-time employees; $60,725 spent in professional and consulting fees in 2018

Continued

TABLE 3.2 *Continued*

Organization	Year registered with the Government of Canada	Annual revenue	Charitable program (or expenses*) annual budget over five-year period	Salaries/salary ranges and other compensation
Vancouver Moving Theatre Society	1983	$345,547 in 2014; $707,489 in 2018	$326,823 in 2014; $705,091 in 2018*	Two full-time positions at $1 to $39,999; $357,442 compensated for 250 part-time jobs; $2,292 paid in professional and consulting fees for 2018
Vancouver Native Health Society (includes the Positive Outlook and Sheway programs)	1992	$6,994,844 in 2014; $7,318,169 in 2018	$6,389,477 in 2014; $6,424,166 in 2018	Seven full-time positions at $40,000 to $79,999 and three at $80,000 to $119,999; $4,385,677 compensated for 59 full-time positions and 76 part-time positions; $101,562 paid in professional and consulting fees in 2018

Academy and the Sarah McLachlan School of Music (respectively from $40,000 to $79,999 and from $80,000 to $119,999 in 2018).

Overall, organizations in the Downtown Eastside generate their revenues to varying degrees from governments, donations, gifts from other charities, and sponsors. Figure 3.2 shows that 3 of the 10 organizations studied derived over 75% of their funding from government sources for each of the last five years their financial statements are publicly available: PHS Community Services, Vancouver Moving Theatre, and Vancouver Native Health. Churches also receive government funds for anti-poverty work. For the Carnegie and various other community centers locally, the City of Vancouver government pays some or all of their operating costs.

However, aid organizations offering music in urban poverty are often unstable— prone to underfinancing, lack of fiscal regulations, misuse of funds, and susceptibility to funding cuts. In the Downtown Eastside, various music programs at aid organizations as well as the organizations themselves were terminated during my research and, increasingly so, during gentrification in the neighborhood, which privileges upwardly mobile classes' use of city space as opposed to the poor's. The Health Contact Centre closed in 2012 (shutting its workers out with little notice), and the Residential School Healing Centre ceased in 2004 because its Canadian federal government funding ended. The music jam at the Health Contact Centre had ended in 2008, but facilitator Peggy Wilson left her sheet music there so any people with instruments would have charts whenever they wanted. The 2012 closure meant definitive discontinuation of music-making there as Wilson went to pick up her songbooks (text message from Peggy Wilson, June 18, 2019). The music jams at First United Church as part of the Residential School Healing Society's outreach programming also ended as the healing society closed. The First United Church building housed popular music jams once more in the 2010s, funded by the Carnegie Community Centre's outreach programming for recreation, and then again these were discontinued (emails from Kristine Lawson, June 10 and 19, 2019). For another example, in 2017, the administration at The 44 or Evelyne Saller Centre, funded by the City of Vancouver, chose to shut down music there. At the Downtown Eastside Women's Centre, a music jam happened once monthly in the early and mid-2000s. In 2019, popular music there consisted of one concert and women's sing-along all year, cohosted with other organizations, while weekly meetings for Indigenous traditional hand drumming took priority (WISH Drop-In Centre Society, Vancouver Youth Choir, and Atira Women's Resource Society, 2019; see Harrison, 2019).

Of 10 organizations quantified in Table 3.3, 7 were still open at the time of writing in 2019. The Health Contact Centre, the Positive Outlook branch of the

TABLE 3.3

Irregularity and instability of aid-focused organizations in the Downtown Eastside and their popular music programs

Years	Frequency	Organization	Organization open in 2019?	Music program(s) open in 2019?
1996–ongoing	Twice weekly, multiple programs	Carnegie Community Centre	Yes	Yes
Sporadic: e.g., 2003, 2004, 2006	Once monthly	Downtown Eastside Women's Centre	Yes	No
1990–2017	Once weekly	The 44/Evelyne Saller Centre	Yes	No
Sporadic: e.g., 2003–2004, 2013–2016	Once weekly	First United Church	Yes	No
1995–ongoing	Twice weekly	Gathering Place	Yes	Yes
2001–2008	Twice weekly	Health Contact Centre	No	No
2013–ongoing	Once weekly	Instruments of Change	Yes	Yes
1999–2000; 2004–2006 (sporadic)	Once weekly	Positive Outlook (program of Vancouver Native Health)	No	No
2001–ongoing	Once weekly	Sheway (program of Vancouver Native Health)	Yes	Yes

TABLE 3.3 *Continued*

Years	Frequency	Organization	Organization open in 2019?	Music program(s) open in 2019?
2000–2004	Once weekly	Residential School Healing Centre	No	No

Vancouver Native Health Society, and the Residential School Healing Centre closed due to the withdrawal of health funding from major government funders (provincial British Columbia [BC] and federal Canadian). The City of Vancouver has taken over various floundering organizations before closure, for example, The 44/Evelyne Saller Centre. Only 4 of the 10 organizations still hosted popular or Indigenous music in 2019, even though they offered such initiatives earlier. Organizations and programs that have had a diverse array of funders, and have been entrepreneurial in getting grants from governments and foundations as well as donations and funding from sponsors, are much more successful at surviving and thriving compared to institutions and projects with one or two main funders, which increases vulnerability to closure due to repurposing or removal of funding. Arts entrepreneurship is the purview of arts administrators, who lead, for example, the performing arts companies and private arts education institutions.

For funders as well as administrators of the aid or service organizations, making popular music jams and therapy happen for Vancouver's poor is not necessarily a priority. Furthermore, there seem to be few or no enforced controls or laws regarding continuous and stable service provision specifically for the Downtown Eastside's vulnerable population. Even though community-based nonprofits may be set up to meet the needs of urban poor, typically they are not directly accountable to the poor (see Mitlin and Satterthwaite, 2007). Decisions are made by and accountability lies with people in power positions including in funding bodies, the nonprofits, and even investors—whoever controls the money (see Fraser and Kick, 2007).

On the other hand, there is almost constant neighborhood discussion among arts funders and administrators about whether and how to prune so-called overlaps in areas of funding. Consolidation of and dialogue on resources have been attempted. In 2003, arts administrators and artists working in the Downtown Eastside tried to form a Downtown Eastside Community Arts Network that would share in planning, organizing—including securing funding—facilitating, and creating arts. Unfortunately, the network never took off.

To sum up, making popular music in jams and music therapy sessions emerged over about four decades through continuation, especially the relative stability of the repertoire, genres, musical behaviors, and dominant value of inclusivity. By contrast, the organizations in which this popular music scene unfolded were the opposite: inconstant as a whole. During my research period characterized by ongoing gentrification of the Downtown Eastside, over half of the popular music jams and music therapy sessions that I visited regularly were closed, rendering them inhospitable to urban poor making music. Urban poor then not only were disenfranchised from rights and privileges due to poverty but also became disenfranchised from the capability to make music in those programs. In turn, they were deprived of human rights that can circulate through the music-making and capabilities that developed there.

II

Human rights and capability development in musical moments

HUMAN RIGHTS ACTIVISTS undertake what anthropologist Sally Merry describes as acts of translation when bridging international human rights discourses to local cultural contexts. This kind of venularization, Merry writes, is often undertaken by "people in the middle," who "translate the discourses and practices from the arena of international law and legal institutions to specific situations of suffering and violation." The intermediaries "work at various levels to negotiate between local, regional, national, and global systems of meaning. Translators refashion global rights agendas for local contexts and reframe local grievances in terms of global human rights principles and activities" (Merry, 2006: 39). With regard to the Downtown Eastside popular music scene, such translators may be facilitators of music jams and music therapy sessions, urban poor advocating for their own rights, or myself as a pro–human rights academic. Through acts of translation, activists can frame human rights in local cultural moments. After Merry, I will define frames, a term she adapts from social movement theory, as "ways of packaging and presenting ideas that generate shared beliefs, motivate collective action, and define appropriate strategies of action (Snow et al., 1986; Tarrow, 1998)" (Merry, 2006: 41).

Over the coming chapters, I explore framings of human rights—especially the human right to health, women's rights, and the right to self-determination—vis-à-vis jams and music therapy practices using popular songs in the Downtown Eastside. Facilitators of the jams and music therapy sessions translate, for example, what the mention of health or women in the aims of a nonprofit may mean for human rights (i.e., the right to health or women's rights) in the music they organize. Through interviews with them and their event participants, I examine whether anything is gained or lost by Downtown Eastside framings of human rights in musical moments, musically, culturally, and in terms of human rights themselves. Or does such framing offer an overarching functionalist justification to the music-making or a way of understanding particular facilitator approaches? I identify self-determination as a major issue faced by urban poor within service organizations and when collaborating with facilitators. An interesting aspect that facilitators, music participants, and myself as a researcher navigate is when human rights might be in conflict.

4

THE HUMAN RIGHT TO HEALTH: AUTONOMY

IN THE DOWNTOWN Eastside, popular music facilitators have framed how one might attain the "right to the highest attainable physical and mental health" (International Covenant on Economic, Social and Cultural Rights [ICESCR], art. 12) in different ways. For example, facilitators often say that the inclusive repertoire protocol and choices promote participants' health and well-being *in general* (e.g., interview with Peggy Wilson, October 13, 2004; interview with Ken Tabata, June 7, 2005). This argument is difficult to critique. Everybody is welcomed to music sessions, which provides an experience of belonging. Experiencing belonging is also a capability. According to the premier international medical database MEDLINE, over 9,300 public health publications, including comprehensive statistical studies, attest to the health-promoting influences of specific aspects of social networks, especially social capital and social cohesion. Social capital refers to "social networks, norms of reciprocity, and trust in neighborhoods or communities that develop through social cooperation, and which can be used" (Harrison, 2019: 3; see Daykin, 2012); social cohesion involves individuals cohering into a group. Specific qualities of social networks reduce overall morbidity and mortality as well as benefit health in the broad definition proposed by the World Health Organization (WHO) in

Music Downtown Eastside. Klisala Harrison, Oxford University Press (2020). © Oxford University Press.
DOI: 10.1093/oso/9780197535066.001.0001.

1948—"a state of complete physical, mental, and social well-being and not merely the absence of disease or infirmity" (WHO, 2019). Thus, this idea voiced by music facilitators could not be considered hearsay or medically insupportable.

This logic also extends observations already made by scholars of music and health. Taking support from medical science studies, many have advocated for the importance of social connectivity to human health and to salving health and well-being problems (see Harrison, 2019). Music therapy scholar Evan Ruud lists ways in which people can bond and belong through music (Ruud, 2012, which builds on Ansdell, 2010). Music psychologist Stefan Koelsch and music therapist Thomas Stegemann (2012) discuss the possibility that music can fulfill human beings' need to belong and to form and maintain enduring interpersonal attachments. Doing so can increase health and life expectancy, although there are many specific requirements about the kinds and qualities of social connections forged. Social cohesion can strengthen confidence in reciprocal care and trust that opportunities to engage with others in the same way will emerge in the future (Koelsch and Stegemann, 2012: 440–441). The mechanisms by which connecting socially can promote good health have to do with how social relationships can buffer physiological reactions to stress (West and Ironson, 2008). University-trained music therapists working in the Downtown Eastside have absorbed at least some of these health studies findings and draw on such knowledge streams when they interpret inclusive music-making as healthful in this way or, indeed, others. A trope that socializing through music can be good for you circulates among different types of music facilitators.

Quantifying concrete health effects of the music programs is beyond the scope of this study, yet it is relevant to the human right to health, if not trite within music scholarship, to remark that facilitators found it important that participants develop social connections via music-making. Peggy Wilson, music facilitator at the Carnegie Community Centre, Health Contact Centre, and Gathering Place, observed:

> I've seen people make friends that . . . you just know they haven't had a friend and so . . . I'm going to cry now. Like at the Contact Centre, you know that people have just been going around. . . . [She's crying.] It's funny because I never cry. . . .
>
> I love it because you see people build social [connections] that you know they haven't done maybe since they were in a really low grade in school. Because the majority of people that are coming to the jams haven't graduated from high school, like even the people who are so smart. . . .

I love it that people have made friends and people that would never really talk to each other, they now call each other by name. Even when the music jams aren't going on, they might go out into the main room in the Contact Centre or wherever and do other things together and start sort of forming . . . sub-groups from the main music group. I think it's relieved a lot of loneliness for people. (interview with Peggy Wilson, October 13, 2004)

During popular music-making at the service or aid organizations, participants who were friendless have made friends and talk with people and call people by name whom they might otherwise not have.

Participants have identified making social connections and friendships via music-making in a group as important too. They have emphasized their capabilities to forge social relationships. I interviewed music participants at The 44, among other organizations, on the friendships and social connections they had formed via music-making. Some emphasized that their possibilities for social connections broadened and the ones they had already had deepened when they jam-hopped, through making music with different and the same people in various neighborhood groups. Most musicians said that they largely restrict their friendships formed in the jams to the jams (interviews with Christopher, October 19, 2016; Connie, October 19, 2016; Nancy, October 19, 2016; Robert Chippeway, October 26, 2016). A minority didn't. One participant had gone on trips and for dinner with some people with whom she plays music (email from Stephanie Swenson, September 1, 2017). Some friendships built in music sessions move from being light affiliations to being so close that two participants, Marcus B. Roy and Joanne Shuttleworth Roy (deceased 2016), even married—twice. Jam participants performed at Johanne and Marcus's 2011 wedding reception (handwritten letter from Marcus B. Roy, November 5, 2016; email from Stephanie Swenson, December 21, 2016).

Popular music facilitators may translate the "right to the highest attainable physical and mental health" (ICESCR, art. 12.1) into musical practice in a more socially specific way too. Some frame music as promoting what I will identify as individual autonomy and, therefore, according to the discourse of the health equity movement, indirectly and implicitly, the human right to health. Autonomy refers here to an experienced sense of control over one's own life situation, and not feeling controlled by other people. The health equity movement focuses political and mass public "attention on the distribution of resources and other processes that drive a particular kind of health inequality—that is, a systematic inequality in health (or in its social determinants) between more and less advantaged social groups, in other words, a health inequality that is unjust or unfair" (Braveman and Gruskin, 2003: 255). While the music facilitators are familiar with the human right to health and generally aware that the health equity movement exists, I have not heard them use the word "autonomy" specifically. In naming as autonomy what facilitators describe, I create an analytical frame that, in turn, connects with human rights discourse.

The music therapist at The 44, or the Evelyne Saller Centre, Stephanie Swenson, explained that what I will call autonomy-promoting qualities of her practice distinguished it from approaches taken broadly by many workers in Downtown Eastside service or aid organizations:

> A lot of people come into the Downtown Eastside [with the attitude that] "I'm going to help you." The only way that you are going to help somebody is by changing them. You shouldn't change them. You would be trying to control them. [It is important] for a person to come in and be completely non-judgmental and be with somebody. That person could have been a lawyer, two years ago, or somebody who worked on a tugboat, or someone who worked on a fishing boat who supplied your salmon that you ate for ten years. They just happen to be in a difficult situation right now. You don't know a person's background [before they enter a music therapy session or a popular music jam]. He or she could have had a very traumatic event where she lost her family in a fire. (interview with Stephanie Swenson, September 28, 2004)

Peggy Wilson echoed Swenson in saying that it was important methodologically, if one wanted to promote autonomy, not to judge participants in a musical moment, and to encourage the participants to accept one another as they are then: in the jam setting "either you are accepting each other or else don't be there with others. It's almost like you have to be accepting of one another or your presence isn't really going to work regardless of what you're thinking" (interview with Peggy Wilson, October 13, 2004). On the other hand, a music facilitator at the Carnegie Community Centre, Stephen Edwards, explained that he tried to give individuals control over their own personal spaces of musical expression by being as encouraging as possible of what they each contributed musically and sonically to music groups (interview with Stephen Edwards, October 25, 2016). A music therapist at the Positive Outlook program of the Vancouver Native Health Society, Jeffrey Smith, elaborated in an article on music therapy in "Canada's poorest postal code" that attributing control to participants over their own musical moments ideally "provided them with a safe space for creative expression and self-care" (Smith, 2007: 105). Wilson also saw it as her job to mitigate any conflicts that emerged in and around music-making and that threatened the sonic and social autonomy of others, to allow autonomy to flourish once again. In one music program, Wilson was alert to "people on harder drugs really slagging [criticizing or insulting abusively] the alcoholics a lot and vice-versa. Or the people who aren't addicted slagging the people who are" (interview with Peggy Wilson, October 13, 2004). Wilson reflected, "I watch people work their 'stuff' out with each other. I kind of try and let people work it out, but sometimes you have to step in and draw the line. That's hard" (interview with Peggy Wilson, October 13, 2004). In such ways, music facilitators framed musical moments in terms of autonomy, then thought about how to promote and sustain it, including by making interventions during music jams and music therapy sessions.

Lacking autonomy is widely recognized, in medicine, as a public health risk for all social groups. Lack of autonomy (similar to low socioeconomic status, see Harrison, 2013b) impacts the body as a psychosocial stressor that can generate physiological stress reactions. Experiencing lack of autonomy precipitates the release into the body of stress hormones and initiates complex neuroendocrine responses (West and Ironson, 2008: 432). Reactions in the body to psychosocial stress are complex and various but include a faster build-up of atherosclerotic plaque in the coronary arteries (and thus increased risk of heart attack), a tendency to suffer from central obesity, more damaging levels of high-density blood fats, and an increased likelihood to be resistant to insulin (Wilkinson, 2000: 36). Chronic stress negatively impacts the brain, thymus gland, and other immune tissues as well as the circulatory system, adrenal glands, and reproductive organs. It can devastate health.

Autonomy is among various key concepts of the health equity movement, associated with human rights discourse. The final report of the WHO's Commission on Social Determinants of Health (CSDH), which centers its argument on health being a human right, motivates the health equity movement by stating, "The right to the conditions necessary to achieve the highest attainable standard of health— Article 12 of the ICESCR—is principally concerned with disadvantaged groups, participation, and accountability and lies at the heart of the health and human rights movement (Hunt, 2007)" (CSDH, 2008: 158).

Urban poor experience dramatic erosion of a sense of autonomy because they experience being controlled by aid organizations and government bodies that support them. Swenson observed that lacking a sense of control over one's life has a particular manifestation in the socioeconomically depressed neighborhood. Although Swenson honed in on government-funded organizations, feeling control over one's life situation also is at issue in aid organizations funded by a range of public and private sources:

The Downtown Eastside is in some respects institutionalized in itself because there are so many different government organizations down there. It has that sense to it. There is a lot of controlling being done about what you can and cannot do, if you are on [financial] assistance [from the government] or if you need to seek out help through a government organization. There is always a factor of control. (interview with Stephanie Swenson, September 28, 2004)

Parallel situations can be found in other poor urban neighborhoods across Canada and other nation-states struggling in different ways to meet needs of the economically most vulnerable (McKnight and Kretzmann, 1996). The poor are at the mercy of not only economic forces but also the nonprofit community-based organizations and their workers that help them to survive day to day. There are an estimated 174 social service agencies in the Downtown Eastside (City of Vancouver, 2013: 66; more recent data not yet available).

Lacking autonomy indeed becomes an issue for the poor who get financial assistance from the government. Individuals may feel controlled by conditions put upon them, through government employees, for receiving funds from government agencies. If one receives employment insurance in Canada (when being unemployed), one must report regularly in person or via Internet, on one's unemployment status to the Service Canada branch of the Canadian federal government. For receiving welfare or disability assistance in BC, one must make status reports to the province's Ministry of Social Development and Social Innovation. People on income assistance in BC can apply for different funding supplements, but each and every one requires an application. For example, if a person has no other way to purchase an essential medical device, he or she can apply to the ministry for preapproval for the provincial government to purchase it. Such controlling of everyday life activities extends to many areas of one's life. If a person receives income assistance, he or she can keep a certain amount of money earned through work (at the time of writing, $200 per month for a person on welfare in BC; $800 per month for one on disability assistance). However, if the ministry has reason to believe that a welfare recipient has trouble spending his or her money wisely, it may elect to have the money administered, which most of the time means paying one's welfare check to one's landlord. People on welfare may be asked to sign an employment plan and follow what it says (Istvanffy, 1977, 2012). Government employees do welfare-related monitoring over the telephone or in person.

Urban poor also experience having their behavior monitored when accessing free social services at the nonprofit community-based organizations. Even though behavior monitoring can be justifiable (e.g., sometimes for security reasons), it further reduces the poor's senses of autonomy or control over their own life situations. The nonprofits monitor urban poor assiduously. At the main doors of the Carnegie Community Centre, one of the organizations where I feel *least* monitored, security guards track all clients' entrances and exits, in part to maintain the center's rules of conduct. These rules—also enforced inside the building by employees and community volunteers—prohibit drug and alcohol use, dealing drugs on the premises, verbal abuse or harassment, verbal threats and threatening behavior, fighting, different kinds of assault, willful damage to property, and theft, for example. These rules currently punish misconduct as listed in Table 4.1, although some punishments have been more severe in the past (dealing drugs

TABLE 4.1

Rules of Conduct of the Carnegie Community Centre

Conduct	Consequence: Not allowed in the building for
Behavior indicating alcohol/drug use	One day
Consuming alcohol/drugs on premises	One day
Dealing drugs on the premises	One month
Participating in drug activity and seeking entrance	One day
Nonthreatening, disruptive behavior	One day
Verbal abuse and/or harassment	One day
Escalated verbal abuse and/or harassment	One week
Verbal threats or threatening behavior	One week
Fighting on premises	One month minimum
Common assault on premises	Two months minimum
Sexual assault or abuse	One year—police involved
Sexual offenses involving children	Permanently—police involved
Willful damage to property	Two months and payback arrangements made
Gambling	One day
Theft	Determined by situation and if police involved
Refusal to leave for one of the above	Must see security coordinator

Carnegie Community Centre (2014).

carried a six-month minimum ban from the center from 2002 to 2014). While the restrictions may seem reasonable in a community center, I experienced others that sometimes left the impression of monitoring the miniscule. These included peddling; panhandling; soliciting or gambling; yelling, running, and roughhousing; sleeping or appearing to sleep; taking off shirts or shoes; playing music through speakers; and bringing bicycles and animals into the organization.

Rules and enforcement procedures differ from organization to organization. However, like at Carnegie, the organizations often actively involve urban poor in the monitoring; for example, volunteers can gain credit toward free food at an organization's canteen or another small reward. Thus, the effect of an institution monitoring and enforcing behavior extends to urban poor monitoring and enforcing one another's behaviors.

Swenson, after pointing out that the Downtown Eastside was "institutionalized," positioned her own music therapy practice in opposition to the autonomy-eroding institutional contexts experienced by urban poor. She thought of her practice as helping urban poor to manage life in institutions. Swenson's position contradicts the sense of being controlled that a person experiences when entering a service organization to make music. Although outreach programs have existed where people make popular music outdoors (before the 2004 Safe Streets Act, especially at the local Oppenheimer Park or on sidewalks), most music-making takes place within the buildings of organizations, and via musical behavior that does not in any way threaten their rules of conduct. It is common that human rights activism, in this case promoting an interpretation of the right to health, does not challenge structural contexts that erode that right (Merry, 2006: 48). Music facilitators must work within organizational requirements and they receive compensation when doing so.

Initiatives by music facilitators to enhance autonomy also exist within a contradiction involved in their attributing control over the life situations of people whose musical activities they guide. Because the facilitators *facilitate* autonomy, their efforts themselves control, at least to some degree, spontaneous expressions of autonomy by music participants. The autonomy experienced by the poor in these kinds of institutional and musical contexts can only ever be partial. Nonetheless, exercising autonomy is a capability that facilitators encourage for and with urban poor.

I will focus further on some outcomes of Stephanie Swenson's practice at The 44, and how these in turn may be framed as enhancing the human right to health or not in the abovementioned and other ways. Until the center shut down its music program in 2017, Swenson encouraged participants in the music group there to take control over their own lives when making music. In a group setting, individual participants could choose to narrate the psychological impact on stress reduction of their musical experiences, and discuss how they interacted with the musical sounds of others in the group. Psychological processing of stress through music and interacting with people through music are musical capabilities.

Participants reported that, through making music, they felt able to express the stresses of their life situations. One participant said that music allowed her to express stress about being diagnosed with hepatitis C, coping with memories of severe sexual abuse, and fighting cancer. Seeing a psychologist is typically expensive and unaffordable for the poor in BC;[1] therefore, she had difficulty getting psychologist appointments. Marcus B. Roy said that making music "gives you more ideas, more relief because you can exert it [your feelings, yourself, your problems] into the music and it comes out." Joanne Shuttleworth Roy summarized: "Stress relief" (interview with Marcus B. Roy and Joanne Shuttleworth Roy, September 30, 2004). As chronic stress negatively affects health, mental experiences of stress released through music-making can also be interpreted as promoting health and therefore the human right to health. Much research has found that music reduces stress (Baltazar et al., 2019). Via stress reduction, music can support the human right to health.

Experiencing mental control over one's life situation through creating music to emotionally and psychologically process a personal and stressful problem of course had specific manifestations in musical sound. One participant said that he jam-hopped in the neighborhood with two friends, and then one of the friends committed suicide. The second died after falling through a window in a drug-related conflict. He said, like Joanne, that he used the music to release mental and emotional stress, but only when he "drums to the melody":

Sometimes I drum to the lyrics and sometimes I drum to the tune. When I drum to the tune, I am using the song to express my emotions. I can't drum with everyone when I express my emotions. Sometimes my feelings don't match what other people are doing. (Harrison, 2008: 88)

For this drummer, experiencing autonomy enough to express himself sometimes necessitated avoiding groupness to the extent that he did not sync his drum rhythm with the sounds of other instrumentalists. His capability to interact with

---

[1] Seeing a psychologist can be costly in BC because this is not funded by the province's medical services plan. Psychologists' fees may be paid, however, by extended health benefits offered by some employers.

others through musical sound, and any benefits to health and the human right to health that such social connectivity might entail, seemed somewhat blocked. In an anecdotal explanation, the participant suggested he had experienced trauma after the deaths of his friends, but also due to a major accident. His jaw was a mass of scar tissue, and one large scar ran across his entire face.

The different means of pursuing the right to health—through autonomy, stress reduction and social connectivity—intermingled in the reported musical moments. The music therapist had a responsibility to manage health promotion, which could include these several means. This again points to autonomy being a quality that a group leader cannot unproblematically "attribute" to group members due to the power dynamics of leadership.

Like other facilitators, Swenson encouraged participants to experience and express control over their life situations through music repertoire selection. Being able to select a song and enjoy musical preference are also capabilities. Together with participants, Swenson created and continuously added to The 44's songbook of photocopied song lyrics and chords contained in a black binder. Multiple songbook copies and music stands ensured that each participant got to use one and experienced his or her own physical space for making music, as music facilitator Stephen Edwards put it. Then, during sessions, Swenson ensured that participants had space and time to speak about why the songbook's songs were important to them. The narration was perhaps less autonomous than the song selection because as detailed below, participants again made statements that could be considered therapeutic, for example about the songs reducing stress at local deaths and disappearances. The music therapy context and therapist arguably cued these narrations. At the same time, the narratives indicate that participants supported their health and human right to health via unprescribed grieving through music. This often spontaneous use of popular music, and musical behavior for and of grieving, are widespread in the neighborhood.

Swenson started making the songbook by compiling songs that honored individual participants in music therapy and their contributions there. She added the Rolling Stones' "Wild Horses" after she noticed that Joanne had a nice voice and could sing all the lyrics to the song, as Joanne said:

And then the following week, that's when we put "Wild Horses" in the book because I was singing it while helping Stephanie put things away that day and she says, "Holy smokes. Have you ever got a nice voice." She says, "You know all the words to that song." So I wrote them out very quickly for her on a paper towel and the next week it was in the book. (interview with Marcus B. Roy and Joanne Shuttleworth Roy, September 30, 2004)

The songbook celebrated individual musicianship also by including Paul Revere and the Raiders' "Indian Reservation," to which percussionist Ron Score played in the music sessions tamboa, a tuned slit drum, with particular skill. Musicianship, of course, is a human capability.

Stephanie, at the behest of music therapy participants, also added songs to the songbook because of their popularity in the group. Two examples are Pink Floyd's "Comfortably Numb" and the Eagles' "Hotel California." People who enjoyed performing these songs can be individually identified since the number of participants in music therapy ranged from around 3 to 15, as participants Joanne and Marcus explained:

> JOANNE: And then when this fellow, [name withheld], when he was with us in our crazy bunch that we were, right, that's when we started getting into doing a lot of Pink Floyd with him and Rolling Stones. [The Stones'] "Sympathy for the Devil" and "Get Off My Cloud" and . . .
>
> MARCUS: "Jumping Jack Flash."
>
> JOANNE: Yeah because he was into all of that, so Stephanie put that in the book for him, right? And [another man] he liked that song, "Unchained Melody," and he was into a lot of B. B. King, [he] was, right. So we put a couple of B. B. King, and "Unchained Melody," and a couple other songs into the book for [name withheld].
>
> MARCUS: [The Blues Brothers'] "Flip Flop and Fly."
>
> JOANNE: That was Joanne's, gray-haired Joanne's. She loved that one. (interview with Marcus B. Roy and Joanne Shuttleworth Roy, September 30, 2004)

The songbook includes one song because a music therapy participant co-composed it. In addition to music performance, composition is another capability of musicianship. The musician, Larry McCully (Photo 4.1), wrote the lyrics and then Stephanie created the melody and chord chart (see Figure 4.1). "In the Cool of the Night" describes a prostitute working the streets where McCully lives.

In music therapy, the narrations of song choices happened after someone chose to play the song in counterclockwise order going around the song circle and before the group played the song. When participants shared why the songs were important to them, the result was logical but striking. It was

PHOTO 4.1. Larry McCully sings at The 44. Note the thickness of the songbook, whose songs memorialize participants.
Photo by Manon Tremblay, 2016.

logical because most of the musicians talked about how each of the songs in the book represented individual participants in music therapy (my narrator of pop stars' deaths being an exception), which the songs did. It was striking because as participants narrated their song choices from the songbook in the mid-2000s, I experienced an imagined community more stable than the one I in fact observed.

Joanne, Marcus, and Stephanie were still involved in music therapy, but "gray-haired" Joanne as well as others (listed earlier in Joanne and Marcus's quote anonymously as "this fellow," "another man" and "name withheld") no longer lived in the neighborhood. The songbook's songs represented a sample of the Downtown Eastside's social fabric, which continually shifts due to migration, death, and unstable roles of individuals in community—changes made more poignant by a sense that people just disappear. If one doesn't meet an individual where or when one expects to, one may not know whether the person has moved, has died, has become ill, has lost interest in a given community context, or is "partying." Many people circulate through the community anonymously or using pseudonyms for identity effect, to obscure difficult pasts or to protect themselves. This gives the

"In the Cool of the Night"

lyrics by Larry McCully and music by Stephanie Swenson

```
C                        Am
There she struts, the lady in the cool of the night.
C                        Am
A lonely lady camouflaged beneath the darkness,
F            G
Beneath the neon lights.
       C                Am
In the cool of the night where evil seems to grow,
D
Watch out for this woman,
       Fma7            G
She'll haunt ya, scar you to the bone.


       C              Am
In the cool of the night, where darkness falls.
D                Fma7      G
Down on the corner, in the streets, and in your halls.
       C              Am
In the cool of the night where lust fills the air,
D                Fma7           G
Just as sure as we exist, like a cold blank stare.


       C                Am
In the cool of the night there's evil all around.
G                F
I must find a place where I can make my stand.
G                F
Get myself together in search of the promised land.
G                Fma7
Evil seems to dwell in the cool of the night.


       C
In the cool of the night
            Am
There is a hooker decked out in white.
G                    F
Looking for something to make her feel right.
G
A lonely lady so cold
       Fma7          G  C
deep in the cool of the night.
```

FIGURE 4.1. A song co-written locally then inserted into a songbook that celebrated and memorialized participants

impression of disappeared identities before people actually leave. The rapidity with which people come in and out of focus in one's individual experience feels unsettling. Joanne told me that she worried when her best friend in the neighborhood, who joined her and Marcus on their honeymoon, disappeared. Then she re-emerged in Washington State several months later. Many people die, violently, as the participant who drums to the melody recalled and as I recorded in one fieldnote:

A First United Church volunteer told me that a man from Senegal has died. A car hit this man, with a history of drug dealing, around 2am last night. His head hit the pavement and he bled to death. He had no drugs on or in him. His hair was tested, showing no trace of drugs, which meant that he must have been clean, the volunteer said, guessing that he had stopped dealing. Also, I learned that the really tall and beautiful transvestite woman who I often see has died. She had been on the street, warning others of some bad cocaine, which was grey. Soon after, she smoked some rock and passed on. (fieldnote, June 9, 2004)

Some violent deaths are accidents, but many others emerge from poverty-related issues, such as risks of the drug and sex trades. Experiencing homelessness or insecure housing, mental illness, and substance misuse also makes people vulnerable to violence. It is common to see high or drunk people wander into traffic. One day I saw a decapitated corpse lying under a semi-truck; a person had wandered into the middle of Main Street.

As people's absences left social holes in the music therapy group, narrating the missing individuals took importance. We see this in the following transcription of a conversation between music numbers at music therapy:

JOANNE: Yeah. So, what are we doing here, "Bye Bye Love," darlin'? Kli?
KLISALA: 8a.

Joanne announces again the song's number in the songbook, which is sequenced. She gets everyone's attention and we almost proceed. She stops us.

JOANNE: R.C. used to like this song. He used to like this one.
KLISALA: Who was R.C.?
JOANNE: R.C. used to come years and years ago. Tall drink of water of a man, long hair, and he wore nothing but Montreal Canadiens clothes, like, everything.
KLISALA: Oh, yeah. That's funny.
JOANNE: I'm sure his underwear was even that too.
KLISALA: Really?
JOANNE: Yes, everything he wore was in those colors—red, blue, and white.
KLISALA: Wow.

JOANNE: Oh yeah.

MARCUS: 8a.

JOANNE: He used to like this one.

This process of sharing memories of people gave the songbook value to longtime members of the group. Songs in the songbook soon represented new members too.

Remembering individuals through song took special importance for participants when someone disappeared from the jam in a way that other therapy participants found traumatic—for example, due to illness, death, or intensifying substance misuse. In an interview, Joanne and Marcus recalled songs associated with people who had come but gone in tragic ways.

> JOANNE: You know, there are so many songs that remind me of people that have come and gone. You know, there is this fellow. I think his name is Noah or something like that. Anyways, he liked Guns & Roses, right, so we put "Patience" and "November Rain" in there for him, right. And then there was another young fellow. What was his . . .? Leo, tall Leo who is a crackhead now. He used to play a lot at Carnegie, in fact, years ago. Really, really tall fellow, Caucasian.
>
> KLISALA: Ooohhh. Bald?
>
> JOANNE: Kind of balding, yeah.
>
> KLISALA: Guitar player.
>
> JOANNE: Guitar player. He used to be a *phenomenal* guitar player. Now he's so cracked out.
>
> KLISALA: Is that, what . . .? He said he was doing crystal meth.
>
> JOANNE: Same thing.
>
> MARCUS: Yeah, that too.
>
> JOANNE: But anyways, when he used to come to the group in '96, '97, and '98, he was into the country stuff. So we put [Kenny Rogers's] "Ruby" and [Willie Nelson's] "Momma Don't [Let] Your Babies Grow Up to Be Cowboys."
>
> MARCUS: [Kenny Rogers's] "Lucille." CCR [Creedence Clearwater Revival].
>
> JOANNE: "Lucille." All them kind of songs. . . . And then we had a Native [or Indigenous] fellow . . .
>
> MARCUS: . . . [who played] guitar, electric guitar . . . Blues: of course [CCR's] "Proud Mary" came in the book.[2] "Sitting . . .

---

[2] Creedence Clearwater Revival incorporated influences of the swamp blues of southern Louisiana in the late 1950s and early to mid-1960s.

JOANNE: "Sitting [on] the Dock of the Bay"—Otis Redding.

MARCUS: Oh man, he could play that guitar.

JOANNE: Yeah.

MARCUS: And he died of sclerosis of the liver.

JOANNE: And HIV complications.

As Joanne and Marcus talked to me about musical moments important to them because they memorialized people who had come and gone, I sensed that these musical moments held the most emotional weight for them. They also said that the musical moments were stress-releasing (interview with Marcus B. Roy and Joanne Shuttleworth Roy, September 30, 2004).

In sum, Stephanie Swenson encouraged participants to select songs, some of which she put in the songbook if they weren't already there. During music therapy, she provided social space for them to narrate songs that they chose from the songbook. If an individual represented by a song was gone, participants remembered and talked about that individual. Joanne, Marcus, and other music therapy participants narrating song choices in memory reflects anthropologist Carolyn Nordstrom's understanding that "if people are defined by the world they inhabit, and the world is culturally constructed by the people who consider themselves part of it, people ultimately control the production of reality and their place in it" (Nordstrom, 1995: 136), an analysis that Swenson agreed with when I showed her this text (email from Stephanie Swenson, January 9, 2017). Nordstrom in her analysis of the war in Mozambique (after Portuguese colonizers left in 1975) remarks that war's violence unmakes the world for those who experience it and witness it. She maps how Mozambicans employ creative strategies of trade, healing, and sculpture to survive war, emphasizing that the strategies are truly creative, not only mimetic. Remaking social worlds through creative acts, including musical expression, is particularly a feature of contexts of violence, disease epidemics, or other situations where social fabric decays with unusual rapidity (Nordstrom, 1995).

When participants in music therapy at The 44 were given the chance to choose the repertoire and narrate it, they spontaneously replicated patterns of music-related behavior that flourish throughout their neighborhood. People commonly perform songs in memory of missing and deceased participants in local music therapy sessions and jams elsewhere. About the Carnegie Community Centre's song circle, Peggy Wilson said:

There the one fellow on [a local CD titled *These Are the Faces*] who has passed on and he's got originals, so. We were all good friends with him, but Mike still plays some of his songs because they did a lot of music together. So that was Dave McConnell. . . . There's quite a handful now who aren't with us anymore, and once in a while we will pull out their songs. (interview with Peggy Wilson, October 13, 2004)

Wilson remembered deceased people who had selected the same songs to perform in jams every week, and the songs when chosen later might evoke their memory, although as a facilitator she did not formalize this tendency (interview with Peggy Wilson, October 13, 2004).

At another service organization, Sheway, music therapist Carol Wiedemann frequently tells her clients that they wouldn't be alive if they weren't creative:

> The reason that most of those people are still surviving and still alive is because they are very creative. They have to be creative just to survive. So when people tell me they are not creative, I say those people are the most creative. (interview with Carol Wiedemann, May 24, 2005)

In situations of turmoil, people may use music creatively as a survival tool. Psychological coping and survival is ultimately what playing songs in memory is about. Playing songs in memory can enable grieving, in turn promoting the mental health and right to health of living musicians. Wilson noted that grieving permeates the playing of songs in memory of deceased individuals also at popular music jams at the Carnegie Community Centre (interview with Peggy Wilson, October 13, 2004). Life expectancy is lower for urban poor than the more affluent (see Harrison, 2018). In the mid-2000s, for instance, life expectancy for men in the Downtown Eastside was 10 years lower than the Vancouver average, and for women, it was 5 years lower (66 years for men and 69 years for women; City of Vancouver, 2005). There is no organization that pays for celebrations of life or funerals for deceased indigent poor. Therefore, playing songs in memory of the poorest of the poor, in jams and music therapy sessions, takes more importance for friends who grieve them than it otherwise might. In rare cases, for long-time volunteers or community members actively involved with the Carnegie, that organization holds a celebration of life. Locals will almost always perform songs and music in memory of that individual (email from Rika Uto, November 5, 2019). Songs performed in Carnegie popular music jams, held in the same auditorium, could be thought of as extending that practice.

At The 44 and elsewhere in the neighborhood, a specific aspect of grieving through music emerged. In musical grieving, "the successful resolution of grief lies not in letting go, but in internalizing and incorporating aspects of the lost person" (Silverman and Klass, 1996, in Garrido and Garrido, 2016: 61; see also Davidson and Garrido, 2016). Downtown Eastside musicians accomplish this when they repeat a musical action that a deceased person performed in the past. This happened at the 44 when people played a popular song that a deceased person enjoyed performing, for example. Keeping "something of [a deceased] person alive in us" (Garrido and Garrido 2016, 59) is present in perhaps a still more intense way when local singer-songwriters compose songs about community members who have died and even about their deaths as well as perform and record these songs. One example is the gentle folk ballad "Three Dragons," by Carnegie music facilitator Earle Peach, which he recorded for a local CD *These Are the Faces*. The song memorializes a man who died from alcoholism (and drinking a Chinese cooking wine called Three Dragons). Composing a song about someone involves deeply taking into oneself information about that person; performing and recording the song are other instances of "keeping alive" something of the deceased. One way in which music allows for a living person to maintain a connection with the deceased is through "acting as a trigger for memories of the deceased and for bringing back vivid images and feelings associated with the deceased (Caswell, 2011–2012; DeNora, 2003)." Narrations of song choices at the 44 allow for this, for instance. Music researchers Sandra and Waldo F. Garrido note, "Given its emotive and symbolic powers, music therefore has the potential to be an even more effective tool for creating continuing bonds with the deceased than material objects" (Garrido and Garrido, 2016: 61). A main point missed in music psychology and sociology studies of grieving is that the performative aspect of music-making can facilitate re-enactment of many dimensions of the social beingness of a deceased person, beyond feelings or images, for example the deceased's physical movements and actual musical sounds that they had made. I have described that phenomenon. Being able to use music to grieve in such ways is another capability.

In this chapter, I documented how the poor together with facilitators of music groups develop music culture through playing popular song hits and other commonly known songs. I suggested that aspects of friendship, remembrance, and inclusiveness that extend to playing commonly known songs, especially in classic rock, pop, and country genres, have been sustained if not initiated to a large degree by indigent poor.

Playing songs in memory furthermore has had the potential to support urban poor's mental health through grieving the early deaths of poverty. Taking a deceased individual into one's body by performing musical sounds and actions that she or he had enables successful grieving and promotes grief-related mental wellness. When participants in The 44's music therapy remembered someone who had died by performing his or her favorite songs, they celebrated these deceased people. They remembered them as unique individuals, as they also wished themselves to be celebrated and remembered. The music therapy participants exercised the capability to remember and mourn individuals and their uniqueness. Therewith they could also feel their own individuality.

Participants also supported their general health when they, in an expression of autonomy, choose their own songs in song circles. In music therapy, whose context carries the social norm of engaging in "therapeutic" talk which a therapist controls, they volunteered narrations of song choices, I argued, semi-autonomously. Certain songs reminded them of music group members who had died or disappeared, they said. The participants also continuously engaged in different forms of social connectivity, which for an individual reason could be blocked even in the social act of group music-making. Overall, Downtown Eastside popular music jams and therapy sessions have nurtured urban poor's autonomy as it relates with their social connectivity and grieving processes, all of which can promote health. In so doing, they arguably nurtured the poor's human right to health.

5

HARM REDUCTION

ALICE[1] USUALLY DOESN'T look people in the eyes and skulks, gracefully, into a room. She looks me in the eyes today. She bends her extremely thin, rain-coated body in strange 45-degree-angle contortions, sometimes talking to herself, sometimes to me. Her eyes keep moving upward, as if to some distant realm. "Bad hair day," she whispers, keeping her crocheted black-and-pink hat on, removing her gloves (one of which she eventually cannot locate, although it is next to her umbrella in plain view). Alice's eyes dance on the filigree on the ceiling of the Health Contact Centre. She is gone. On another occasion at The 44, a high man who isn't a regular at music therapy turns a program's synthesizer into a party toy, while simultaneously taking musical instruction from the music therapist. The man is shaking, his eyeballs rolled back in his head, his eyelids fluttering, and his reflexes very slow, so I am a little surprised when he plays diverse, sampled sounds on the synthesizer and preprogrammed melodies in order to be comedic. He commands the attention of the room, improvising mime to the various sounds and dancing to the melodies. The man is very thin, has no teeth, and looks extremely ill in addition to suffering from addiction. In that moment, he seems to defy sickness or death in a way that seems hilarious and fun for him.

---

[1] This is a pseudonym.

Music Downtown Eastside. Klisala Harrison, Oxford University Press (2020). © Oxford University Press.
DOI: 10.1093/oso/9780197535066.001.0001.

Many local popular music sessions include people with varying backgrounds of addiction: from active addicts, to people with the dual diagnoses of addiction and mental illness, to people who happen to live around addiction because they are poor and the Downtown Eastside offers low rents in Vancouver's downtown core. At the most extreme, addicts participating in music-making have horrific substance misuse problems, using heavy-duty substances. These include, most of all, cheap, store-bought mouthwash and rubbing alcohol, and drugs bought on the street such as crystal meth(amphetamine), cocaine, or heroin—in addition to cannabis, which has been legally available at Canadian dispensaries since 2018 but is available cheaper illegally, and alcohol from government liquor stores or privately owned beer-and-wine shops. Some people in the music jams who struggle with dual diagnoses misuse substances in order to self-medicate for the mental illness or to counteract the side effects of prescribed pharmaceuticals (Smith, 2007). Others misuse to cope with stressful life events and psychological traumas. An overall purpose is to reduce negative affect and increase positive affect, essentially changing how one feels (Heiderscheit, 2009: 140).

When people come high or drunk to music therapy or jams (if they can enter an organization in that state of being), or if they frequently misuse substances, music facilitators may frame and justify their hosting popular music as harm reduction. This framing avoids acknowledgment of the possible, purposeful use of music and psychoactive substances together—which participants neither voiced in sessions I attended nor interviews I conducted, and facilitators do not discuss. Research shows that music can enhance drug use experiences because music and psychoactive drugs (including alcohol) have common forms of emotional processing in the limbic system in the brain (Fachner, 2006: 82–84). Playing or listening to music during drug use makes emotional processing of the brain feel more intense and, with cannabis, can change auditory perception (Fachner, 2006: 90). For a participant who otherwise dwelled in depression and edginess, my synthesizer story suggests different emotional processing of music than a sober one. So does the example of a summer music jam at the Health Contact Centre, where a local songwriter attended so high that he let his genitals hang out of his sports shorts for at least an hour. He strummed his guitar, eyes closed, with a big smile on his face.

Harm reduction developed in 1920s Great Britain and in 1970s Europe as an alternative to existing moral and legal frameworks for dealing with substance misuse (Marlatt, Larimer, and Witkiewitz, 2012: 10, 37). David Purchase, director of the North American Syringe Exchange Network, describes harm reduction as an attitude involving a humanitarian stance rather than a fixed set of rules. As psychologists

G. Alan Marlatt, Mary E. Larimer, and Katie Witkiewitz write, "This overarching attitude has given rise to a set of compassionate and pragmatic approaches that span various fields, including public health policy, prevention, intervention, education, peer support and advocacy. These approaches aim to reduce harm stemming from health-related behaviors . . . that are considered to put the affected individuals and/or their communities at risk for negative consequences" (Marlatt et al., 2012: 6). Harm reduction focuses on reducing the harms caused by and to people misusing substances; it aims to improve the quality of life of individuals, communities, and populations negatively affected by substance misuse.

Harm reduction, when targeting individual substance misusers, my focus here, means offering some sort of activity that reduces their ability or likelihood to harm themselves. Types of addiction addressed most by the field are alcohol; drugs such as cannabis, opiates, amphetamines, cocaine, and steroids; tobacco; and high-risk sexual behavior. Articles in the journal *Harm Reduction* reflect the field as being most concerned with drug and alcohol misuse, to a lesser extent with tobacco use, and to a still lesser extent with high-risk sex.

The Downtown Eastside features well-known harm reduction projects, especially North America's first medically supervised safer injection site, called InSite, and the North American Opiate Medication Initiative study, which trialed heroin-assisted treatment for people with severe heroin addiction (Stoicescu, 2012: 172–173). Yet various local low-threshold service organizations institute harm reduction for drug addiction through needle and syringe exchange programs, opioid substitution therapies (such as methadone and buprenorphine), and the distribution of safer crack cocaine kits.

Harm reduction also is used in arts therapy, including by music therapists (Ghetti, 2004) and visual arts therapists (Wise, 2009). There, harm reduction means engaging therapeutically, via music or other arts, with addicted people in any way that could be said to reduce harm caused to them by their addiction. Arts may also be used to address harms caused to whole populations by addictions.

Framing local music-making as harm reduction takes the perspective that there's no evidence that people misusing substances and making music at the same time can't benefit in a healthful way from music psychologically, emotionally, or physiologically. Various music facilitators think about music programs as a way to reach, for harm reduction purposes, people with deep and chronic addiction who take part in the illicit drug trade. Music therapist Jeffrey Smith writes:

> The harm reduction model recognizes that abstinence based strategies are often impractical and ineffective when applied to the street-entrenched drug

scene. Because many individuals use substances as their primary means of coping, some of the hardest to reach individuals are not in the contemplative stage of recovery and will avoid organizations that insist on abstinence requirements. (Smith, 2007: 108)

In locations where addictions concentrate, harm reduction fits well within low-threshold support programs that make no or minimal demands on the addictive behaviors of users. Harm reduction does not exclude people if they are high or drunk and misuse drugs, alcohol, or other substances. For this reason, it also suits the popular music culture, which emphasizes inclusion, in Downtown Eastside community and health centers.

Framing the popular music practices as harm reduction is, to a great extent, a human rights framing by association. Harm reduction strongly relates with human rights in that media, activists, and academics use human rights discourses to motivate it. Media, including of nonprofit organizations, frequently refer to human rights when arguing for harm reduction. Harm Reduction International (HRI) states on its web pages that it "advocate[s] against human rights abuses committed in the name of drug control and promote[s] the full realisation of the human rights of people who use drugs and those affected by drug use" (HRI, 2017). HRI has published reports promoting harm reduction, including "Harm Reduction and Human Rights: The Global Response to Drug-Related HIV Epidemics" (HRI, 2009) and a biannual "Global State of Harm Reduction" report. The Eurasian Harm Reduction Network, a network of harm reduction programs across 29 countries also promotes harm reduction policies via Internet media and publications. The International Federation of the Red Cross and Red Crescent Societies (IFRC) advocates harm reduction, stating on its website: "interventions exemplify human rights in action by seeking to alleviate hazards faced by the injecting drug users, where needed, without distinction and without judgement. The IFRC advocates harm reduction for one very simple reason: It works" (IFRC, 2019).

Some definitions of harm reduction refer explicitly to human rights. In the academic journal *Health and Human Rights*, Elliot et al. quote the definition of the International Harm Reduction Development Program, a network that claims to promote debate on drug policy:

Harm reduction is a pragmatic and humanistic approach to diminishing the individual and social harms associated with drug use, especially the risk of HIV infection. It seeks to lessen the problems associated with drug use through methodologies that safeguard the dignity, humanity and human rights of people who use drugs. (Elliot et al., 2005: 115)

Articles defining harm reduction sometimes identify drug use as a "human right":

> Harm reduction is defined as . . . an ideology viewing drug use . . . **not only as inevitable, but as simply a lifestyle option, a pleasure to be pursued, even a human right**. . . . [H]arm reduction ideology has politicized drug issues. . . . The only beneficiaries of politicized drug policies are the members of the drug legalization movement. (Mangham, 2007, quoted in Hathaway and Tousaw, 2008: 13; emphasis in original)

The beneficiaries of drug use as a human right would be drug users and participants in the drug legalization movement.

Academic publications on harm reduction furthermore discuss the logic of connecting harm reduction with human rights. The interdisciplinary team of Richard Elliot (lawyer and executive director of the Canadian HIV/AIDS Legal Network), Joanne Csete (a public health scholar), and Evan Wood and Thomas Kerr (both scholars of medicine) explain linkages that permeate media, activist, and academic engagements with the topic. First, "harm reduction's raison d'être is the fulfillment of the human right to enjoy the highest attainable standard of physical and mental health" (Elliot et al., 2005: 115). Harm reduction proponents not only concern themselves with harms directly related to substance misuse but also discuss denials or violations of human rights experienced by drug users from "torture to the blatant denial of health care, from harsh sentences of imprisonment to extrajudicial execution" (Elliot et al., 2005: 116). Second, Elliot et al. claim that securing human rights is necessary for harm reduction work. After physician Alex Wodak (1998: 38–39), they argue that prohibitionist drug policy leads to infringements of various human rights because when a population is negatively stigmatized and goes underground, it becomes difficult to provide medical services for them. Third, the authors conclude therefore that "human rights norms point toward harm reduction, rather than prohibition, in policy responses to drug use" (Elliot et al., 2005: 116–117). Many academic articles on harm reduction explicate human rights justifications existing in truncated forms in media and nongovernmental organization discourses. Others critically investigate such moral investments of harm reduction and elaborate how human rights may be used in political arguments for social change and policy reform (Hathaway, 2001; Keane, 2003: 227–229). Academic work also traces the relevance of harm reduction to specific policies and laws of human rights (Ezard, 2001).

Some music facilitators, when framing their music jams and therapy sessions as harm reduction, echo the service philosophies of the organization in which they work, if that takes a pro–harm reduction stance. The Vancouver Native Health Society's Sheway program (the workplace of music therapist Carol Wiedemann) and its Positive Outlook program (the workplace of music therapists Jeffrey Smith and Jeffrey Hatcher) have had harm reduction in their philosophies. Another example is the Health Contact Centre (City of Vancouver, 2001), whose jams Peggy Wilson facilitated. First United Church, where Hatcher held music therapy sessions of the Residential School Healing Centre takes a harm reduction stance (bc211, 2018).

Various local organizations that host music have incorporated harm reduction gradually over the past couple of decades, formally or informally, as well. Increased funding for harm reduction, to address a current opioid overdose crisis, markedly increased the interest of some organization administrators. In other cases, administrators adopted harm reduction to serve street-involved drug users (Photo 5.1). For example, the Health Contact Centre—co-funded by the Carnegie Community Centre and Vancouver Coastal Health—started as the Carnegie's Street Program. An 18-month pilot program from 1999 to 2001, the Street Program happened in tents at Main and Hastings Streets, a hotspot for drug dealing and

PHOTO 5.1. In the mornings, health and safety workers from the nonprofit organizations patrol the streets of the Downtown Eastside. Here, workers attend to two drug overdoses.
Photo by author, 2019.

the intersection at which the Carnegie locates. This outreach program included music jams at least once to twice a week. Music facilitator Peggy Wilson explained Carnegie administrators' logic behind her bringing instruments out from the center and facilitating popular music jams rain or shine: "one of the big ideas with bringing the jams outside under the tents was that a lot of people who you see outside are barred from coming inside the Carnegie" due to being obviously high or drunk, or less often due to a criminal offense that happened inside the community center (interview with Peggy Wilson, October 13, 2004). In 2001, the Street Program moved indoors to the new Health Contact Centre (City of Vancouver, 2001) and took an official harm reduction stance.

Within this context of increasingly prevalent harm reduction, it makes sense that music facilitators who do and don't work at an organization with a formalized harm reduction philosophy have understood their hosting music as addressing the harms of addiction. Stephen Edwards, facilitator of the Carnegie's music program from 2006 to 2017, said that music-making reduces some of the harms of living around substance misuse. Edwards didn't specify what those harms were, but they could have been any of the physical, psychological, societal, economic, and individual issues listed as harms to be reduced via harm reduction by Canada's drug strategy and British Columbia's (BC's) Ministry of Children and Family Development's Addiction Services program guidelines.[2] He explained:

It's therapy for the [participants] just to come in and, especially the afternoons, anyone can come in and play and maybe they just want to hit the drums for a while or whatever, okay. With me [before I became music director] too, it was like you get to sing and you're letting out some emotion. They get encouragement from that too. It's good for them. There's little cliques [of friends]. And a lot of people have developed musically. I give them pointers and help them to learn stuff. (interview with Stephen Edwards, October 25, 2016)

---

[2] Canada's drug strategy and BC's Ministry of Children and Family Development's Addiction Services program guidelines have defined harms to be reduced by harm reduction initiatives, as follows (in MacPherson, 2001: 60):

- Physical harms include death, illness, addiction, the spread of disease such as HIV/AIDS and hepatitis, and injury caused by drug-related accidents and violence.
- Psychological harm can include fear of crime and violence and the effects of family breakdown.
- Societal harm refers to breakdown of social systems.
- Economic harm includes the large-scale impact of the illegal drug trade and enforcement efforts as well as economic harm to individual users and society, including costs of decreased and lost productivity, workplace accidents, healthcare harms, and business and neighborhood economic development.
- Harms to the individual may be physical, psychological, spiritual, social, and economic.

Edwards evoked emotional release, increased self-esteem, and connecting socially through music-making, all benefits discussed earlier of music jams and therapy using popular songs. The capabilities to shift emotional states, experience self-esteem and connect socially through music were understood as harm reduction. The first two capabilities could minimize certain negative psychological effects of substance misuse like stigma, whereas social connectedness can offer social support for coping. These several capabilities could support the mental health of addicted people and their human right to health.

Earle Peach, who facilitated a variety of music initiatives at the Carnegie from 1984 to 2007, elaborated on how people built their self-esteem through music-making. He acknowledged individuals who improved their mental situations using "therapeutic" music in popular music jams that were not technically music therapy:

There were other people who literally came out of their shells. I'd have people who would come in and just watch for six months. And then they would sit on the stage. And they would start singing along, but under their breath. And then I would sit beside them and play guitar while they sat there. And then, one day, I'd hand them a microphone and they'd start singing into the microphone. And like, two weeks later, they'd be up on the stage singing in front of everybody. And then you couldn't get rid of them. That happened a few times and you know, I think life changed for those people. The good thing about being able to [be a music facilitator] for a longer time like that was being able to see gradual changes of people, and how people grew and also how important people were within this community. You know, there were people I think that we still need to pay some tribute to, people like John Ryan and Bharbara Gudmundson, who is still around. And Tom Lewis, who is dead; Dave McConnell is dead; and oh, Harvey Bowers. There is this whole collection of faces, most of whom passed and [are] gone, right. A guy named Conrad who knew two or three songs, one of which was [the folksong and cowboy music standard] "Red River Valley," which he invariably sang. I got used to people not singing right in 4:4 bars; it's just, when they are ready to sing the next line, you change the chord, you know, that's the way it goes. And Conrad, who died of cancer. Conrad Eberle actually and he died in Prince George and I was on tour with a group going up through there at the time and I saw him in the hospital. I went into his room and he's lying there in the bed and, uh, it was obvious that he was having to do conscious work to draw every breath. Like, you know. And when you think about that, that's like, desperate, right. And I looked at him and I said, stupidly, "Conrad, how are you?"

And he looked at me and said, "Couldn't be better." [laughter] He was just like that. (interview with Earle Peach, October 8, 2004)

If people changing in a positive way reduced, in any number of ways, their suffering due to addiction or being in a neighborhood that struggles with substance misuse, facilitators might interpret this as harm reduction.

Another music program facilitator at the Carnegie Community Centre, Ken Tabata, observed that the music jams specifically prevented depressed musicians from going further into depression, according to their testimonials. He thought about their examples as depression alleviation and suicide prevention. When addiction or witnessing addiction accelerated depression into suicidal tendencies in severe cases, he viewed music-making that addressed this as a kind of harm reduction. Tabata said:

If you are really playing music, if you are really in the zone and everything is connecting, it is nice; it's therapeutic. I think that's the importance of [music in the Downtown Eastside]. If somebody comes in [to the Carnegie] and plays and feels good, right, just even if they're making tons of mistakes and whatever, they're just, it just feels so good to play for half an hour or an hour. And they go out and they are feeling good, rather than, if not, they would be feeling just shitty, shitty, shitty, shitty. It just raises the level of how people feel. There's some hope. It's not all negative and despair. You might not kill yourself.

And that's *real*, that's not just saying that. I think there are people that go in there and they're just at that level where they just might kill themselves, right. If it wasn't for the music program, I think a lot more people would have.

Yeah. That's no joke. It's that real. And even people that don't go every week, but just some people come in off the street, right? And they go, "Can I just play? Can I just play?" And I go, "Yeah, yeah. Why don't you play guitar on this set here?" And they just play and they, and then it's like, "Oh, man." They might be in a bad situation right now, but you can just see where they had been at one point, right. In such a better situation or you can just see how connecting with their soul makes them feel like a whole human being again rather than all just chopped up or something. It makes a big difference. It makes a big difference. (interview with Ken Tabata, June 7, 2005)

Music therapist Jeffrey Hatcher, working for the Vancouver Native Health Society and in First United Church with their official harm reduction agendas, added that intravenous drug use related with depression, desolation, and desperation:

A lot of the gloom and depression [in health centers offering music] comes from the response to fearing for their own health. That's how it seems to me. There's also the isolation [for example] of having HIV and having no family, not many social supports, and your family is far away or they're not interested in you. A lot of [musicians I work with] have totally fractured families and where they came from, like, they can't go back there and they don't know anybody there anymore. Isolation, depression, all [those] things, and fear. (interview with Jeffrey Hatcher, March 24, 2004)

Although socio-musical activities have not been comprehensively studied in relation to suicide yet,[3] for over 120 years the scientific literature has discussed the claim that connecting socially can prevent suicide. Émile Durkheim demonstrated that an excess of suicides occurred in societies undergoing dislocation and weakening of social bonds (Durkheim, 1951 [1897]). How music slows alpha and theta brain waves, increases brain chemicals like endogenous opiates (producing senses of happiness and well-being: see later), lowers heart rate, and reduces stress are all well documented in the music and medicine literature (see MacDonald, Kreutz, and Mitchell, 2012). They could all be relevant here—and if addressing harms of addiction, they could all be considered harm reduction and therefore relate with the human rights entangled in harm reduction discourse. In addition, music therapists treat depression (Hendricks, 2001), whereas psychological harms related to substance misuse constitute one of the harm categories targeted by Canada's drug strategy (the others being physical, spiritual, social, and economic harms—see note 2). If music-making alleviated depression and discouraged suicide among Downtown Eastside urban poor, it promoted their health, well-being and arguably their right to health.

Linking music and human rights, especially the fulfillment of the human right to enjoy "the highest attainable standard of physical and mental health" (Elliot et al., 2005: 115; International Covenant on Economic, Social and Cultural Rights [ICESCR], art. 12.1), thus has suffused facilitators' justifications of popular music-making for and with people negatively affected by addiction. This includes facilitators working at nonprofits that do and do not espouse a harm reduction approach. Any under-researched benefits of music to suicide prevention are part

---

[3] Studies of music and suicide relationships so far have taken music therapy perspectives (e.g., Jensen, 1999), focused on deaths of individual artists (e.g., Jones, 1995), and involved quantitative surveys of populations (e.g., Rustad et al., 2003), for examples. For a literature review, see Stack, Lester, and Rosenberg, 2012.

of what is lost when jams and music therapy using popular songs are shut down during intensifying gentrification.

When music facilitators frame the popular music-making they host as harm reduction, they also may be understood as constructing a "collective social action frame," as social movement theorists have theorized it. Here frame and framing mean the result and action of locating, perceiving, identifying, and labeling an event or occurrence in a way that makes it persuasive within and beyond a social movement. A frame is informed by discussions, debates, negotiations, and renegotiations going on within that movement. Therefore, it is an active, processual phenomenon that involves agency and contention (Benford and Snow, 2000: 614).

The collective social active frame idea is pertinent when music facilitators discuss their practices in terms of harm reduction yet work in organizations that do not formally condone the approach. It is particularly relevant for music facilitators who framed their events as harm reduction from 2006 to 2015. In that period, Canada's prime minister, Stephen Harper, removed harm reduction from Canada's national drug strategy. (The strategy mentioned harm reduction in its initial version of 1987, plus revised versions in 1992 and 1998; Cavalierri and Riley, 2012: 385). Harper reportedly said, "if you remain a drug addict, I don't care how much harm you reduce, you are going to have a short and miserable life" (in the *Winnipeg Free Press*, quoted in Hathaway and Tousaw, 2008: 13), following a refusal to renew the license for the local safe injection clinic InSite, a decision later successfully challenged in Canada's Supreme Court. Despite a lack of government support, which also meant funding, many Canadian activists continued to use harm reduction, to discuss among themselves its significance, and to organize and develop arguments when lobbying government for harm reduction policy and money. Downtown Eastside music facilitators claiming to implement harm reduction in that period were among those activists.[4]

In music therapy at nonprofits with harm reduction philosophies, facilitators would point me to participants who would comply with telling stories about how music helped them recover from addiction—essentially how music had not only served as harm reduction but eventually also "cured" addiction. Some of these

---

[4] In 2015, Canada's next prime minister, Justin Trudeau, reinstated harm reduction as a key national policy. Subsequently, the national government increased funding for harm reduction to address the opioid crisis including deaths from fentanyl, a drug 50 times stronger than heroin (Kassam, 2017). So far, $7 million CAD of annual funding, for 2017 to 2022, from the national Harm Reduction Fund has been limited to preventing HIV and hepatitis C transmission through the sharing of drug injection and inhalation equipment (Government of Canada, 2019c). With music not targeting these kinds of aims (according to facilitators' own words), music facilitators calling their activities harm reduction points to a broader scope of the harm reduction movement.

same participants returned to misusing substances after telling me these stories, but still, they expressed conviction of them at the time. Stewart Wilson, for example, said:

> Before I got [to music therapy], I had a serious life of drug addiction and crime, and I was lost. I didn't have anything or know anything. I always wanted to be able to make melody lines, like, do what they were supposed to do, like make them talk, make a guitar talk. I had always wanted to be able to do that and finally when I got here somebody was there to teach me. And I never looked back, you know. My life has been music, music, music now. It has totally helped me to stay clean today. My focus is no longer on the bad habits. It's all good habits. And that is because of music. (interview with Stewart Wilson, March 8, 2005)

Wilson, and his music therapist, thought about music-making as possibly preventing addiction and its future harms. Addicted people developing the capability, through music, to stop being addicted would strengthen their health, their right to health and any other human rights violated by the harms caused by addiction.

The possibility that music-making can replace drug use is supported by studies that show that hearing music can generate chemicals in the human brain that resemble compounds in certain psychoactive drugs. In this way, music listening could compensate for a biological inadequacy that drives addiction. Norris (2000) found that the brains of people with substance abuse problems have difficulty producing naturally slow alpha and theta brain waves. Slow alpha and theta brain waves help the brain to produce endogenous opiates, endorphins, and dopamine, which give people a sense of happiness and well-being. Using drugs or alcohol generates these slow brain waves, as can music listening and participating (Crowe, 2004: 326–327). Music listening, at least, also can stimulate endorphins (Prince, 1982; Scarantino, 1987). This is one interpretation of the slogan "music is my drug of choice," frequently heard in the neighborhood, as well as a lived experience of certain musicians who have slowly exchanged the experience of misusing substances and their concomitant harms for, instead, making music (as detailed in Hatcher, 2004). All in all, harm reduction, in seeking to prevent diverse kinds of harms associated with addiction, builds capabilities for individuals to prevent those harms.

I will now explore how harm reduction unfolds in Carol Wiedemann's music therapy practice at Sheway vis-à-vis how her practice simultaneously boosts a number of different human rights while taking different, simultaneous approaches to the human right to health. In music, the arts and culture, multiple human rights may be implicated and engaged at the same time, as can multiple ways of pursuing one human right.

The nonprofit Sheway is a partnership governed by four different health organizers and service providers: the Vancouver Native Health Society, the Vancouver Coastal Health Authority, the Ministry of Children and Family Development, and the YWCA of Vancouver. It describes itself as a pregnancy outreach program (Sheway, 2019b) and has a locally unique philosophy:

> The philosophy of Sheway services is based on the recognition that the health of women and their children is linked to the conditions of their lives and their ability to influence these conditions. Hence, Sheway staff work in partnership with the woman as she makes decisions regarding her health and the health of her child. (Vancouver Native Health Society, 2003: 24)

The organization offers health and social support services to Indigenous women dealing with drug and alcohol issues and who are pregnant, have had a baby within the past 18 months, or whose child or children are in foster care (which means that the government has placed the baby in another family).

Sheway, including its music therapy, has responded with a harm reduction approach or philosophy to difficult circumstances faced by new mothers with backgrounds of addiction. Carol Wiedemann said:

> At Sheway, people can be anywhere in their addiction. They can be in the middle of their addiction. They can be accessing resources to detox, to go into treatment, to be completely healthy. They can be at all levels of the recovery process. It's definitely harm reduction at Sheway. (interview with Carol Wiedemann, May 24, 2005)

Sheway was formed by a group of social and health care providers as a response to a report documenting that 40% of infants born to mothers in the Downtown Eastside area were exposed to alcohol or other drugs in utero (Lock et al., 1993, in Sheway, 2019b). The rate of low birth weight was 33% and government authorities removed all of the infants from their mothers' care. At the same time, hospital workers were identifying an increasing number of socially high-risk pregnant women who were ready to deliver and misused drugs and alcohol. They and their babies had poor health outcomes (Sheway, 2019a). Sheway therefore developed the aim "to help the women have healthy pregnancies and positive early parenting experiences" (Sheway, 2019b) through offering prenatal care and other supports; promoting the health and nutrition of mother and child; providing education, referrals, or supports to help the mothers decrease drug and alcohol use or stop using entirely; and supporting the mothers in their capacity as caregivers.

Women in need of these services have attended music therapy at Sheway since 2001. A lot of these women are pregnant and have a toddler or two. Carol Wiedemann, as Sheway's music therapist, uses music-making together with the mothers in efforts to support their journeys in and toward healthy parenting.

Many women accessing music therapy at Sheway still struggle with their babies being placed in foster care, in addition to substance misuse. Losing custody is likely to happen if a woman has a file with BC's Ministry of Children and Family Development. A woman may have had one, two, or more children already taken away and government authorities have documented her substance misuse. If this is a first child, though, there would have been no reason to involve the ministry previously. However, if the woman has a social worker or is recommended by a health worker to voluntarily contact the ministry to get support, then the woman may do so. Women living in poverty who are pregnant or who have young children will need a place to live, a living allowance, supplies for the baby, and other support to raise a child that the nonprofit offers.

What Sheway does is fill a gap in the government system, especially for those women who have a file at the ministry. Staff work with these women toward a plan for them and their families. The ministry tends to take away all children birthed to one woman if she has had children taken away in the past, even if she has stopped using alcohol or other drugs. The ministry deems taking away the baby to be best for the new child. Sheway workers fill in the blanks that ministry workers don't have time to. For example, they may document what a mother or couple have accomplished in terms of addictions treatment, how long she or they have been sober, what they are going to do in the future, and where they are living now, but promise drug testing every week and facilitate a ministry visit to evaluate their housing situation. When the government allows a woman to keep her baby, she is living in poverty, and therefore needs support (interview with Carol Wiedemann, May 24, 2005). That is where extensive support offered at Sheway comes in: food, clothing, toys, and supplies for the baby, as well as drug and alcohol addiction counseling, music therapy, and medical care staffed by doctors, nurses, pediatricians, psychologists, occupational therapists, and music therapists. Sheway works in close collaboration with a special unit of BC Women's Hospital dedicated to mothers using substances and babies exposed to those substances, where the women may give birth.

Music therapy happens in a common area of Sheway, where the mothers can socialize with their babies and their partners. For women who access Sheway services and care for their babies at home, music therapy undertakes important tasks of mentoring and teaching parenting. For women who have had their babies taken away and put in foster care, Sheway and its music therapy may be a context where "visitations" with the baby happen. During a visitation, a mother whose birth child has been placed in foster care gets to visit with her child. She may have a goal of trying to get her child back from foster care. Sheway staff can advocate for the mother to this end while working in collaboration with the Ministry of Children and Family Development. Sheway employees might recommend to the ministry reinstating custody, for example, if a mother demonstrates the ability to lovingly care for the baby, abstains from drug and alcohol misuse, and accesses a range of social support services for low-income parents, such as those provided by the center. Regaining custody would reduce the psychological harm—affecting both the women and their partners—of having one's baby taken away due to alcohol or drug misuse, which supports Sheway's mandate of harm reduction. The women's partners are also welcome at music therapy if they attend together with the mothers.

The women I met at Sheway expressed keenness to protect their ability to be mothers and appeared highly collaborative in attempts made by the music therapist to guide loving care of babies and to promote access to Sheway services. For women who have had their babies taken away due to substance misuse, music therapy supports the meeting of the requirements to regain custody—except for abstinence—through a harm reduction approach. Via music therapy and other programs, the mothers work toward reducing harms involved in having their babies taken away, ideally resulting in regaining custody. The music therapist, echoing ministry requirements, when possible suggests addictions treatment, which does not qualify as harm reduction.

Music therapy at Sheway, in taking a harm reduction attitude to the mothers' situations, acts upon the harm reduction discourses promoting the "right . . . to the enjoyment of the highest attainable standard of physical and mental health" (ICESCR, art. 12.1). Since the mothers struggle with being able to take care of their own children, music therapy also supports the human right of "provision of assistance to parents and legal guardians in the performance of their child rearing responsibilities including the development of institutions, activities and services for the care of children" (Convention on the Rights of the Child art. 18.2; OHCHR, 1996–2019b).

How Carol Wiedemann as a music therapist supports the mothers in loving parenting and accessing Sheway services may also be framed as supporting different approaches to the human right to health, as well as additional human rights via developing specific capabilities of the women. I received substantial feedback from Wiedemann in a dialogic approach to writing this chapter, during which she said she found the human rights framing important. Due to restrictions around research permissions at Sheway nowadays, she also asked that this chapter reflect her practice in the mid-2000s.

Taking different approaches to the right to health, Wiedemann's music therapy practice—like Swenson's—on the one hand promotes clients' autonomously choosing music repertoire as much as is possible within the format of a formally organized music program. I discussed earlier how the capability to choose songs and thereby exercise autonomy bolsters health and arguably the human right to health. Wiedemann said:

> They know that they can come to me and say, "Hey, let's play that song because it will change what's going on" or "We haven't played anything for the kids. Why don't we play some lullabies" or "Why don't we play something these kids are really going to like." So then it becomes really focused on the children. I really like it if I'm not the one making all of those decisions. It's really not ideal if I'm doing all of that. (interview with Carol Wiedemann, May 24, 2005)

Wiedemann said, like Swenson, that it is ideal for her if the women self-direct (autonomously direct) their repertoire choice and how they use music therapeutically.

The repertoire that mothers at Sheway choose to sing largely consists of mass-mediated popular songs that are emotional and have a good story, quite often love songs. Children's songs are also performed sometimes.

The mothers most often choose a song that relates to their own lives. In the mid-2000s when I conducted fieldwork at Sheway, popular song examples included Celine Dion's "My Heart Would Go On" and Kid Rock and Sheryl Crowe's "Picture." Women come into the organization still today wanting to sing and requesting popular songs. Wiedemann said, "I have a couple regulars as it were and they will come in and say, 'I want to sing this song today'" (interview with Carol Wiedemann, May 24, 2005). The music therapist has also introduced on-the-spot songwriting as music therapy.

On the other hand, Wiedemann simultaneously pursues the right to health through using music to facilitate therapeutic emotional work, and social connectivity on which she provided a special perspective. According to her, choosing songs is emotionally therapeutic for the women when the songs resonate with their lives as people who have loved (sexually), of which their children are one result. "Picture," for example, is a sung dialogue between a man and a woman about losing love, but at the end of the song, they get back together. Wiedemann commented:

> It's got enough sadness and people just love it, but it's got the happy ending. That one I think is very socially appropriate because it has a lot to do with a lot of relationships [locally]. It's very real. (interview with Carol Wiedemann, May 24, 2005)

I described earlier how the Downtown Eastside has an atmosphere of social transience when people move, disappear, die, or party for a long time. The socially transient aspect of getting sucked into partying affects people's close relationships if they physically or mentally "aren't there" for others. "Picture" combines the themes of transience, drugs and alcohol, and love relationships. The man sings about living his life "in a slow hell . . . fueling up on cocaine and whisky" while sleeping with different girls in a hotel. The woman sings that she has been waiting for the man "on heartaches and cheap wine." They have put away one another's pictures; they can't stand to look at them when lying with other lovers. Wiedemann noted, "They just love that one. They want to hear that song because someone's bummed out about somebody and they want it all to work out at some point" (interview with Carol Wiedemann, May 24, 2005). It's therapeutic, Wiedemann said, "The music provides a safe container for the women to do emotional work. It offers that safety" (interview with Carol Wiedemann, May 24, 2005).

Wiedemann offered new angles to connecting socially through music, one being that subtle feelings of sharing experience with others, even people who aren't physically present, like a songwriter, can be important to social connectivity:

> You can walk in[to Sheway] and hear a song that hopefully has some relation to your life. It's just like hearing a song on the radio and you think, "Wow." Maybe it gives you a feeling of connection—connection to the other women, connection to somebody. That somebody knows how you feel, or is kind of there with you even though you don't have to talk to them. It creates that bond of someone being there. So I think it really makes it a lot more comfortable for people to sit there and be part of the environment. And sometimes it is really fun too, if people are singing and hanging out. (interview with Carol Wiedemann, May 24, 2005)

A music therapy participant feeling that a lyricist or singer of a popular song "understands" his or her situation, even though he or she probably never knew the songwriter or singer personally, can be important to feeling social connected. The participant resonates with the song on the level of shared humanity, or if the song parallels his or her life.

The women connect with one another implicitly, as well, through unspoken recognitions that they each identify with songs, perceivable, for instance, through the emotion they put into singing or through body language. Nonverbalized senses of commonality, Wiedemann says, can facilitate a comfort level that then allows the mothers to connect socially, actively, and overtly with one another and her. This can happen through singing and verbally, beyond music-making, when hanging out together. Wiedemann, when she discusses with the mothers, encourages them to access Sheway's resources, including prenatal support services; health and nutrition help for pregnant women, nursing mothers, and their babies; addictions treatment or treatment referrals; and other parenting supports like housing assistance.

Such practical help offers the mothers opportunity to strengthen specific human rights identified as typical of harm reduction by public health scholar Nadine Ezard (2001). The medical assistance creates "conditions which would assure to all medical service and medical attention in the event of sickness" (ICESCR, art. 12). Harm reduction also works to minimize harms associated with intravenous drugs, for example, of bloodborne virus transmission, which in turn indexes the human right to "prevention, treatment and control of epidemic and endemic diseases" (ICESCR, art. 11). Support given to a mother with an addiction background and her child strengthens their human rights to an "adequate standard of living, including adequate food, clothing and housing" (ICESCR, art. 11).

Via music and other resources, Sheway offers "assistance to parents and legal guardians in the performance of their child rearing responsibilities" (CRC, art. 18.2). If a mother says to Wiedemann, "Hey, do you know this song?" Wiedemann views the request as an opening to create a relationship that supports harm reduction and her human rights. Wiedemann either plays the song and then starts a dialogue, or goes home and figures out how to perform the song for the next music therapy session. She said:

> Hopefully by the next week I'll "have it," and hopefully that encourages them to come back, if that's an issue for them. Maybe they're not consistently coming. Or if they are coming, it starts a relationship through the music and that's one of my biggest goals, having a relationship built with a lot of the women, so that from that place I can either support them from where they

are or I can help them find the resources they need, even within Sheway. (interview with Carol Wiedemann, May 24, 2005)

Wiedemann feels that the better the relationship she can have with the women, the better she knows how to use music therapeutically with them, in ways addressing their personal medical histories (interview with Carol Wiedemann, May 24, 2005). From the basis of relationship and dialogue, Wiedemann has also been able to introduce the mothers to a nutritionist or other Sheway experts as appropriate.

Relationships between Wiedemann as a music therapist and the mothers have also been built around improvising song lyrics. Wiedemann fosters humor and a sense of fun when co-creating the words. She said:

> We'll start playing a blues song and get people to start putting in words. And then it is really fun because then it is in the moment and it's really applicable to whatever is going on, but then there is a lot of humor and laughter and, yeah, everybody really relates to humor. So, it helps a lot. One day there was a song about going to the doctor—everybody's there to see the doctor and just about making fun of that. You know, it's really fun. (interview with Carol Wiedemann, May 24, 2005)

On another occasion, the women made new lyrics to Tracy Chapman's "Give Me One Reason," which starts with "Give me one reason to stay here/And I'll turn right back around." The new lyrics also centered on accessing Sheway's assistance, for example, free lunches and free clothes. The free lunch lyric was: "Karen makes really good lunch now/So we're all going to have us some." Other lyrics mentioned shopping in the free clothes area at Sheway. Making song lyrics about what Sheway offers is another way to promote the accessing of those resources.

Bringing people together when making music around a common theme helps to alleviate isolation, but because it is "fun," it might also help alleviate, at least for a moment, mentally oppressive experiences of negative stigma of poverty. The capabilities to use music to alleviate isolation and musical fun to reduce negative stigma promotes mental health and the human right to health. Wiedemann sometimes included in music-making Sheway's psychologist, who sang opera and played guitar. Incorporating him into a "fun" activity together with the women might help them to overcome a negative stigma attached to seeing a psychologist especially in the lower and middle classes in Canada.

For those mothers working toward regaining custody, Wiedemann said that their participation at Sheway needs to be about self-change. When singing and making music at Sheway, she finds that the mothers express and work through troubled feelings about parenting. When mothers are on visitation with their babies during a music therapy session, for example, the women may use music to "work on stuff" related to that situation, especially, as Wiedemann said, "about bonding with their children and dealing with the feelings that are coming up about how they feel about being a parent" (interview with Carol Wiedemann, May 24, 2005). She added:

> There is this overwhelming belief sometimes that they have no right to know their children and be a parent to their child because they have addiction problems. And because they are poor. And because they live in the Downtown Eastside. And because they are single. [They feel these pressures from] society and themselves, dealing with their own guilt of using when they were pregnant. A lot of them have to deal with that guilt.
>
> Okay, so you've made mistakes when you're pregnant and then you have the child, and then the ministry says, "Okay, well, we're going to put the child in foster care for a while. And you're going to have to jump through all these hoops to prove that you could possibly, maybe, be a good parent." It's pretty hard to believe that you'd be a good parent. And you have to believe that first before you can convince everybody else. So that's really setting up the walls so high and then telling yourself, "You are going to be able to jump over them." (interview with Carol Wiedemann, May 24, 2005)

Making music is useful for mothers who need to overcome an overwhelming feeling that they are unfit to parent due to substance misuse often in utero as well as being poor, living in the stigmatized Downtown Eastside, and being single. Often through music at Sheway, the mothers work to overcome all four of these mental obstacles and be in a psychological position to be able to convince the authorities that they can parent. The capabilities to express oneself through making music, take in therapeutic guidance regarding parenting during music-making, and then self-reflect are key. As Wiedemann says, "if they have a way of turning some of those feelings around" and feel and think "that things can change," then the mothers have a better chance at taking actions that would help them to regain custody. These are the capabilities developed through music and song which the mothers can use to assert to the ministry that they can enjoy, with their child(ren), the right to an "adequate standard of living, including adequate food, clothing and housing" (ICESCR, art. 11). Through relying on Sheway services, they should be able to secure adequate resources to raise children. In the musical process, special work on connecting with one's feelings is needed for people with addictions. Wiedemann commented:

I know that sometimes when one of the girls is singing, some of the other girls are really watching her and really relating. And it's not even her song, it's some song from the radio, but she chose it, she's putting her feelings into it and then it seems to be safe for other people to express their feelings, or to have feelings even. Because in addiction, you are not always connected to your feelings. So if the music can make you feel something and [experience] a safe container, a safe space for those feelings, that's doing a lot of work. That's really good. (interview with Carol Wiedemann, May 24, 2005)

Wiedemann also argues that self-expression helps the women to overcome psychological barriers relating to the damage or harm caused by their past addictive behaviors, especially when it comes to bringing up their children.

Freedom of expression is described in the legally justiciable International Covenant on Civil and Political Rights: "Everyone shall have the right to freedom of expression; this right shall include freedom to seek, receive and impart information and ideas of all kinds, regardless of frontiers, either orally, in writing or in print, in the form of art, or through any other media of his choice" (art. 19.2). Freedom of expression makes possible the therapeutic parts of music therapy that involve self-expression. The women tell that they feel safe to express themselves at Sheway particularly because it is a female-driven environment. Wiedemann recognizes that marginalization of women in the Downtown Eastside is something that needs to be protected against and actively worked against. In the social dynamic in the Downtown Eastside, especially among homeless and the most vulnerable, she noted, men frequently take over social spaces while the women are left without voice or opportunity for expressive possibilities—the capability to express themselves (email from Carol Wiedemann, October 24, 2016). Women's human right of freedom of expression is blocked. Wiedemann feels happy that the women using Sheway's services have chosen to create for themselves "a really protective, nurturing kind of environment [that] feels really safe. It's like a little oasis." Yet "if it's not, people deal with it right away. It's not even staff, it's the women who protect their space" (interview with Carol Wiedemann, May 24, 2005). This, in turn, evokes another human right, "the right of everyone . . . to security of person," whose appearance in the International Convention on the Elimination of All Forms of Racial Discrimination (art. 5b; OHCHR, 1996–2019e) references violence and bodily harm.

For mothers whose babies are on visitation during music therapy or who bring their children there, freely expressing themselves via making music may also enable bonding with the children in a way that demonstrates loving parenting and the capability for mothering. At Sheway, music therapy also may involve education on and modeling of parenting by the music therapist.

Music therapy at Sheway uses modeling as a safe and effective approach to learning. Wiedemann emphasizes that her making music together with the mothers and their children can model or informally teach ways of relating to one's child that perhaps the mothers never experienced before in their lives. Maybe the mothers were never sung to as children. Wiedemann says that teaching the mothers about singing to their children through modeling this behavior can provoke questions such as "Why would you think it's important to sing to your own child?" and "Why is it important to sing to your baby?" Singing to one's baby can calm the dyad. It can also enable bonding and be a great way for children to play, interact, and learn. Music can give the parents ideas about new ways to interact with their children. Wiedemann also uses music to model how parents can instill positive learning experiences in their children. She acts in an encouraging way about what these children do musically. She commented that the mothers "are really trying to be good parents, but a lot of the time they're single parents and they didn't have a good model to follow, so they're trying to figure out what that means 'to be a good parent'" (interview with Carol Wiedemann, May 24, 2005). Children usually like music. The mothers seeing the children enjoying music can also act as a hook that encourages them to attend music therapy again and learn more. Yet at the same time, Wiedemann does not consider her practice behavioral music therapy, which aims to cue ideal behaviors. The practice, in my view, does aim to prompt desired behavior when using music as a calming effect or using musical interactions between the therapist and child to get the parent and child to behave similarly. Wiedemann countered:

> It doesn't have to be a set course; it doesn't have to be "this is what you have to do." It just happens organically and then it gets past people's blocks about what they need to learn or how they learn for adults, much less what they pass on to their kids. (interview with Carol Wiedemann, May 24, 2005)

Levels of formal education in the Downtown Eastside tend to be low. Thirty-eight percent of residents over age 15 have not finished high school (compared to 17% in Vancouver overall); 38% have a postsecondary certificate, diploma, or degree (compared to 60% in Vancouver overall; City of Vancouver, 2013: 38). Homeless and street-involved people have mental blocks about formal education. They are used to feeling that they are stupid and unable to understand things, since this is a sentiment that people suffering from poverty commonly experience as being expressed to them by more privileged and educated classes everyday (interview with Jim Green, December 8, 2004).

Informal education particularly, such as making music in the communal space at Sheway, is essential for avoiding ingraining social exclusion, which can result from low education and is one of the social deprivations of poverty. Encouraging education supports the human right to education, which is inscribed in the legally justiciable ICESCR (art. 13.1) and the United Nations' legally justiciable Convention on the Elimination of All Forms of Discrimination against Women (art. 10).

Music-making involves learning something new about musical sound and its meanings as well. It involves developing capabilities of musical performance. Although the women tend to sing only, with the music therapist playing guitar and singing, the therapist encourages them to play guitar. Often when she takes a break, she will leave her guitar in the organization's common space. Sometimes, she says, "someone who is maybe too shy to say that they would love to play guitar will see it just sitting there and then they'll just pick it up and they'll play it. Lots of times when I know someone might want to play it, I'll just leave it there and walk away" (interview with Carol Wiedemann, May 24, 2005). The guitar has never been stolen.

Music learning sometimes happens through humor and fun involving the children. On one occasion, I noticed a little boy singing while playing with a toy farm. As the toddler intoned "Old MacDonald Had a Farm," I accompanied him on violin. Then, through playing another tune, I attempted to evoke musical genres associated with farms and rural communities. I fiddled the bluegrass tune "Bile Them Cabbage Down," also known as "Boil Them Cabbage Down" and "Bake Them Hoecakes Brown." This simple song, sometimes characterized as a traditional old-time piece or an American breakdown, is particularly reminiscent of rural life in Oklahoma, Arkansas, southwestern Pennsylvania, and northeast Alabama. Like "Old MacDonald Had a Farm," listeners stereotypically associate "Bile Them Cabbage Down" with rural communities. My playing with the idea of a stereotype became a joke that I shared with surrounding adults.

Music therapy often involves education. The role of education in music therapy was theorized, for instance, by Herbert Bruhn (2000), who maps the relationship between music education and music therapy according to musical function. He discusses didactic and psychoprophylactic music therapy techniques that integrate music education, in contrast to some clinical music therapy approaches that do not integrate music education in any way (see Robertson, 2000). At certain times in the music therapy practice, what Bruhn calls the educational share of music therapy outweighs the therapeutic share. For musically gifted children over the years, Wiedemann has worked with clients to develop applications to the Sarah McLachlan Foundation, which provides funds for older children to take music lessons. The therapist also arranged for children to take music lessons at Saint James Music Academy, which offers free music lessons to children living in the low-income neighborhood of the Downtown Eastside. She teaches toddlers visiting her practice something about singing songs. Wiedemann notices the rapidity with which toddlers learn in her practice, which is "very hands-on—they know they can come up and play the guitar; we can play songs; we can interact."

In conclusion, framing musical activities as harm reduction is in many ways a human rights frame because interrelated media, activist, and academic discourses justify harm reduction in terms of promoting human rights. Facilitators of jams and music therapy using popular music in Vancouver's Downtown Eastside often call their practices harm reduction when the organizations in which they work have harm reduction in their service philosophies, and even when they don't. With harm reduction's raison d'être being the right to health, music facilitators discussed with me how they saw harm reduction they undertook through music as promoting the health of urban poor. They developed, in participants, the capabilities to use music to release emotions, experience self-esteem and connect socially. Shifting emotional states and enhancing self-esteem through music could minimize certain negative effects of substance misuse (e.g., stigma); connecting socially can offer social support for coping with addictions contexts. Thus, the capabilities can support health and the right to health. The facilitators suggested that music-making helped to alleviate depression and prevent suicides of severely depressed people. If so, (the capability of) using music in this way supported the participants' health, well-being and human right to health. Although some participants were high or drunk while making music, which research finds to enhance drugs' emotional effects, facilitators did not describe this contradiction as undermining any healthy effect of music. Over the past two decades, they have increasingly adopted harm reduction as a collective social action frame within the context of the harm reduction movement in Canada.

In musical moments facilitated using a harm reduction approach, I observed and framed multiple human rights including and beyond the human right to health. I illustrated this through my ethnographic case study at Sheway, a nonprofit where a music therapist assists Indigenous mothers with backgrounds of substance misuse to regain custody of their children who live in foster care. If successful, regaining custody reduces psychological harm to the mothers of losing their babies, thereby strengthening their mental health and arguably their right to health. Toward regaining custody, the mothers must demonstrate suitable parenting skills, sobriety, and access of Sheway's social support services—all documented by Sheway staff for the appropriate government authority. Although the mothers clearly face limits to their autonomy in this situation, Sheway furthers the human right of provision of assistance to parents regarding performance of childrearing. The music therapist, after creating relationships with the mothers via making music with them, encourages them to access Sheway's support services. The nonprofit's medical services promote the human right to access of medical service and attention in case of illness; addiction treatment opportunities promote the right to prevention, treatment, and control of diseases, such as those spread through sharing drug paraphernalia; and other services address the mothers' and children's rights to food, clothing, and housing, for instance. The music therapist describes her practice as having a range of therapeutic benefits to the mothers made possible by exercising their capabilities to express themselves through music and therefore their right to freedom of expression. She also promotes the mothers' right to education through undertaking informal education that uses musical behavior to model healthy parenting. For their part, the mothers themselves create a social space for music therapy that feels safe, which enacts their right to security of the person. The music therapist also takes simultaneous approaches to supporting the right to health: she encourages the mothers to choose songs to play themselves, slightly increasing their autonomy, and nurtures the mothers in connecting socially amongst themselves through music. This ethnographic example demonstrated that multiple human rights can circulate among participants in single musical moments, as can different musical approaches to one human right.

The musical moments and activities related to them, connected with multiple human rights, support many kinds of capabilities, at Sheway: acting autonomously, connecting and forming relationships with other people, and connecting with one's own feelings. They supported the capabilities of self-expression when doing internal therapeutic work, and of creating a safe place. For the mothers, they also modelled capabilities of parenting. These capabilities respectively supported the human right to health; the human rights of "adequate standard of living, including adequate food, clothing and housing" (ICESCR, art. 11), freedom of expression, and security of the person; and, for the mothers, the right to education.

6

WOMEN'S RIGHTS

THROUGH CASE STUDIES of two projects promoting human rights of women through popular music-making, this chapter asks: what is the relationship between the human rights deficit contexts that activist music initiatives emerge in and react to, and the human rights promoted through planned musical actions? The case studies are the women-centered projects of a once-weekly music program called Women Rock and an annual protest called the Women's Memorial March. My ethnographic accounts suggest that one needs to be careful in assuming that the human rights actually promoted within formally organized cultural practices are precisely the same rights as those drawn attention to in activist discourses or observations used to motivate those actions, and with the same intensity, for the same reasons or for the same people. Any of these factors may be different and change over time.

The Women Rock project is a once-weekly class that started in 2014, in which women learn to perform popular music, thus developing their musical capabilities. Former flute professor Laura Barron and singer-songwriter Leah Abramson initiated Women Rock within the Vancouver-based not-for-profit corporation Instruments of Change, directed by Barron. The program responds to what they understood as discrimination against various rights of women in the Downtown Eastside.

Music Downtown Eastside. Klisala Harrison, Oxford University Press (2020). © Oxford University Press.
DOI: 10.1093/oso/9780197535066.001.0001.

The two initiators based Women Rock on their volunteer experiences at music camps with "girls" and "rock" in their names—Barron at the Rock 'n' Roll Camp for Girls in Portland, Oregon, and Abramson at Girls Rock Camp Vancouver. These programs teach girls how to play popular music instruments in bands with a view to developing girls' self-esteem and positive senses of self in the face of sexism. The Rock 'n' Roll Camp for Girls, for instance, uses music to "promote respect and do[es] not tolerate racism, sexism, homophobia, or other discriminatory behavior or expression" (Rock 'n' Roll Camp for Girls, 2012). Women Rock was piloted in the Greater Vancouver area in a multi-level-security jail and in a transition home (Instruments of Change, 2012a, 2012b). About these pilots, Barron commented, "I felt such tremendous appreciation from the people I worked with, and a real sense that they weren't always accustomed to being valued. Bringing dignity to people who don't take basic rights for granted—that is a privilege, and a really powerful thing" (interview with Laura Barron, October 21, 2016). After raising funds to host women's songwriting programs in Vancouver-area prisons, Barron, together with board members of Instruments of Change, has been successful in fundraising for the nonprofit. The organization, therefore, can hire teachers at professional artist rates and pay other costs of the Women's Rock program in the Downtown Eastside, including providing weekly lunches for participants (Photo 6.1). The

PHOTO 6.1. Women Rock teaches musical skills—here reading music—and provides lunch to participants.
Photo by author, 2016.

Carnegie Community Centre (funded by the City of Vancouver) gives Women Rock a space without charge as well as musical instruments and equipment.

Many women in the Downtown Eastside feel particularly excited about Women Rock because, compared to men, they have experienced a lack of opportunity to perform music and to learn how to perform music. In preliminary research before setting up Women Rock, Barron said she "heard infinite stories from women in this neighborhood about feeling marginalized and feeling at open mic nights and other music programs [that] those were male-dominated, non-safe spaces for them, and that it was very important for them to be able to develop [musical] skills and expression, [and] to have a women-only space" (interview with Laura Barron, October 21, 2016). For her, this paralleled needs met by Portland's Rock 'n' Roll Camp for Girls program "for girls who probably didn't fit into their school environments—who didn't have a traditional way of expressing themselves in the world. However, suddenly, when they were amongst their peers, all kinds of alternative girls finally found a safe place to be themselves" (interview with Laura Barron, October 21, 2016). In her informal research in the Downtown Eastside, Barron heard the "same kinds of stories." Women told her about instances when they approached an open mic night and "literally, a man grabbed the mic from her." Others relayed tales of being "asked to leave or just not offered a chance to have their moments at the mic." She also said that many women spoke of "feeling invisible or ignored. Some women even felt that their songs had been stolen at times" (interview with Laura Barron, October 21, 2016). In addition to these reports, local women talked to me about sonic harassment during some music jams. Women expressed discomfort with singing and playing instruments together with men playing amplified instruments, whom they experienced as sometimes turning up their amps so loud that the women were drowned out (see interview with Nancy, October 19, 2016).

These Downtown Eastside women felt that they were not given enough chance to perform compared to men, which challenged their human right of freedom of expression. This also could be interpreted as compromising their right to "the freedom indispensable for . . . creative activity" (art. 15.3) outlined in the International Covenant on Economic, Social and Cultural Rights (ICESCR), which is legally binding, including on gender equity. The ICESCR states that the "States Parties to the present Covenant undertake to ensure the equal right of men and women to the enjoyment of all economic, social and cultural rights set forth in the present Covenant" (art. 3). Laura Barron summed up that facilitating basic rights was "pretty much" what's moved all the work that she does with Instruments of Change (interview with Laura Barron, October 21, 2016).

The discrimination expressed by Downtown Eastside women emerges from a specific local history. This includes the intensity of musical engagement being lower for women than men in the mixed-gender jams and music therapy I observed. Almost all of their male participants played an instrument and sang, or attempted this, over the past several decades and more. In the early and mid-2000s, I found that most women did not play a musical instrument, although they frequently sang—except at The 44/Evelyne Saller Centre, which had more female participation. The pattern remained consistent in the early 2010s but had shifted by the mid-2010s toward slightly more women playing an instrument while singing. For example, in autumn 2016, one woman performed at an open mic night at the Carnegie Community Centre while at The 44 about two of five music-makers were female. However, no women played a musical instrument at an open mic session at a local church; men played five acoustic guitars, sometimes together with one acoustic bass guitar, two djembes, a harmonica, a shaker, and other percussion. After most audience members had left for a free lunch served at the church, one woman started to sing. The female singer, who had no audience other than a black Labrador-cross dog wandering into the room, myself, and my mother, was accompanied by only two men, one on guitar and one on djembe, compared to the 10 and more instrumentalists heard together with the earlier, male singers. Today, the tendency of excluding women from music-making still exists in contexts that do not actively seek to address it.

Women Rock's lead facilitator, Geetha Subramaniyam, commented that "every woman who comes into Women Rock, they're like 'Oh, no men?' and it's not that they hate men, it's just that they have had so many experiences where they've been shoved out and elbowed and kind of put second, put down because the men are playing" (interview, October 26, 2016). She commented that the sexism was so bad that she as lead facilitator "had a lot of men coming into the [teaching] room trying to tell me how to do my job. . . . Usually it's like, 'Oh hey, do you know what you're doing there, girlie?'—that sort of attitude—and so I go, 'Yes, I do know what I'm doing. Can I please ask you to leave now because I have a class to teach?'" (interview with Geetha Subramaniyam, October 26, 2016). In the Downtown Eastside, seeing a group of women playing instruments is so unusual that a bunch of men and women will stand, staring, mouths literally gaping, outside the glass doors of the teaching room at the Carnegie Community Centre. Some men, Subramaniyam says, seem to "feel that they're more entitled to the instruments than the women" and may interrupt the group in a way that is best to deal with together with the Carnegie's security staff. To assuage distractions, it is possible to draw a curtain across the door. Carnegie regulars, though, have become more and more supportive of Women Rock; the Carnegie's arts and education programmer, Rika Uto, expresses intense support by arranging the cost-free space for the program.

The challenges and discrimination expressed by local women suggest that they have not experienced, as much as men, "the right freely to participate in the cultural life of the community, to enjoy the arts," cited in the Universal Declaration of Human Rights (UDHR, art. 27.1) and the right to "participate in all community activities" cited in the United Nations Convention on the Elimination of All Forms of Discrimination against Women (CEDAW, art. 14.2(f); OHCHR, 1996–2019a). The latter requires state parties like Canada to "take in all fields, in particular in the political, social, economic and cultural fields, all appropriate measures, including legislation, to ensure the full development and advancement of women, for the purpose of guaranteeing them the exercise and enjoyment of human rights and fundamental freedoms on a basis of equality with men" (art. 3).

Why women in the Downtown Eastside feel that they need a safe space to make and learn music, and why Women Rock uses only female teachers and is a women-only program, has its specific history in the Downtown Eastside too. In addition to feeling sonically repelled by male performers turning amplifiers up to very high levels, women in their childbearing years, particularly, experience widespread sexual harassment. In and through the popular music events not detailed in this book, sometimes one male participant or a few males would sexually target a female participant. If women experience harassment when trying to make popular music, will they willingly put themselves in the same situation again? When I sent this text for a community ethics review at the Carnegie Community Centre, one commentator gave a markedly disagreeing view when suggesting that most local women respond passively to sexual harassment. The reviewer asked if it is a mark of privilege to name sexual harassment and rally against it, as many local women do neither.

The sexual harassment can be mild or intensive. It is usually mental or emotional but can aim toward being physical. I will use examples from my own experience so as not to humiliate other women. On one occasion, a musician ordered me to pick up my violin's shoulder rest (which he was borrowing) from in between his legs, which I described in a fieldnote:

Danny is always asking to use my violin and I always say no. As I played, he came and sat beside me. He kept begging, like a little kid. He has no teeth and sparkling eyes. A hand-rolled cigarette dangled from his mouth. I gave in. He played a scratchy version of "Rubber Dollie," mostly double stops. My violin shoulder rest fell off my violin and into Danny's crotch because he had positioned the instrument on his chest. He told me to get the shoulder rest. Then he wanted me to take my fiddle back. (fieldnote, August 13, 2004)

A more intensive example of sexual and mental harassment happened when one popular musician wrote sexualized poetry about me, using my distinctive first name, slightly misspelled but still recognizable, in an issue of the *Carnegie Newsletter*, disseminated in hard copy for free and on the Internet. I made an unsuccessful request to the male editor asking him to stop publishing the poetry; similar poetry about me appeared in the next newsletter. Local artist and activist Diane Wood stepped in and prevented any publication of similar poetry in the newsletter in the future. She immediately succeeded in getting the online love poems about me removed from the Internet. Still, the increasing advances of this young man also during popular music-making caused me to feel so uncomfortable that I rarely attended popular music-making when I knew he would be there. I approached two music therapists about the harassment. They responded that I did not have a right to criticize locals for anything since I was a researcher, and that the harasser was not dangerous.

Another possible example of harassment pertinent to all women accessing one music therapy practice could be interpreted in a pornographic drawing. A music therapist had fixed the drawing on the wall of his health center office, next to a black electric guitar. A regular male participant in music therapy had made the colorful picture. It showed a woman with long, black, flowing hair and one breast exposed. She wore a garter belt on each leg and a green halter-top, but no underwear. She crouched—a passive expression on her face, eyes closed—with her legs open, showing her genitals. Her exposed breast and vaginal and clitoral areas were highlighted in silver ink. The silver female genitals were the main visual focus. I wondered whether flowing lines depicted the genital area as having been gauged or sliced open. Text around the drawing read: "PICK UP AN AXE [slang for electric guitar]—BECOME A MAN MY SON! LEARN TO PLAY GUITAR . . ." (underline and caps. in original). Participants in music therapy could see the drawing as the therapist's nearby office door stayed open during music-making. If any drawing could be sexually threatening to women wanting to play guitar, this was it. Music therapy, as said, often includes music education and it did in this practice.

Female musicians in the Downtown Eastside largely not being exposed to as many opportunities as men to learn to play and perform popular music challenged another "basic right" (interview with Laura Barron, October 21, 2016): their right to education. The CEDAW directs "States Parties [to] take all appropriate measures to eliminate discrimination against women in order to ensure to them equal rights with men in the field of education and in particular to ensure, on a basis of equality of men and women . . . access to studies," such as in "technical" education and "all types of vocational training" (art. 10; OHCHR, 1996–2019a), of which music-making is one example.

Women Rock therefore engages professional musicians to teach music performance knowledge to local women. The participants develop and exercise their capabilities for learning. This expands upon rare music lessons specifically for women locally. One of the Women Rock meetings I attended included a group music lesson: a singing warm-up that focused on tone-matching while singing slowly up and down a major scale and while exploring resonance in the head, throat, and chest; a workshop on the basics of guitar tablature, including how this corresponds to practically playing a guitar including a riff from "Ghostbusters," the *Ghostbusters* movie theme song by Ray Parker Jr.; setting up an audio system with microphones and speakers; and then practicing and cycling through singing "Ghostbusters" while taking turns playing the guitar part to a drum-set accompaniment by one participant. During the rehearsal, Subramaniyam taught the women how to "count in" to the chorus's phrase "I ain't afraid of no ghost." She coached the drum kit accompaniment. Subramaniyam together with a second instructor, Chloé Ziner, coached the guitar performance as well as vocal pitch-matching in the group. Another session, taught by Barron and Subramaniyam, involved a lesson in beginner music theory, then beginner piano chording through learning a new song. In the theory lesson, the women learned definitions and sounds of the terms scale, major, minor, solfège (sonically simplified in that syllables were not modified in natural minor), flat, sharp, natural, chromatic, melody, harmony, tonic, and dominant. The women learned a major scale from C to C. They were also taught the major-scale notes that make up a major chord (1, 3, and 5). Next, Barron demonstrated a piano accompaniment to "Lean on Me" by Bill Withers using chording. The women practiced the major chord sequence, sitting side by side so that they could each play in a different octave with one hand while singing the song's melody (Photo 6.2). Next, the group practiced performing Elvis Presley's "Love Me Tender." Subramaniyam staged the performance so that one participant would walk on stage whistling the beginning of the song. Then the group sang two of the song's four verses, the second louder than the first. The group hummed the song a third time to "ooooo."

In a group interview, the women expressed gratitude for being able to learn music and performance, and described why learning music was important for them. I will share some of their statements before putting these in dialogue with

PHOTO 6.2. Women Rock participants learn piano basics. The mural behind the women was painted by Richard Tetrault and commissioned by Vancouver Moving Theatre. The mural foregrounds, lower left, Indigenous guitarist Ricky Lavallee who often played in Downtown Eastside popular music sessions, and lower right, an Indigenous female drummer from the Women's Memorial March. The other artists worked in presentational music events in the neighborhood as it gentrified into an arts district, explained later.
Photo by author, 2016.

the inequities and rights deficits that initially motivated the Women Rock program. One Indigenous participant, Taninli, said:

I didn't learn music before this. I always wanted to, believe me I always wanted to. I didn't have enough money, my mom never ever did have enough money, and society told me that I wasn't good enough, and I believed it. I believed it because they said that I was never going to amount to much in life. I was going to end up barefoot and pregnant with a dozen kids, and you're going to end up nothing but an alcoholic and living in the streets. And I believed it. But I timidly walked through these doors, scared shitless, excuse my lingo. It changed my life. If you [had] ever seen me, two-three years ago, I couldn't look at you in the eye. Meeting so many friends here, it's amazing. I just can't say enough about it and learning more and more about myself every day, and learning [music] until I can be comfortable in my own skin, rather than what people told me. [They] treated me like a dog, like I was nothing but a speck of dirt to sweep in the corner and be forgotten about. So I have you people to thank, for being a part of my life and making that change, and accepting me for who I am, and that's a proud [Indigenous] Indian woman. I belong here. I wished the program had been offered at the residential schools so my people would not have had to go through years of torment. (interview, October 25, 2016)

Learning to perform music, in addition to offering an educational possibility, boosted self-esteem here too. It helped one woman to overcome psychological barriers of being socially and economically underprivileged, and of having grown up with structural discrimination. She particularly referenced residential schools, to which Indigenous Canadian children were forcibly removed from their families from 1831 to 1996. The schools are infamous for abuses and for enforcing cultural assimilation through forbidding children to practice their Indigenous cultures, including musics and languages (Haig-Brown, 1988; Milloy, 1999). Another Indigenous woman, Theresa, added:

I came here because I wanted to learn more about music and to sing with other people and to learn how to read and write music because in school, when I went to elementary, they didn't really help me and it was a similar thing where the teachers in school just made you feel you were wrong and didn't help me to understand it. Instead they just "let it fall by wayside." Since kindergarten I wanted to do this and I thought of Elvis Presley who was a musical genius who never even learned how to read and write music, but he was one of the best singers in the world and he was part Native Cherokee [6.25% according to online Elvis fan clubs]. And Native [Indigenous] people have such beautiful music and traditional music. I wanted to learn to sing the Coast Salish [Indigenous] anthem and I sing along with the radio. [Singing] is such a huge part of Native people's lives. . . . Yeah, so I'm glad that I came here. I've only been here twice, but Geetha Subramaniyam has really tremendously helped and I'm very thankful. She explains it very well and is very friendly and open and other people have been. So that's why I returned even though before I wouldn't sing very loud, but now I'm saying to people, "You've got to sing louder! We're being overpowered by the instruments and our human voices should be equal!" (interview, October 25, 2016)

The women expressed their self-esteem musically through projecting self-confidence—one said that women's singing voices should be at least as loud as instruments in popular music performances. In performances, the women some-times dress up in colorful outfits (one wearing a feather boa) and self-confidently make jokes. They show off and share musical skills (capabilities) that they have learned in Women Rock after experiencing capability poverty as girls when it came to learning and knowing musical skills. The women building self-esteem through music contributes to their mental wellness and arguably strengthens their human right to health.

A new Canadian from China, Anita, commented that she felt grateful that Women Rock gave her a chance to learn some music theory and play a musical instrument:

Before I didn't know any music theory. Then I know here I can learn how to play the instrument. I'm so excited so I can join. And I thank you all the in-structor here Laura[1] and Geetha and some teacher here. I feel well happy and I get very well relationship with all of our members and I like all of you. So I want to continue. (interview, October 25, 2016)

Another participant of Chinese heritage who did not feel comfortable speaking much English nodded enthusiastically, adding, "I like music, but I don't know music. I come here and I learn about this." An Anglo-Canadian participant, Heather, expressed appreciation at being able to learn to play a musical instru-ment, for example, guitar, which she had not had the opportunity to learn before:

I've always loved music ever since I was a little girl. I remember when I was in kindergarten and I did three song solos onstage. So I could sing already when I was 5 and I was in a . . . choir when I was 10 years old. I took piano lessons from age 11 up to age 18. I had this hope that I could become a con-cert pianist, but my teacher dashed my hopes. She kind of said you're not really that good or whatever. I was very disappointed. I switched teachers. I've been in amateur choirs or church choirs a few times . . . but when I came

---

[1] Use of first names in the interviews is reiterated here. The Women Rock participants asked to be called by their first names in this book, with one exception.

here I was very excited because I love electric guitars. I always wanted to play one and I got an opportunity here and I want to continue to learn. I'd love to try drums although it's very complicated. . . . Here I feel very encouraged and very comfortable [to learn]. It's not stressful. Learning classical music, I always had to learn my two songs every week and practice them really hard and my teacher would always be really disappointed in how I did. But here it's like whatever I do is okay. (interview, October 25, 2016)

Another Anglo-Canadian musician who came from a low-income background, Angela, started to learn guitar performance in her 40s. However, she experienced poor training in technique, developing carpal tunnel syndrome. Women Rock was a place where she could explore new guitar techniques that didn't harm her. She enjoyed taking piano lessons and improving her singing in Women Rock before her untimely death in 2019:

I'm Angela and what a long strange trip it's been. . . . I was wanting to do music when I was seven. My mother had worked as a domestic for billionaires and I was excluded from doing music. I got to watch the other kids take piano and learn music, but I had to stay in the kitchen and they wouldn't let me participate. So that was my first exposure and I didn't really understand what classism was or I didn't really have an analysis at that time. I just knew that really it was really painful; it really hurt. So, my music career was stunted and I didn't get the opportunity. When I was in my 40s, I [decided] to learn music because I'd been held back for so long, that I took up guitar. I started guitar lesson[s] with a classically trained professional and nobody instructed me on the proper guitar to buy, so I ended up starting with this really huge guitar. I was so overzealous to make up for lost time that I was practicing every night for like two hours and I was holding a guitar that was not the right guitar for me. So what happened was over a three-year period I developed carpal tunnel. I was so excited and not given proper instruction with body dynamics. What's been really inspiring about coming to Women Rock is I'm actually now learning alternative ways to even make a few little sounds with my hands. One thing that I was exploring with guitar is playing it lying flat on my lap because it doesn't hurt my fingers that way, but it's actually meaning you're learning guitar in a whole new way. If I hadn't participated here in Women Rock I wouldn't have thought about that. I'm also doing a little bit of piano training with Geetha once a month so that's exciting, but here in Women Rock I mainly want to focus on becoming a more polished singer. (interview, October 25, 2016)

A common history told by four of the seven women I interviewed was that they came from socioeconomically depressed backgrounds (see also interview with Connie, October 19, 2016). Two of the six women were Indigenous and had struggled with learning or had been unable to learn music performance in residential school. The threats to and obliteration of the women's human right to education, including capability development in and through music, started early in their life courses.

All of the women participating in Women Rock agreed that music education was important for them today. Women interested in the Women Rock program before it started had expressed a need "to be able to develop [musical] skills and expression, [and] to have a women-only space" (interview with Laura Barron, October 21, 2016) due to local histories of gender discrimination, which Barron framed as transgressing various human rights. When I interviewed the female participants about Women Rock sessions, they also highlighted problems with achieving music education as children due to feeling put down in their childhood homes, at grade schools, or in classical musical lessons; structural discrimination experienced in society as poor or Indigenous people; and their childhood families not having enough money for them to take music lessons.

Reasons given by participants in Women Rock for why music education was important to them spoke to the program doing deeper work than perhaps initially expected, through addressing long histories of marginalization. Taken together, the stories collected by Laura Barron, Geetha Subramaniyam's observations, and the testimonials the women shared during Women Rock spoke to an almost life-long timeline of age-, class-, ethnicity-, and gender-related discrimination against such women by authority figures of children like parents and teachers, by people of more affluent classes, and by men. Laura Barron commented on this book text, "I always understood that marginalization in adulthood [is] an extension of marginalization experienced throughout [our] lives"; discrimination against the women was "one motivation for initiating our program . . . corroborating explanations of a parallel marginalization that has echoed throughout their lives" (email from Laura Barron, September 5, 2019).

Local women tend to talk about sexual harassment as a fact of everyday life, which wasn't an issue that they felt important to represent in their life stories. For the facilitators, sexual harassment was as important a subject of discussion as capability development. Urban poor participants presented Women Rock as being more about capability development for them. This may serve as an example of different actors in a human rights intervention emphasizing different reasons for the intervention.

Barron and I conversed in the final stages of preparing this book about how her program's outcome of reducing gender discrimination, which she highlighted in a 2016 interview with me, did not adequately represent how Women Rock came to address societal injustices beyond sexism, especially classism and racism. These, she argued, drew in a wide array of human rights and capabilities deprivations, and constituted important motivations for her work by 2019. She felt that the program's addressing intersecting discriminations across gender, class and race broadened its initially intended rights impacts through addressing marginalization as a blanket concept, while my analysis attended most to the program's initial focus on women's rights and the marginalization of women, as advertised on the Instrument of Change website:

Women Rock! This empowering music program provides a safe and inclusive, women-only space where participants learn to play rock instruments, form bands, manage gear and write songs. Consequently, they build their confidence, creativity, collaboration and communication skills. (Instruments of Change, 2012a)

The title of the program and brief Internet description highlight women, not intersecting oppressions, as a motivation for capability development. I wondered—in general about any musical interventions on human rights—about the interplay between self-representation, public representation, other communication, interpretation, and revisionism of human rights goals, and to what extent reasons given for promoting human rights before a cultural intervention may amplify, complement, or contrast those reasons articulated as important from the intervention's start to finish, over time, by different people who engage it (emails between Laura Barron and Klisala Harrison, September 5, October 13, 2019).

Analysis of reasons for human rights promotion, over the course of interventions, can identify additional depths and layers of need. One can learn from the women's stories that the intersection of music with classism, racism, and sexism is a structural problem that hits children particularly hard who today are adults living in poverty, creating in them a desire for adult music education. In the Downtown Eastside, Saint James Music Academy also responds to this. Since 2007, it has offered free music education to children (today, 170 children). The academy started due to drastic cuts to music education in public schools, then families living in poverty not being able to afford after-school music lessons for their children. Until Women Rock started, though, not much attention was given locally to adult women who had suffered structural discrimination growing up and continued to experience marginalization in the urban poverty context for example, of popular music-making.

In Women Rock, a safe space to learn is encouraged by teaching strategies that are always encouraging and never negative. Group teaching involves helping the women individually, yet not shutting anyone in the group out. In other words, the teachers work against marginalization at a micro-level. The women participating, even if they maybe haven't finished high school or don't speak English very well yet, seem to always be able to access and replicate something from the little building blocks of information that the teachers have discussed and demonstrated from different perspectives. Geetha Subramaniyam, who has a bachelor's degree in behavioral neuroscience and has researched learning, acquisition, and retention, spoke to me about her teaching philosophy. The women expressed that they had experienced psychological suffering of marginalization that impeded their progress—and Subramaniyam worked with this productively, as she might any other kind of learning block:

> I'm really interested in removing barriers, so when I tutor I always try and see what's the blockage and take that away rather than trying to push the person through. Because I always believe there's more than one way to do anything. So the same with music too. You don't have to sit with your Royal [Conservatory of Music] book and learn the theory or anything right away. On the first day of Women Rock [each semester], Laura sets out what she calls an "instrument petting zoo." That's a really cool [concept] because you just go there, you don't have to know anything about [music], but you still get to absorb a little bit and then you get interest[ed] and then you [can] get over the hump of whatever obstacle in learning that you have. (interview with Geetha Subramaniyam, October 26, 2016)

Subramaniyam's approach has had impressive results musically, on which she commented, "I find that a lot of the women, I teach them three chords [and then] they go learn another six on their own, and just fiddle around—because I told them, 'There's no such thing as a mistake in music, and if you find something that sounds like a mistake, then you can just play it differently next time'" (interview with Geetha Subramaniyam, October 26, 2016).

Through such teaching approaches, Women Rock successfully fosters various human rights one can identify in deficit in most local popular music jams and music therapy programs, Sheway's music therapy for mothers excluded. Women specifically are given a chance to make music together and therefore to freely express themselves. Supporting their freedom of expression is complemented by a strengthening of their "freedom indispensable for . . . creative activity" (ICESCR, art. 15.3), which women do not experience if they are to some extent excluded from music jams and therapy sessions. The program, by offering a space for women to make popular music, promotes the women's right to "participate in the cultural life of the community, to enjoy the arts" (UDHR, art. 27.1); advances the women's right to development and advancement in a cultural field (CEDAW, art. 3); and takes a step "to eliminate discrimination against women in order to ensure to them equal rights with men in the field of education" in a local context (CEDAW, art. 3). Subramaniyam said that Women Rock was particularly having a gender equality–promoting impact in the community, slowly. Participants, she said, are starting to have the confidence to "learn a bunch of songs so then [they] can go to open mic and read the chords, read the charts and at least go if somebody tells you, 'Hey do you know what you're doing,' [they'd] be like, 'Yes, I do know what I'm doing'" (interview with Geetha Subramaniyam, October 26, 2016).

When one compares the human rights deficits identified before the Women Rock project, in the Downtown Eastside generally, with what has happened in the music workshops, Women Rock meaningfully supports certain capabilities and rights in more depth than the other local programs accessed predominantly by men. For instance, Women Rock has done more collective songwriting with the women than any other local music program. This has developed the women's capabilities to create new songs. Led by professional songwriter and project co-initiator Leah Abrahamson or another teacher, the songwriting arguably promotes, in a deeper way compared to singing covers of songs, the right to freedom indispensable for creative activity as well as freedom of expression. The women start songwriting by brainstorming topics, ideas, metaphors, descriptive language, lines, and rhymes. Then the teacher will play chords and ask the women what kind of musical scoring they want. Figure 6.1 shows, for instance, the music of "Dreaming of My Future Home" written by Women Rock participants in 2016. It is up to the women to say if they want the song to be faster or slower, as well as what they intend the song's mood and genre to be. The first song that the women wrote, "Firekeeper," is about women's empowerment. Each woman contributed two lines of lyrics. When the group learned how to sing the blues, a participant who had emigrated from China told the group that when she was six or seven years old, government officials seized her family's furniture, including the piano. The group wrote a blues song, "Back at It Again" that mentioned her piano being taken away. The words of the chorus are:

What do you want? / I want to play my piano
What do you want? / I want to play my piano

Why? / Why? / Because I like the / Music

When I was six years old / My piano was taken

Now I have the chance to learn back, take back, play back / At Women Rock!

Lyrics of another song, "I Found Me," speak to a sense of hope and positivity at being able to survive difficult experiences (Figure 6.2).

The songwriting process also develops the capability to create artistic products, which has the potential to strengthen human rights having to do with gainful employment, for example, a person's right to "the opportunity to gain his living by work which he freely chooses or accepts" that is aided by "technical and vocational

"Dreaming of my Future Home"

by Women Rock participants with Geetha Subramaniyam

FIGURE 6.1. Women Rock participants undertake guided songwriting, which promotes various human rights.

"I Found Me"
collaboratively written by the participants in Women Rock

The butterfly wings spread wide.
Hold my head high, fighting to survive.
Searching for a hero to fill the void.

CHORUS
Over the sea, to the mountain tops.
At the end of the earth, I found me.
The only place I could be.

Not sure what my life has ahead,
But I feel the faith inside of me.
I believe I can overcome it all.

CHORUS

Walking on the beach, enjoy the light.
It makes me happy. I like the beach.
I want to dance. I feel like jumping.

CHORUS

I was walking around feeling lost.
Bright new clothes, too much cost.
Garbage at the bus stop, food on the road.

CHORUS

Trudging down the road, I see the past.
moving right along, I stumble and I fall.
I pick myself up and shed a single tear.

Slowly I step toward the unknown.
With a lightened heart, I see the golden sun.
Finding my strength, I can go on.

CHORUS

FIGURE 6.2. Participants in Women Rock collaboratively writing, and publicly performing, songs such as "I Found Me" ultimately strengthens the role of women in the local popular music scene.

guidance and training programmes . . . and techniques to achieve steady . . . cultural development" (ICESCR, art. 6). Such songwriting, by women only, can also be interpreted as resistant to the gender dynamics of "hit" songs of classic rock, pop, and country so frequently performed in the jams and music therapy sessions elsewhere in the neighborhood. In a survey of popular songs performed at The 44/ Evelyne Saller Centre in 2004, for instance, represented by Table 6.1, one sees a predominance of male recording artists (for additional surveys, see Harrison, 2008).

Only 8 artists or bands out of 49 are all-female; one band has mixed male and female members. Four songs were cowritten by a man and woman and two songs were written by a woman (see Table 6.1's footnotes), yet 42 were written by men, while "House of the Rising Sun" is of uncertain authorship (not noted in the table for sake of space). Performing such a male repertoire emphasizes men's freedom of expression, freedom indispensable for creative activity and employment-related human rights. Songwriting at Women Rock developed these human rights for women.

As a result of musical training (Photos 6.3), including prominently songwriting workshops, the women have become sought-after performers in the neighborhood, for example, at music events of the University of British Columbia's (UBC) Learning Exchange program and the Downtown Eastside's annual Heart of the City Festival. The women performing their own songs give their shows a unique edge. Barron commented that

> they feel really flattered and excited by [the invitations]. They've all really faced performance anxiety demons. [Performance] has been a big by-product of the work and now they're looking for performance opportunities. (interview, October 21, 2016)

The women became increasingly interested in performing music and began to think that arts professionalization could be possible for them.

Women Rock has increasingly pursued this direction of enhancing the women's capabilities to create their own performance artworks and to perform publicly over the years. By 2017, Women Rock also offered individual lessons to women on keyboard, bass, guitar, and drums. A wrap-up concert included powerful solos, especially on drum kit. Barron commented that an increased focus on artistic performance has had to do with the women being capable of performance, on the one hand, and her believing that performing could bring the women additional benefits, on the other:

> At first we never made performance a requirement of the program. We really always just addressed each individual and their need or interest in doing [music]. Invariably, even the ones that said, "No, no, no, no—I just want to do this for fun. I'm never getting on any stage," by the time they had a bunch of cool songs learned or written, and it came time for the end of that three- or four-month program, they were all ready to go on stage and they all rose to the occasion like so often happens in performance contexts. So, I'm a big

TABLE 6.1

A survey of repertoire played at The 44/Evelyne Saller Centre (2004 survey dates: February 24, June 3, June 16, August 18, August 25, September 15, September 29, November 24)

	Song	Recording artist	Gender
1	"A Hard Day's Night"	The Beatles	Male
2	"A Horse with No Name"	America	Male
3	"All My Loving"	The Beatles	Male
4	"And It Stoned Me"	Van Morrison	Male
5	"As Tears Go By"	The Rolling Stones	Male
6	"Bad Moon Rising"	Creedence Clearwater Revival	Male
7	"Behind Blue Eyes"	The Who	Male
8	"Black Magic Woman"	Santana	Male
9	"Bridge Over Troubled Water"	Simon & Garfunkel	Male
10	"Cat's in the Cradle"[1]	Harry Chapin	Male
11	"Comfortably Numb"	Pink Floyd	Male
12	"Drift Away"	Doby Gray	Male
13	"Everybody Hurts"	R.E.M.	Male
14	"Flip, Flop and Fly"	Big Joe Turner	Male
15	"Folsom Prison Blues"	Johnny Cash	Male
16	"Hand in My Pocket"[2]	Alanis Morissette	Female
17	"Have You Ever Seen the Rain?"	Creedence Clearwater Revival	Male
18	"Help Me Make It through the Night"	Sammi Smith	Female
19	"Help!"	The Beatles	Male
20	"Here Comes the Sun"	The Beatles	Male
21	"Homeward Bound"	Simon & Garfunkel	Male
22	"Hotel California"	The Eagles	Male
23	"House of the Rising Sun"	The Animals	Male
24	"I Can See Clearly Now"	Johnny Nash	Male
25	"I Should Have Known Better"	The Beatles	Male
26	"Imagine"[3]	John Lennon	Male
27	"Kansas City Blues"	Janis Joplin	Female
28	"Knockin' on Heaven's Door"	Bob Dylan	Male

Continued

TABLE 6.1 *Continued*

	Song	Recording artist	Gender
29	"Lean on Me"	Bill Withers	Male
30	"Let It Be"	John Denver	Male
31	"Lookin' Out My Back Door"	Creedence Clearwater Revival	Male
32	"Moon Shadow"	Cat Sevens	Male
33	"Mr. Bojangles"	Bob Dylan	Male
34	"Mr. Tambourine Man"	The Byrds	Male
35	"My Sweet Lord"	George Harrison	Male
36	"No Woman No Cry"	Bob Marley	Male
37	"Norwegian Wood (This Bird Has Flown)"	The Beatles	Male
38	"O Siem"[4]	Susan Aglukark	Female
39	"Oh My Darling, Clementine"	N/A	N/A
40	"Something"	The Beatles	Male
41	"Sweet Home Alabama"	Lynyrd Skynyrd	Male with female backup singers
42	"The Rose"[5]	Bette Midler	Female
43	"These Boots Are Made for Walkin'"	Nancy Sinatra	Female
44	"Unchained Melody"	The Righteous Brothers	Male
45	"Walkin' after Midnight"	Patsy Cline	Female
46	"What's Up"[6]	4 Non Blondes	Female
47	"Wild Horses"	The Rolling Stones	Male
48	"With or Without You"	U2	Male
49	"Your Cheatin' Heart"	Hank Williams	Male

[1] Cowritten by Sandra and Harry Chapin.

[2] Cowritten by Alanis Morissette and Glen Ballard.

[3] Cowritten by John Lennon and Yoko Ono.

[4] Cowritten by Susan Aglukark and Chad Irschick.

[5] Written by Amanda McBroom.

[6] Written by Linda Perry.

PHOTO 6.3. Members of Women Rock rehearse.
Photo by author, 2016.

believer in the benefit of process, but I am absolutely committed to the benefit of performance as well and product. They both serve very different roles. (interview, October 21, 2016)

By 2017, the program also actively supported one of their most dedicated and involved participants, Taninli Wright, to develop a one-woman play about her personal life story, including her independently walking across BC in 1997. Her Messenger of Hope Walk advocated for improving education of Indigenous, Asian, and special needs youth. Wright's show enjoyed a variety of public performances by the time of writing, including at the Firehall Arts Centre, a professional venue, as part of the 2019 Heart of the City Festival. Thus, Women Rock has worked toward a different human right—to employment of choice and development toward employment, in Wright's case as an actor—than those identified as rights deficits before Women Rock started. Wright's play also took still further the right to freedom of expression and the value of "giving voice": it is a one-woman show in which a Downtown Eastside woman shares profoundly personal experiences from her childhood, including racism, violence, and structural violence. She turned "trauma into triumph" through the play (text message from Taninli Wright, August 28, 2017). Wright's development toward employment as an actor ended in triumph as well. After performing in various other theater productions around Vancouver, television and movie scouts discovered her. She performed, for instance, in season four of the TV show *Outlander*, shot in Scotland in 2018, in addition to various films.

In sum, Women Rock, by supporting multiple human rights, is successfully targeting the rights deficits identified before two women started organizing the program. As well, it facilitates one of these rights more deeply than other comparable projects locally—the right to freedom indispensable for creative activity—and promotes other human rights—for example, the opportunity to gain a living through freely chosen work—that were not initially targeted. Women Rock strengthens the first right by supporting its participants' capabilities to participate in local, popular music-making, which is dominated by men and from which therefore they felt deterred; and, when so doing, to learn (more about) music theory and performance and to create new songs. The program promotes the second human right when nurturing women's capabilities to work in the arts as performers.

The second ethnographic example, the Women's Memorial March, names a Downtown Eastside protest organized each Saint Valentine's Day, February 14th, in honor of Indigenous women who die each year due to violence and foul play. Over 60 women from the Downtown Eastside have gone missing or been murdered since the 1980s (City of Vancouver, 2013: 85). One infamous case was that of pig farmer Robert Pickton, convicted in 2007 for the second-degree murder of 6 women and charged in the deaths of another 20 women. He received six life sentences without parole (Organization of American States [OAS], 2014: 34). The City of Vancouver states that one-third of the missing and murdered women taken from the Downtown Eastside are Indigenous (City of Vancouver, 2013: 87); police report that many are involved in survival sex work and use drugs (OAS, 2014: 33). The march is organized by a women-only committee—a small collective of a maximum of 20 people on which I have served. It meets in the fall and early new year at a local organization like the Downtown Eastside Women's Centre or Carnegie Community Centre. However, no organization officially sponsors the march.

According to one media advisory released by organizers, violence issues that the march works to raise awareness about include "not just physical violence but the violence of HIV/AIDS, homelessness, poverty, addictions, and lack of medical care. The women's lives and deaths are swept aside because of where these women lived [in poverty], what they do for money [including prostitution], or who they were. These women are not nameless, they are not faceless, they are human beings deserving more than what they got" (Media Advisory, 2005). This aim is supported by and part of human rights activism relevant to and led by Indigenous women.

When I helped to organize the march in the mid-2000s, march organizers often referred to the Native Women's Association of Canada, which for long has understood discrimination against Indigenous women and girls, including violence, as a human rights issue (Native Women's Association of Canada, 2015). Indigenous women who die in urban poverty in Canada struggle with human rights problems such as "the inherent right to life" (International Covenant on Civil and Political Rights [ICCPR], art. 6.1; OHCHR, 1996–2019c) and the right to a "standard of living adequate for . . . health and well-being [including] housing and medical care and necessary social services" (UDHR, art. 25.1). In the mid- to late 2000s, the Native Women's Association of Canada led a national, grassroots campaign called Sisters in Spirit, which drew attention to the ongoing issue of missing and murdered Indigenous women. Rights information from the Sisters in Spirit campaign and the Native Women's Association of Canada was discussed during organizing meetings for the Women's Memorial March in the mid-2000s; I still have a Sisters in Spirit poster given to me during one of these discussions.

International human rights actors have also engaged the issue of missing and murdered Indigenous women of the Downtown Eastside. At the behest of grassroots organizers such as those of the Women's Memorial March, contacts at the Organization of American States or OAS (2014) researched and published a *Report of the Inter-American Commission on Human Rights on Missing and Murdered Indigenous Women in British Columbia*, focused on two case studies of the Downtown Eastside and Prince George. The OAS is a regional security organization based in Washington, DC, whose purposes according to its 1948 charter include promoting regional peace and justice, as well as member nations' solidarity, cooperation, sovereignty, territorial integrity, and independence. Its most powerful member, the United States, has dominated decision-making to resolve various conflicts and security threats, yet in various cases has compromised with Latin American countries (in which the United States nonetheless has hegemonic influence; see Shaw, 2003, 2004). The OAS report analyzes the issue of Indigenous Canadian missing and murdered women according to the OAS's American Declaration of the Rights and Duties of Man (from 1948). The declaration has been accepted as legally binding by the Inter-American Court of Human Rights and the Inter-American Commission on Human Rights, especially for OAS member states that have not ratified the American Convention on Human Rights (in force since 1978), including Canada and the United States. The commission, which decides which cases are admissible to the Inter-American court, operates through hearings on human rights violations initiated by nongovernmental organizations (NGOs) and private actors that document them—not nation-states, although collaboration with nation-states in the documentary process often results in the most fruitful results politically, especially following a hearing result (Buergenthal, 1997: 711; Padilla, 1993). With NGOs and private actors as the main instigators, the OAS and Inter-American human rights system could be interpreted as institutions that defray legal responsibilities from states to nonstate actors, meanwhile leaving the appearance of human rights leadership, or distracting from ostensibly US geopolitical pursuits undertaken via the OAS. This is not to dismiss all OAS initiatives. The report of missing and murdered women of Indigenous Canadian heritage states that 88% were mothers (OAS, 2014: 18) whose life experiences of structural discrimination following colonialism rendered them vulnerable. It emphasizes that the missing persons cases have not been handled with due diligence to prevent, investigate, prosecute, and punish perpetrators of the violence (OAS, 2014: 72), which has led to imagined and real impunity, allowing the problem to grow. It also questions to what extent Indigenous women and girls have enjoyed protection of the following rights in the declaration:

> [to] life, liberty and security of [the] person (Article I); equality before the law and enjoyment of the rights and duties established in the Declaration without distinction as to race, sex, language, creed or any other factor (Article II); protection of honor, personal reputation, and private and family life (Article V); measures of special protection in the case of children and pregnant and nursing women (Article VII); preservation of health and well-being (Article XI); and resort to the courts to ensure respect for one's legal rights, together with a simple brief procedure whereby the courts will protect the person concerned from acts of authority that, to their prejudice, violate any fundamental constitutional rights (Article XVIII). (OAS, 2014: 57)

The report concludes that "the numbers of missing and murdered Indigenous women are particularly concerning considering that Indigenous people represent a small percentage of the total population of Canada" (OAS, 2014: 11), with Indigenous women being "eight times more likely to be murdered than non-Indigenous women" (OAS, 2014: 49), while stating that "the police have failed to adequately prevent and protect Indigenous women and girls from killings, disappearances and extreme forms of violence, and have failed to diligently and promptly investigate these acts" (OAS, 2014: 12).

Following decades of activism and public pressure to live up to international human rights obligations (OAS, 2014: 76), the government of Canada launched in 2016 a two-year National Inquiry into Missing and Murdered Indigenous Women and Girls. It remains to be seen to what extent "underlying factors of discrimination that originate and exacerbate the violence" are addressed in Canada (OAS, 2014: 123), which the report recommended along with the national inquiry. Further public engagement with the issue is needed in Canada, as well as elsewhere in North America where the issue of missing and murdered Indigenous women has not been addressed comprehensively. Yet related activism can only be considered international: American protesters, including at a women's march protest in January 2019 in Washington, DC, have brought the issue to mass and news media attention via the performance of a "Women's Warrior Song" used in Vancouver's Women's Memorial March since the 1990s (Women's March, 2019).

The Women's Memorial March protest starts with an indoor gathering of families, friends, and community members of the missing women and then moves to an outdoor protest that anyone can join—the more people the better. The indoor event features an opening prayer, musical performances (by local, popular singer-songwriters and by singer-drummers of historical Indigenous genres), musical recordings, and the reading of poems and speeches by family members of the deceased. The event acknowledges the missing women's lives and facilitates grieving, which can be considered a type of spiritual, emotional, and psychological cleansing. As people exit the theater, smoke from a smudge passes over them. Smudging is an Indigenous North American ritual of Plains origin in which sacred healing plants (tobacco, sage, cedar, or sweetgrass) are burned toward cleansing. The focus on cleansing mirrors stories about the origins of the protest, as well as rituals during the outdoor protest (described further later). As Diane Wood writes:

> In 1991 a woman was murdered on Powell Street in Vancouver. Because of the way the woman was murdered her family, people of the Coast Salish [Indigenous] territory, did a cleansing ceremony at each of the sites her remains were found [in order] to cleanse her Spirit and allow it to travel to the Star Nations to rejoin her ancestors.
>
> This woman's murder in particular was the catalyst that moved women in the community into action. Out of a sense of hopelessness and frustration that no one was listening, and feeling like they needed to show the larger community that violence against women—especially in this area—had to stop, the women organized a march. (Wood, 2004)

The ceremony before the march preserves a space for community grieving that is less possible in a public march context.

The organizing committee has chosen the musical recordings played with particular care so as to respect the intention of gathering around missing and murdered women. These recordings have included popular songs about local missing women, such as "Missing" (words: Susan Musgrave; music: Brad Prevedoros) and "The Streets Where You Live" (by Wyckham Porteous, Gary Durban, and John Ellis). A particular favorite has been "Missing," whose lyrics mention missing women by name, in line with a goal of the march to recognize the women as human beings with names and faces (Figure 6.3).

Jack Cummer, a resident of Nanoose Bay, BC, coordinated the creation and re-cording of "Missing" in 2002, after police found the remains of his granddaughter Andrea Jonesbury on the pig farm of Robert Pickton, who later was convicted of serial homicide. Jack Cummer linked up with Susan Musgrave through mu-tual contacts and asked her to write the song's lyrics. After hearing guitarist Brad Prevedoros perform at a Vancouver Island resort, Cummer asked Prevedoros to ar-range the song. Cummer intended the song to be a memory of his granddaughter and in memory of all missing women in the world (email from Jack Cummer, May 23, 2005). On a web page containing a newspaper article with the song lyrics, Musgrave commented about the resultant commercial single recording of "Missing," which features singer Amber Smith:

It really feels like a tribute. It feels like something honoring those women, giving them a kind of a voice, I guess, of their own, a stance of their own, that's positive. It isn't depressing, it's life-affirming, actually. (Culbert, 2006)

The proceeds from CD sales of the single, now no longer sold, went toward the Haven Society in Nanaimo, BC, which administrates a transition house for women who have experienced violence and seek safety as well as various anti-abuse and anti-violence programs for women, men, and children.

The outdoor protest of the Women's Memorial March is led by Indigenous elders walking through Downtown Eastside streets, followed by women drummers and then the other participants, who include community members, family members, and friends of those who have died, as well as rights activists of all ethnicities, genders, and ages. Banners and quilts artistically representing murdered and missing women appear prominently; some participants wear placards with the women's faces on them. The female elders leave red roses and tobacco, a healing plant in their traditions, at places where a woman was murdered. They leave yellow roses and tobacco at sites where women were last seen. Purple roses are also used; according to Indigenous women organizers, purple is the color of healing. The march stops at about a dozen street locations in the Downtown Eastside including hotels, community centers, and parks. At each stop, the elders conduct a healing ceremony in which the location is smudged. During these ceremonies, the march

"Missing"
lyrics by Susan Musgrave; music by Brad Prevedoros

Missing's a word that can't begin to describe
the way I miss you more each day;
You left to chase the wind on high
and the rain rained down to stay.

Will they remember me when I'm gone, you said,
when I've kissed goodbye to pain;
Or will their lives just carry on
in the small hours of the rain.

You may be lost in the eyes of the world,
but how can I set you free;
When there's a whole empty world in my aching heart,
you're the missing part of me.

Ruby Anne Hardy, Jacqueline McDonell, Jennie Lynn Furminger, Sarah de Vries
Heather Bottomley, Andrea Joesbury, Marcella Creison, Dawn Teresa Crey
Elaine Allenbach, Debra Lynne Jones, Angela Arseneault, Lillian O'Dare
Mona Wilson, Michelle Gurney, Cindy Beck, Laura Mah
Sheryl Donahue, Wendy Allen, Julie Young, Teresa Triff

CHORUS 1
How far from home is "missing"?
In our prayers you're close beside us every day;
When you left to chase the wind so high,
the rain moved in to stay.
Will they remember me when I'm gone, you said,
when I've kissed goodbye to pain;
Or will their lives just carry on
in the small hours of the rain.

You may be an orphan in the eyes of the world,
can we ever love anyone enough?
You'll always have a home in our loving hearts,
You're the missing part of us.

Sheila Egan, Rebecca Guno, Angela Jardine, Brenda Ann Wolfe
Georgina Papin, Sherry Irving, Helen Hallmark, Tanya Holyk
Leigh Miner, Inga Hall, Patricia Johnson, Yvonne Boen, Tiffany Drew
Julie Young, Janet Henry, Dorothy Anne Spence, Ingrid Soet, Elaine Dumba, Sherry Lynn Rail
Jacqueline Murdock, Olivia Gale Williams, Catherine Gonzalez, Heather Chinnock

FIGURE 6.3. Song lyrics memorializing missing and murdered women from the Downtown Eastside.

CHORUS 1

How can we believe in a merciful world
that could never believe in you enough?
Take what strength you need from our fearless hearts,
You're the missing part of us.

Taressa Williams, Diana Melnick, Kathleen Dale Wattley, Catherine Maureen Knight
Wendy Crawford, Elsie Sebastien, Marnie Lee Frey, Stephanie Lane
Frances Young, Nancy Clark, Cindy Feliks, Dianne Rock
Kerry Lynn Koski, Sereena Abotsway, Andrea Borhaven, Maria Laliberte
Yvonne Abigosis, Verna Littlechief, Dawn Lynn Cooper, Linda Louise Grant

CHORUS 1a
Missing means you're gone, I can't find you;
My dear one, I'll never hold you again.
You left to chase the wind too high
and the rain can't wash my tears away.
[last 4 lines of CHORUS 1]

You may have disappeared in the eyes of the world,
but when I close my eyes I'll always see
your name, the way you smile, inside my wishful heart,
The missing part of me.

FIGURE 6.3. Continued

halts and its protesters are silent—there is no song. Since the 1990s, the Women's Memorial March has spread to cities across Canada as well as the United States (see Feb 14th Annual Women's Memorial March, 2019).

In the protests, advocating for Indigenous women and their rights is done to almost constant music: the "Women's Warrior Song," by Martina Pierre of the Lil'wat First Nation in western BC, who gives the march permission to use the song. The protesters sing the melody to vocables only; however, Pierre also created Coast Salish language verses to the song—one of which is in support of women, another of which recognizes the ancestors, and another of which acknowledges the future, our children. The "Women's Warrior Song" came to Martina Pierre during a 1989 logging blockade against the logging of an old Indigenous graveyard along Lillooet Lake, BC (Diana Billy, personal communication, August 9, 2002). A long-time chairperson of the march's organizing committee, Marlene George, noted that the song "honor(s) women as warriors, and that's why we sing that song on the march because the women that died in this community were warriors for sure. Anyone who lives in this community is a warrior because just of the survival alone" (interview with Marlene George, June 19, 2005). The song is sung to steady beats of a hand drum or sometimes a powwow drum.

Protests are interesting events from a human rights perspective because they protest injustices and human rights not being fulfilled, but the protests may not measurably strengthen those transgressed rights, at least immediately. The Women's Memorial March events object to the series of human rights violations experienced by missing Indigenous women and girls. However, when family, friends, and community members of the missing women gather before the march, they can be understood as strengthening their human right to health—mental health—through the "cleansing" and "healing" processes of grieving through music and smudging. This, very understandably, was not the right to health or to life that had been violated for the missing women. During the march that flows from the intimate gathering, as soon as intimates exit a theater onto the streets, protesters exercise rights other than those discussed as violated with missing and murdered women—at least in organizing meetings for the protest and related policy documents. In the moment of protesting, protesters exercise the following rights: "of peaceful assembly" (ICCPR, art. 21); that "everyone shall have the right to hold opinions without interference"; that "everyone shall have the right to freedom of association with others" (art. 22); and that "everyone shall have the right to freedom of expression . . . includ[ing] freedom to seek, receive and impart information and ideas of all kinds, regardless of frontiers, either orally, in writing or in print, in the form of art, or through any other media of his choice" (art. 19: 1–2). Thus, for various reasons—for example, due to the way an event evolves like Women Rock, or the format and genre of a musical and cultural event—musical interventions on human rights issues may actively engage different human rights in practice, and even for different people, than those rights and people that the event initially sets out to address. Any causal relationships between human rights intentions and outcomes—which may well be complex—are important to comprehend when planning and analyzing human rights interventions made through music and culture; they can be quite fluid and may be revised over time by various actors.

7

SELF-DETERMINATION

SELF-DETERMINATION IS AT issue for urban poor participating in jams and music therapy using popular songs in the Downtown Eastside. Whereas autonomy means the amount of control one feels over one's own life and the degree to which one does not feel controlled by other people, self-determination refers to an individual or small group determining one's or its own actions. Self-determination is about independently motivated decision-making and action (Deci and Ryan, 1985). In this meaning, self-determination is a capability.

Self-determination also refers to a human right. The right to self-determination is enjoyed by legally defined peoples when determining their own governance. Human rights law usually discusses self-determination in relation to individuals who band together to form a nation-state, or a people who make a claim to control territories and thereby secede from a nation-state (Burak and Eymirlioğlu, 2005; McCorquodale, 1994). Music and arts scholarship analyzes cultural dimensions of peoples to which the human right to self-determination applies (Donders, 2012), particularly those who can be legally defined as peoples because they share a common economic life, compose a certain number, come from a common historical tradition, experience cultural homogeneity, or speak the same language, among other defining factors (McCorquodale, 1994: 866).

Music Downtown Eastside. Klisala Harrison, Oxford University Press (2020). © Oxford University Press.
DOI: 10.1093/oso/9780197535066.001.0001.

This chapter illustrates how slippery self-determination is to achieve for the severely marginalized, especially the poorest of the poor. The self-determination of individuals and small groups is often interfered with in the popular music scene of the Downtown Eastside. Blocking the capability of self-determination at the individual and small-group level troubles if not prevents urban poor from determining themselves as a coherent, larger group, should they want to.

In this way, the chapter puts in dialogue the capability of self-determination with the human right to self-determination. It extends arts scholarship that studies the self-determination of individuals and small groups (Lee, Davidson, and McFerran, 2016) as well as arts scholarship on the right to self-determination. The latter deals most with marginalized collectives, for example, citizens of oppressed nation-states (Jawad, 2013); and groups facing equity challenges in society, such as people with disabilities (Price and Barron, 1999), minority races (Ritter, 2011), and ethnicities, particularly Indigenous people (Harris, 2004; Newsome, 2008). It resonates with the first article of the ICESCR and the International Covenant on Civil and Political Rights (ICCPR): "All peoples have the right of self-determination. By virtue of that right they freely determine their political status and freely pursue their economic, social and cultural development." The UN Declaration on the Rights of Indigenous Peoples also has as its third article, "Indigenous peoples have the right to self-determination." I think marginalization is also very important to consider in relation to self-determination as a capability.

Individuals and small groups can self-determine to form a larger social unit—including a people of urban poor, hypothetically. Downtown Eastside urban poor share economic circumstances, culturally homogeneous elements that I documented in popular music-making, a cultural history sustained in popular musicking (Small, 1998), and the central use of English. A people cannot emerge, though, if individuals and small groups cannot exercise the capability to self-determine, particularly to form a larger social unit. In this chapter, I describe how the popular music scene of the Downtown Eastside is a social setting that too often blocks the capability of urban poor to determine their own actions. Some popular music jams and music therapy sessions suffocate the self-determination of individuals and small groups experiencing poverty. Both facilitators and participants suppress the self-determination. Other facilitators respond to various self-determination tensions, documented here among music organizers and participants, with the social work method of noninterference adapted to music-making. Many of these examples result in human rights conflicts and violations. Rights conflict and suppression impacts, for example, local songwriters who try to perform their original songs, whose contents I describe.

One way that I see some music facilitators limit and erode the self-determination of urban poor participants involves cooptation. In some cases, music therapists respond to a pressing desire for music performance knowledge and know-how among the poor by providing musical skill development, but in ways that serve their own purposes of music therapy—a main reason that they, as music therapists, are hired by poverty alleviation organizations. This taking-over of a desire of the poor to learn to perform music (better), and transmuting it into therapy, in turn, supports any agenda that an institution has to offer music therapy, but this may not be the agenda of urban poor. The therapeutic aims are often, even typically, not openly and explicitly discussed with the music therapy participants.

In one music group—confusingly called a music jam but run by a music therapist who had earlier called the group music therapy—all of the participants talked about how much they wished to learn to play instruments and sing, or how much they and others had improved—in other words, musical capability development. Participant stories that I collected there were essentially biographical, as in Helen's[1] case:

I've been playing since I was about 15-16, yeah, but I was working in between so I couldn't keep it up all the time. So then I took some lessons too, a little bit and then, it wasn't [for] very long and then I had to move. Then that stopped. Then I started going to, bars and hotels, and that's where I started watching guys playing. So I learned some stuff from them too. A little bit just by watching. . . . This one pub that I used to work just down the street from, I used to go there. I used to have to chase the guys down to learn stuff from them [and] if I couldn't [learn through making music with them], I'd sit there and watch [them]. I was going to leave one night and this one fellow come in. He was just awesome. And I was taking lessons or I'd taken a couple of lessons at the time. The person that was giving me lessons [allowed me to do] my fingering all wrong. I don't even know how I was doing it now. [That night, the performer] showed me the proper way to do an E and an A and a B[7] [chord]—just the basic stuff. And yeah, and then he said, "Just keep practicing, just keep practicing." Like I said, I was working too, so I didn't have a lot of time to play back then. I do when I can but not very often until I came here. (interview, 2016)[2]

---

[1] This is a pseudonym.
[2] Most primary sources in this critique have been anonymized.

Another participant said:

> We do an amazing job for what we've got and when we're only together once
> a week. I've improved. I've learned to play guitar with these people. When
> I first came here I had a hard time doing that, and I've learned to sing better.
> (interview, 2016)

The music therapist, by contrast, saw the desire for knowledge and music lessons,
as well as pride in musical skills gained, therapeutically, as "a way for people to be
able to integrate into the music group setting" (email communication, October
27, 2016; September 1, 2017). For the therapist, the music lessons aimed beyond
strengthening musical skill to also being music-therapeutic—through reducing
anxiety, enhancing interpersonal communication skills, boosting self-esteem, and
increasing mental presence, for example. About the second participant, the therapist commented privately:

> In his case I have used a metronome and taught him to play quarter-note
> beats to the bar, then eighth notes, etc., and have [had] him play both rhythm
> and lead to the metronome and to the rhythm of my guitar. What happens is
> he tries to say, "Yeah, okay," and then not connect to the meter, and wants to
> move on. He has a hearing impairment and throughout his life when people
> speak to him he often responds by saying "yeah" or "okay," without having
> heard what they say. Because of this behavior, it's difficult for him to follow
> instructions and to engage with others in a way that is congruent with what
> is happening in the moment. This creates or increases anxiety for him. I have
> spoken to him about this behavior and we have tried different approaches
> to communicate better. I have found the most successful [approaches to
> promoting congruent engagement in musical moments] have been [to] use
> the metronome and [to] teach him how to develop a sense of time. I have also
> used basic [recorded] drum tracks to get him to play in time. Teaching him
> to hear where the first beat is forces him to use his hearing and become more
> present in the moment. There is still some anxiety around this and it shows
> up with him playing single notes at random when I'm trying to teach him
> something. When this happens, I get him to repeat a task over and over until
> he is comfortable and feeling successful. The results are that his listening
> skills have improved dramatically and he feels more comfortable in his own
> skin. [Other results are] reduc[ed] anxiety; connecting with me and with
> the music; engaging, developing his skills; . . . increas[ing] self-esteem and

self-worth; and becoming more present. (e-mail communication, October 27, 2016; September 1, 2017)

The music therapist described the first participant, Helen, as an example of someone whose self-esteem and confidence grew through music lessons.

> For "The Thrill Is Gone," I taught her a little lick [based on a] b minor pentatonic scale and integrated that lick into two other b minor pentatonic scale positions that she already knew; and she soloed over my rhythm and at the end of our session. I said we would play it in the group. What was really cool is that I'm the only one who has ever sung that song, so when she chose to sing and play that song she was taking a risk. It shows me how much she has grown and that she has developed her self-esteem and feels safe enough in the group to take the risk. (e-mail communication, October 27, 2016; September 1, 2017)

Helen performing B. B. King's "The Thrill Is Gone" within the music group demonstrated her newfound self-esteem and confidence.

In the Downtown Eastside, I have witnessed that most participants go along with any (undisclosed) therapeutic agenda of the therapist if they get, in part, what they want—usually knowledge about how to perform music—along the way. I have mentioned that music therapy may have an educational share (Bruhn, 2000), but what if participants in music-making aren't particularly interested in music as therapy? What if they are more interested in music education that develops capabilities of performance skills when, however, most institutions offering musical services to Downtown Eastside urban poor are not providing that (and to which Women Rock and other educational initiatives responded)? When considering self-determination within a formally organized music group with a leader, we enter a problematic conceptual zone. Facilitating music for a group, at all, limits the capability of self-determination of its participants.[3] Promoting some self-determination can be accomplished by a facilitator codesigning a musical trajectory—as with participants collaboratively making songbooks with music therapists—or a facilitator making clear, ahead of time, what is the proposed musical trajectory, then a participant in music-making choosing whether or not and how to engage with that.

---

[3] The arts health literature grapples with this point. Low individual self-determination has been hypothesized as implying a social context of low autonomy, which, as explained, negatively impacts human health and well-being (Norfield and Nordin-Bates, 2012; Sebire et al., 2016). The hypothesis rings true in my research data.

What I'm describing here, although resonant, differs from musical approaches based on self-determination theory, which explores a range of degrees of individual motivations for action, some of which are controlled by a therapist or teacher.[4] Musical studies of individual self-determination and motivation—found in music education, music therapy, dance studies, sport and recreation studies, and criminology, among other fields—generally do not question or undermine ethical guidelines for professional (health or arts) practices (see Evans and Liu, 2019; Hickey, 2018; Küpers et al., 2014). By contrast, my material suggests potential dishonesty of an artistic leader toward urban poor about the function of art-making. A group leader withholding knowledge about a therapeutic course of action poses problems to group members' self-determination (Slotta, 2017), although I recognize that therapists can be very well intentioned and emotionally invested (Kalir, 2019). To what extent are urban poor participants in group music-making coerced out of the self-determination of their own artistic processes by music therapists?

My purpose here is to draw attention to problematics of what I will call a trade-off dynamic, meaning experiencing the need or compromise of trading off one experience (here, learning musical skills) for another (being treated as a therapy patient). Trade-offs run deep into the lives of many urban poor. One local songwriter told in a public jam about her vulnerability to making trade-offs as a homeless person—how she sometimes traveled to a town near Vancouver to stay with a man who gave her a free accommodation for "cooking" and "cleaning." She said that, one evening, after she sang the Beatles' "The Continuing Story of Bungalow Bill" (lyrics: John Lennon and Paul McCartney), which asks "if to kill was not a sin" and "What did you kill," her drunken host bragged that he had murdered three people. She popped on a nearby tape recorder, recording his statement, but he threatened to kill her if she went to the police. The economic vulnerability of people who experience poverty results in them often being in situations they don't want to be in but that they endure in order to get for no money something they need or want, in this example housing. Some women I made music with, who worked in the sex industry, trade their bodies for survival and/or drugs. The broader violence of economic and class hierarchies creates an atmosphere in which people lower in the hierarchy are vulnerable to making trade-offs, including for musical knowledge and know-how. Making trade-offs manipulates and warps self-determination.

---

[4] More specifically, self-determination theory and particularly its so-called basic needs subtheory hypothesizes several social contexts ("psychological needs") for individual behavior (autonomy, relatedness, and competence) according to whether they are more or less likely to produce self-determination, as well as some cognitive and affective results (Norfield and Nordin-Bates, 2012: 258–260; Sebire et al., 2016: 101).

In many local instances, as well, people experiencing urban poverty want to gain both musical and healthful capabilities through music therapy. I am not saying that music should be either one thing or the other—it can build both musical skills and wellness levels. Granted, music therapy participants who can benefit from psychological and emotional assistance may self-restrict their self-determination, whereas music can take a role in liberating their capability to self-determine. One of the worst qualities of marginalization is that it can lead a person to self-marginalize, which can mean that he or she self-restricts his or her self-determination. About his practice at Positive Outlook, music therapist Jeffrey Smith argued for the redemptive possibilities of music for self-marginalization and, particularly, limiting one's own capability to self-determine: "Some of the individuals who participated had not left the Downtown Eastside for months at a time. One individual had restricted himself to a four-block radius for over two years, feeling trapped in his isolation due to economic and cultural marginalization" (Smith, 2007: 112). Smith interpreted the music therapy participant's traveling to another part of Vancouver to record a track for a CD as helping him to overcome his inability to determine and act on where he wanted to be in a way that supported his musical development (Smith, 2007: 112).

Problematically, some music organizers verbally attack urban poor's preferred popular music genres (e.g., classic rock, pop, and country hits) and, in so doing, any capability to build their own music culture spawning from those—including new song compositions. One politician who organized opera education said of the jams and music therapy sessions using popular music, when arguing for opera and music theater initiatives in the Downtown Eastside:

What have you got [as music in the Downtown Eastside]? Right, well, I play guitar, and I sing [Johnny Cash's] "Oh Lonesome Me" or whatever, [Hank Williams's] "Your Cheatin' Heart." Well, great. I'm a country music fanatic, so let's do that. On the other hand, what other influences can we bring in, without trying in any way to say that this is better than the indigenous cultural component? But if people haven't had the opportunity to be exposed to certain things, they will never, ever know about it. They will never understand it. So, they have lost the opportunity. So, the idea is: how do you make this exposure so people can have an opportunity? (interview, 2004)

Citing musical poverty (Fiol, 2013) as a motivation for music programming that the poor in fact do not control within organizations risks symbolic violence (Bourdieu, 1977) toward musico-cultural formations made by the poor. It is sometimes undertaken, in the Downtown Eastside, by professionals who seek grants to offer programming in musical genres whose performance normally necessitates extended training and that may be associated with higher socioeconomic classes. Music education scholar Vincent C. Bates writes that "recognition of the *rich* musical practices and heritages of impoverished groups and individuals is essential in avoiding the *symbolic violence* of programs predicated on faulty assumptions that people who lack basic necessities also lack culture . . . music in particular" (Bates, 2016: 3; italics in original). We should bear this critique in mind when thinking about a range of music initiatives in the neighborhood that accompany its gentrification (see chapter 8), when they do not stick to or build from popular music genres played by the poorest of the poor, or when they necessitate skill development that, although offered, presents problems with access and benefit for the indigent, the poorest of the poor.

Self-determination is a struggle among different urban poor participants as they try to collaborate in the popular music jams and music therapy sessions as well. This interpersonal struggle emerged aurally as participants in the popular music-making actively excluded songs composed by other participants. Some facilitators supported this practice to the extent that they seemed not to want to, or be able to, intervene.

From the 1980s to 2000s, participants in popular music jams typically used sound and music to protest any performance of a locally composed song (see interview with Ken Tabata, June 7, 2005). If a participant selected a song that he or she had composed but no one knew or wished to learn, and the participant started to play it, social order all but broke down. The other participants would begin talking very loudly and practicing other music—usually a Billboard Top 40 hit or other very well-known song. Often the noise grew so loud as to drown out the sound of the performing songwriter or small collection of individuals attempting to perform the song. Such infighting gradually decreased over the 2010s.

Rejecting original songs repressed the capability of local songwriters to determine themselves to perform their songs in the song circles (see Varga, 2013). However, it exercised for non-songwriters their human rights to freedom of expression (ICCPR, art. 19.2), to freedom indispensable for creative activity (ICESCR, art. 15.3) and "freely to participate in the cultural life of the community, to enjoy the arts" (Universal Declaration of Human Rights [UDHR], art. 27.1). The same act suppressed the same human rights of the songwriters.

What specifically was excluded musically from the popular music jams? Locally created songs in a variety of popular music genres, with a variety of content, but nonetheless displaying certain patterns. The majority of the songs were born in urban poor individuals' heads, homes, and street-living circumstances. Others had been created before the individual came to the neighborhood, especially in songwriting programs in Canadian prisons, or together with a music therapist in a music therapy program.

I know about these songs primarily because an arts district developed in the neighborhood in the 2000s and 2010s (see chapter 8) that increasingly offered performance opportunities for the songs. Examples are performances within Vancouver Moving Theatre's 12-day, annual (since 2004), and 100- to 150-event Heart of the City Festival. The festival features presentations by Downtown Eastside songwriters alongside other artists from the neighborhood and throughout Vancouver. It also has showcased a series of popular music theater productions developed in and about the Downtown Eastside since 2003.

To a lesser extent, digital song recordings initiated by music therapists, jam facilitators, institution administrators, and university employees have encouraged songwriters and their self-determination to write and perform their own songs. Recordings include the CDs *These Are the Faces* produced by the Carnegie Community Centre in 2000 and *The Circle of Song* produced by the Positive Outlook program of Vancouver Native Health in 2005 (Nikleva and Peach, 2000; Positive Outlook, 2005). At the request of Carnegie Community Centre administrator Rika Uto, in 2010 I initiated the Assistance with Music Production project, AMP for short, together with my students from the University of British Columbia and teaching assistant Rodrigo Caballero. AMP was an assignment within an applied ethnomusicology course. The students created digital press kits for local singer-songwriters who elected to be involved. Each press kit included demo recordings (video and/or audio), photographs, a biography, and a MySpace page.

Some of the songs excluded from the popular music jams expressed Christian ideologies. One Indigenous singer-songwriter's compositions, sung to arpeggiated or strummed acoustic guitar, use hymn texts set to new music, or incorporate texts from the Bible that also form the song titles, for example, "2nd Chronicles, Chapter 7, Verse 14–16." His guitar arrangements use just a few chords for each song. This artist croons, with breaks in his voice before the starts of notes, reminiscent of country music styles, at slow tempos. Sometimes, he alternates singing with speaking, conveying different types of emphases—to stress a first-person narrative (important in many Indigenous Canadian cultures) or to mark a change between two different hymn texts set to new music in a medley (e.g., "Help Me" by Kris Kristofferson and the first verse of "Surely the Presence of the Lord Is in This Place" by Lanny Wolfe). In a song based on Psalm 23, the singer-songwriter speaks instead of sings lines in the first person, for instance, "Even though I walk through the valley." The continuation of the line is then sung: ". . . of the shadow of death." He often precedes performances, especially during local church services, with a testimonial about feeling that a Christian god has had a positive and transformative influence in his life.

Other songs expressed Indigenous cultural concepts. Songwriter Frances McAllister, for example, indexed teachings that he learned when participating in ceremonies associated with his Cree ancestry and in rituals of an addiction recovery approach called the red road to recovery. In the red road to recovery approach, Indigenous people connecting socially with one another via music and culture, with an emphasis on spirituality, strengthens aspects of sociality that can effectively aid in addiction recovery. Promoters of the approach view healthy Indigenous socialization as damaged by processes of residential school, foster care, and forced cultural assimilation (Harrison, 2019). McAllister himself stayed in 17 foster homes as a youth, including non-Indigenous homes, where he did not learn about his Indigenous cultural heritage. As a young adult, he ended up in prison. He learned there about his ancestral Cree culture as well as powwow and hand drumming music genres associated with the red road—because by then he struggled with substance misuse.

McAllister wrote about the importance of spirituality in his personal journey toward well-being in his original song "Creator." "Creator" references cultural identity recovery through using the vocables "way" and "hey" in a final verse. The lyrics say that he spent too much time putting his troubles on other people, but now he takes responsibility for his actions. He asks his god to show him "the way," singing that he is coming home to the Creator. With the word "Creator," McAllister suggests that his was an Indigenous spiritual path. He then sings "way" and "hey," vocables heard in powwow songs. Other verses narrate his healing path toward addiction recovery. In the red road to recovery approach, participants typically give verbal accounts of their healing journey, in Vancouver, within talking circles that precede drumming and singing in Indigenous powwow and hand drumming styles (Harrison, 2019). McAllister's lyrics talk about how he is 37 years old and that since his childhood spent in Edmonton, western Canada, he feels he has achieved nothing except a prison record. When I discussed this with McAllister before his 2005 death on the streets due to exposure (to outdoor elements), he always told me that he was a good man; his lyrics tell of his true heart and spirit.

Suppressing the capability of songwriters to self-determine what they performed in music sessions negatively impacted a range of human capabilities and rights beyond the rights to freedom of expression, freedom indispensable for creative activity, and free participation in the cultural life of the community. Since excluding new songs from popular music jams successfully stifled their contents, it discouraged any capabilities and related human rights involved in the creation and performance of those contents. For the two songwriters mentioned previously, composing and performing songs about their religious beliefs constituted religious expression and worship. Music composition developed new manifestations of Indigenous performing art. McAllister, when singing powwow vocables, practiced Indigenous tradition. Undertaking religious expression and worship through creating music (performance), developing new manifestations of Indigenous musical art, and practicing Indigenous musical tradition are all capabilities. Closely related, and compromised, human rights were the right to freedom of religion (ICCPR, art. 18.1); the Indigenous right to develop new manifestations of Indigenous culture and performing arts like popular songs; and the Indigenous right to practice and revitalize cultural traditions (art. 11.1, United Nations Declaration on the Rights of Indigenous Peoples).

Many other songs written by locals but drowned out in the group music-making were highly political. This raises the issue of how the suppression of songwriters' capability of self-determination diminished their civil and political rights as well as their capabilities to exercise those rights. It affected songwriters' ability to speak out against classed hierarchies and inequities that put them at the bottom. In the examples that follow, the rights to freedom of thought and conscience (ICCPR, art. 18.1) and "to hold opinions without interference" (ICCPR, art. 19.1) may be interpreted as exercised when creating the song contents. I speculate that various participants in jams and music therapy did not consciously want to suppress human rights of singer-songwriters, but rather understood themselves as pursuing the dominant value of the sessions—inclusivity—at the cost of newly composed songs. Typically all members of the music session could not practically sing the original songs because they didn't know them. Performing originals could not include all participants.

Political songs included, for instance, "More Money" by Andy Kostynuik (deceased 2016, 63 years). "More Money" criticizes rich politicians who do not assist poor citizens. Kostynuik demands, "Give me more money more money more money money." The question "What for?" is followed by: "To sue the government." Kostynuik's "Suck Hole" addresses an arrested politician rudely with that moniker. The lyrics state that the politician "suck[s] the milk of corporate cows," "you're never finished sucking on my wa—," and that the politician's "time is up, you're finished . . . suck me!" Kostynuik also takes political stances toward illicit drugs and prostitution, celebrating the first in "Loaded and Laid." He commiserates about prostitution with the line "Can't get laid, 'less you're paid" in "This Is the Law."

May Kossoff[5] composed social commentary songs whose lyrics critique war in the Middle East and the treatment of women in Iran. Kossoff also wrote songs

---

[5] This is a stage name.

about women missing from the Downtown Eastside and about homelessness. "Gone from the Downtown Eastside" protests authorities' treatment of women living in poverty, particularly Indigenous women and sex trade workers who go missing. The lyrics express Kossoff's disappointment with inactions of police and Vancouver city politicians, especially an initial lack of comprehensive investigation on what turned out to be murders. Her song about homelessness puts her own situation of living on the streets in global perspective. With rising global inequality, the lyrics remind us, there are more and more homeless people looking for a bed at a shelter or for another safe place to sleep.

Mark Oakley, a local musician who served as a music program facilitator at the Carnegie Community Centre, wrote "Sparkle and Shine," which starts with a repeated electric guitar riff and solo, then continues with a verse that starts:

> You're lookin' for a sparkle and shine
> You're lookin' for a greener tomorrow . . .

The second verse begins:

> You're wishin' for a dollar bill
> You're wishin' for a brand-new car
> You're wishin' for a bloody rich man
> You're wishin' for all you are . . .

The lyrics of "Sparkle and Shine" can be read as criticizing consumer capitalism, almost constantly supported by Canada's governments. It also points out the very human experience of never feeling satisfied.

Other songwriters, whose lyrics and songs are silenced in the jams and music therapy sessions, focus on life on the streets of the Downtown Eastside, sometimes evoking political controversies implied by illicit drugs and police brutality. Local songwriter Shannon Bauman, for instance, sings to her own accompaniment on acoustic guitar one of her original songs featuring its key message: don't leave your friends behind. As explained in concerts, the lyrics emphasize the need to take care of friends who are doing drugs—Bauman lost five friends in one week to fentanyl during the current opioid crisis. She feels that ensuring that friends using are okay (alive) is challenging but important. Another of her songs addresses police violence. Bauman's "That's Life" tells about everyday life on the streets—making friends with a crack cocaine dealer and someone overdosing.

Other songwriters share internal personal struggles of street life. "When Will Peace Find a Way," a country song written by the late Lori Wilson, tells about her being homeless already as a child. The song begins:

A child without a home, without love or understanding
You reach out your ol' hand, try to give me what she's demanding
Doesn't know compassion, doesn't give just change
It's so hard to look at someone like this. How much can someone take?

Wilson commented, "Music has been really fundamental in maintaining my sanity because I went through a lot as a kid," before becoming homeless at age 12. The lyrics continue to reflect on her childhood, stating, "I can't remember ever feeling at ease," "searching for love," but then "I realized that I was always loved." Lori Wilson told me that these lyrics describe "a woman who is trying to seek her womanhood" in extremely challenging circumstances of homelessness (interview with Lori Wilson, March 8, 2005). Lori Wilson's husband, Stewart Wilson, wrote the song "Finding My Way" (Figure 7.1), which tells about his internal struggles with

"Finding My Way"
by Stewart Wilson

I grew up on the streets
Trying to make ends meet
Just a man, living, trying to get through another day

CHORUS
Finding my way, finding my way
Finding my way, finding my way

Nobody cares to help me
I was so young, grew up in a hurry
And the streets seem to say they have won. Stop me from...

CHORUS

Instrumental break

CHORUS

Nobody cares to get out
But wherever I go, black clouds seem to follow
Has the world gone mad? All is lost and sad. Is there any life for me?

CHORUS (x2) . . .

FIGURE 7.1. Songs such as "Finding My Way," by Stewart Wilson, share internal struggles of street life.

growing up on the streets, such as feeling isolated when no one cared to help him, experiencing despair, and feeling "stuck" in a street life of drug misuse (interview with Stewart Wilson, March 8, 2005).

Lori and Stewart Wilson's songs narrated their internal struggles concerning the human right to housing (Universal Declaration of Human Rights [UDHR], art. 25; ICESCR, art. 11.1) since their lyrics reference homelessness (Lori Wilson) and growing up on the streets (Stewart Wilson). Their struggles also involved the right to health. The lyrics reference mental wellness issues (never "feeling at ease" for Lori Wilson; "black clouds" and "Is there any life for me?" in Stewart Wilson's song). Whereas collective struggles toward attaining human rights form a major topic of the nascent music literature on human rights (Peddie, 2011a, 2011b), I have highlighted the really difficult struggles of individual persons toward achieving their personal human rights in their lives, and the pain that this can inflict on them as individuals.

When the jams and music therapy sessions suppress original song lyrics that communicate personal struggles towards human rights, they likewise diminish the telling of those struggles. Excluding such songs conveys to songwriters that not only their musical creations and creative processes, but their personal life stories are unwelcome. Peers and music facilitators further marginalize people marginalized already within society.

Lyrics of apolitical and non-religious original songs, by contrast, avoid hard realities of poverty. Examples include when Women Rock participants wrote about their dreams of another world where everyone is free (in "Dreaming of My Future Home") or about a woman finding her strength and then being able to go on (in "I Found Me"). There are good reasons for wanting to avoid artistic representations that might be considered painful. As I found in a study on songwriting for and with asylum seekers and refugees with backgrounds of trauma, it may be important not to deal with, or to address opaquely, themes associated with trauma so as not to trigger traumatic reactions (Harrison, Jacobsen, and Sunderland, 2019).

Some songs' contents beg questions about the self-determination of the songwriters during songwriting, particularly in the few Downtown Eastside-related cases where a professional songwriter or a music therapist guides the songwriting process. Stewart Wilson's "Finding My Way," created together with a music therapist, represents him not only as homeless but also as a victim of rough street life that may impel him to do something untoward ("Stop me from . . ."). To what extent do highly marginalized people in poverty tell authority figures what they think they want to hear? What does this do to the poor's sense of self-empowerment and capability to exercise self-determination? In Wilson's case, does he truly want to represent himself publicly as a victim?

In music therapy programs and popular music jams, I experienced singer-songwriters occasionally pushing back against perceived authority figures in the music programs, through personal narratives about trying to determine their own actions. I heard such narratives, for instance, during rehearsals of original songs for local recording projects. This was, in my experience, the only time when music facilitators held space for performing original songs and did not tolerate urban poor shutting down such performances. They accomplished this through organizing time slots for individual songwriters to rehearse their original songs. In the narratives, songwriters used their self-determination and freedom of expression, sometimes, to express resentment toward social hierarchies and authorities, and at other times, to lie to perceived authority figures, thus trying to manipulate them or us.

One songwriter talked about the lyrics of a song that he wrote while in prison and recorded for *The Circle of Song*. "In Tribute" expresses pain at his prison inmates dying, discusses shared experiences among prisoners, and states, "Divided we're weak, but united we're strong. . . . Join hands together, for we'll find our strength this way." The lyrics describe a five-day lockdown, while the songwriter was in jail, for an investigation into the murder of an inmate stabbed by another inmate. Lockdown means that prisoners cannot leave their jail cells. The song voices that the inmates, called "comrades and friends," would be strong in solidarity if they stood against their enemies, which in the songwriter's view were the guards, the keepers as he called them—keepers of the keys. While some lyrics correspond to the song's message as the songwriter told it to me (see Positive Outlook, 2005), many others seem inserted only to appease employees of the prison where he wrote the song within a guided songwriting program: the words take a moralizing tone that encourages listeners to pray for prisoners killed in prisoner-to-prisoner violence and for the jailed to change the ways they live. The lyrics do not clearly express the songwriter's message, to resist prison guards, which perhaps would raise the eyebrows of prison authorities. Resisting prison guards was an action that the songwriter wanted to self-determine. Around rehearsing this song in music therapy at Positive Outlook, the songwriter told me that I was a keepers of keys too. I wondered if his saying so was simply acknowledging inequity between us. Or perhaps he perceived me as an enemy, like the guards, someone to oppose and even hate.

Some facilitators of music therapy and popular music gatherings, not detailed in this book, have responded methodologically to the self-determination struggles evident: in music therapy approaches that limit the self-determination of urban poor over their musical learning processes; in lyrical contents generated through guided songwriting, potentially; and in songwriter narratives about striving to determine one's own actions. The facilitators use an approach called noninterference, which explicitly relates with self-determination. Noninterference means that a worker never interferes with the behavior of a client as it is occurring. Some Downtown Eastside culture workers and locals call noninterference a policy, but no local organization formally condones it.

Historically, social workers have used noninterference in Indigenous-focused organizations throughout the United States and Canada (Wax and Thomas, 1961), including addiction treatment programs (BigFoot and Funderburk, 2011: 312). The idea has an Indigenous-related cultural history. Although what follows is a vast generalization and therefore should be approached critically, noninterference proponents have characterized Indigenous people of North America—especially Pacific Northwest Coast First Nations and Sioux peoples—as historically not interfering in other people's activities unless those are foolish or dangerous. Social norms discourage coercive and manipulative actions, physical and verbal. Jimm G. Good Tracks's 1973 article "Native American Non-Interference" explains such supposed norms for non-Indigenous workers making interventions in Indigenous North American contexts. In Indigenous North American organizations, noninterference is motivated by the logic that especially non-Indigenous people making interventions on Indigenous people interferes with the latter's self-determination (Tracks, 1973: 30), which is listed as an Indigenous human right in the UN's 2006 Declaration on the Rights of Indigenous Peoples (art. 3 and 4).

In the Downtown Eastside, the approach can occur in Indigenous-focused organizations. Yet music practitioners working in multicultural organizations also use what can be called noninterference. In those cases, the logic of promoting self-determination can be thought of as applied to the poor as a group, instead of Indigenous peoples—thus engaging self-determination as a capability rather than a human right.

From a human rights perspective, noninterference often goes awry in the Downtown Eastside. I observed a catalog of human rights transgressions supervised by music facilitators who claimed to use noninterference. Here are several examples. On two occasions, noninterference ended in attempted and successful sexual harassment. A third situation strongly violated personal safety.

On the first occasion, I was taking part, as a violinist and participant-observer, in music therapy in which a man with AIDS-related dementia was a client. As I played violin, the client called me a pretty little girl and lady, repeatedly asking me to dance. After he sensed I didn't want to, he left the session. But on his way out, he tried to grab the buttocks of the nearest man. The nearest man quickly moved away. The music therapist never intervened.

The second incident happened in the same music therapy practice. One day during a break from music-making, a male client and electric guitarist asked how I was. I replied that I had a backache with pain shooting down both legs. He said that I should masturbate because orgasms cause women's legs to straighten out. This happened in the office of the music therapist, who did not intervene. Like the first example, I felt this was sexual harassment.

The third incident, which I experienced as psychologically distressing while threatening violence, happened after a music therapist put me together with a client in an office with the door closed so that I could do a recorded interview for a music therapy project and my research. The sound of music therapy just outside the door made hearing and recording the interview a bit difficult—but both were possible if we talked loudly. While staying faithful to the human rights content, I fictionalize and anonymize this sensitive account.

Partway through the interview, an Asian staff member opened the office door with no warning. He opened a fridge in the office and removed free groceries to give to the homeless. After the fifth time that he interrupted us in this way, the music therapy client started to get angry: "Ah, fuck. Man, can we get a break here?" The staff person replied no. Then the music therapy client yelled, "No? Well, fuck you! Asshole!" When the staff member entered again, he told the client to have patience. By the eighth time the staff person interrupted, the client asked, "How about doing one of these packages for me, too." The staff member said he didn't think so. "I think so. I know so," the client bullied.

After a couple more times of interrupting the interview, the worker explained that he could not give free groceries to the client because the groceries came from another nonprofit organization with which the client was not signed up. The client replied, "Bullshit, you are a fucking liar and I'll . . . . I'm just going to put that fucking zipperhead[6] full of mother fucking . . . . Stick it in your ass, you fucking slopehead. I should have killed you when I was in Vietnam."

After voicing that the majority of people receiving the groceries were Asian, the client said to the staff person that he would "put another 45 through [his] pumpkin" and offered to fight him. The client "wouldn't think for a minute to kill" him.

It was only after the client repeatedly threatened to kill the Asian staff member that the music therapist interfered in the situation, saying that the organization had zero tolerance for racist language. He discouraged the client from killing

---

[6] In the incident, the music therapy participant used this terrible derogatory term. The term connotes a zipper-like face wound after someone's head is blown apart by a high-powered automatic weapon; it associates with the Vietnam War.

anyone, saying that it would land him back in the penitentiary. The music therapist told the client, apologetically, that he was barred from the organization. No
one called the police.

After the client left, I chatted with the music therapist on the street, trying to
understand more about what had just happened. He informed me that the client
had been in jail for homicide. I had no knowledge of this when going into a closed
room together with a convicted killer.

Not interfering in a human rights transgression is problematic. It is important to
care about and analyze whether musical approaches violate human rights. In these
examples, noninterference did not uphold the "right of everyone to the enjoyment
of the highest attainable standard of physical and mental health" (ICESCR, art.
12.1) in that they could have had negative psychological consequences. The third
example also could have harmed physical health and even violated "the inherent
right to life" (ICCPR, art. 6.1). According to the ICCPR, people have "the right to
freedom of association with others" (art. 22.1), but never at the cost of "the protection of public health or morals or the protection of the rights and freedoms of
others" (art. 22.2). None of the human rights that I discuss in this book are absolute.[7] The third example also was blatantly racist in a way that threatened the "the
right of everyone, without distinction as to race, color, or national or ethnic origin . . . to security of person and protection by the State against violence or bodily
harm, whether inflicted by government officials or by any individual group or institution" in the UN's International Convention on the Elimination of All Forms
of Racial Discrimination (art. 5b).

In such cases, the term "noninterference" may be understood as a cover for
human rights violations never intended by the social workers who originally developed that approach. In descriptions of Indigenous North American uses, letting
"things happen as they are meant to be . . . was never intended to result in inaction
in the face of grave potential harm" (BigFoot and Funderburk, 2011: 312).

I heard various excuses for rights-violating behavior, mis-justified as noninterference, in the Downtown Eastside. One music therapist argued for supporting
only the actions and concerns of individual people struggling in poverty moment
to moment, regardless of the actions' consequences for any other people. I was told
that it was understandable for music workers to default to noninterference when
they were too tired or overwhelmed to do anything else. The same music worker

---

[7] Examples of absolute human rights are the right of freedom from torture and cruel, inhuman degrading
treatment or punishment, and the prohibition on genocide. The exercise of most human rights like the
right of freedom of expression is limited, as McCorquodale writes, only so much as to protect "the rights
or reputations of others or for the protection of national security, public order, public health or morals"
(McCorquodale, 1994: 874).

argued that human rights violations taking place could signal that workplaces are too difficult for music facilitators:

> In [difficult work]places [in the Downtown Eastside], staff are really in danger. They are at risk for burning out emotionally and professionally, and taking their problems home with them and hypertension. (interview, 2005)

When noninterference violates human rights, it is not used as it has been intended by its pioneers in social work. If undertaken uncritically and without awareness or caring about human rights, doing nothing may have harmful consequences.

Overall, this chapter illustrated how social hierarchies, power imbalances, and, therein, acts of suppression and violence can block the capability of individuals and small groups to experience self-determination. Blocking the self-determination of individuals and small groups troubles if not prevents their coalescing into a larger group so as to form a people. A people is defined by shared economic and cultural aspects, some of which urban poor demonstrate in the Downtown Eastside's popular music scene. Forming a legally defined people allows its members to fight for, and exercise, the human right to self-determination. I probed interpersonal suppressions of self-determination in some popular music jams and music therapy sessions in the Downtown Eastside. I examined a music therapist coopting a music group for his or her own purposes that disallowed the poor to fully determine their own musical processes; the symbolic violence of verbal attacks by some music event organizers on popular song genres performed by the poor, and what that implied for their self-determination of their own music repertoire; the poor suppressing one another's musical self-determination through censoring songs chosen for performance, which particularly affected local singer-songwriters (as well as their capabilities to create new songs and exercise various human rights when so doing); and some music facilitators' use for music-making of the noninterference method, which aims at promoting participant self-determination, but can lead to violations of other human rights if used carelessly.

Many of these examples resulted in rights conflicts. When participants in popular music jams discouraged their peers from performing songs they had composed themselves, this exercised the former's freedom of expression and freedom indispensable for creative activity, but discouraged the same human rights of the songwriters. Doing so also repressed the songwriters' rights to freedom of thought and conscience (for political songs), to freedom of religion (for religious songs), and to hold opinions (expressed through song) without interference as well as, for Indigenous songwriters, their rights to develop new manifestations of

Indigenous culture and performing arts, and to practice and revitalize Indigenous cultural traditions. Human rights being in conflict in everyday life is a phenomenon well-recognized in human rights literature about culture (Donders, 2010: 17; Yılmaz, 2011).[8] Rights conflicts also occur via music.

My research material suggested, for urban poor taking part in the jams and music therapy sessions, their capability to exercise the music scene's central value of inclusivity by performing a song most participants knew trumped performing any original song that participants didn't know (well). The poor also highly valued the capabilities of instrumental and vocal performance.

Rights violations, though, should also be considered on their own terms as a sort of violence. I routinely saw rights threatened in other musical practices not detailed in this book. For example, I saw some music workers belittle and insult people who struggled with disabilities and mental health issues, in one instance telling them that they did not have minds. This could be considered verbal abuse that obstructs a "right to the highest attainable physical and mental health," especially regarding mental illness (ICESCR, art. 12; OHCHR, 1996–2019d). It is an example of "degrading treatment," from which people with disabilities should be protected according to the Convention on the Rights of Persons with Disabilities (art. 15; United Nations, n.d.-b). I saw other music workers not intervene when locals started to fight at a music event. This in some cases threatened rights of health if the fight went far enough. One music therapist working with HIV/AIDS patients strongly encouraged participants to shake hands and belittled those who did not. Participants who had open sores on their hands, whether due to eczema or intravenous drug use, risked blood-borne virus transmission, which threatened their human right to "prevention, treatment and control of epidemic and endemic diseases" (ICESCR, art. 11). Since it was not possible for me to get permission in any community ethics review process to write about rights violations in detail in Downtown Eastside organizations, I can only say that they exist. One must be vigilant about human rights violations.

---

[8] An oft-discussed example of what was called the Danish cartoon affair illustrated the tension between freedom of religion and freedom of expression: *Jyllands-Posten* published a series of 12 cartoons on the prophet Mohammed, which resulted in widespread protests in Muslim countries, a murder plot, and an explosion.

8

THE RIGHT TO THE CITY DURING GENTRIFICATION

AS IMPORTANT AND sometimes troubling as the previously described music projects can be, they can be threatened with complete obliteration during gentrification in such socioeconomically depressed urban neighborhoods as the Downtown Eastside. Gradually since the 1980s, yuppie shops and restaurants, condominiums, and upscale apartment developments (many being built and others in approved city-planning stages) have interspersed the kinds of organizations I describe. This type of development is called gentrification. Gentrification transforms an economically depressed, working-class or "vacant" area of a city (e.g., industrial buildings) into upper economic class, middle-class, and/or commercial use (adapted from Slater, 2012: 173). It has widely emerged in cities in Canada, Australia, New Zealand, and Europe and more sporadically in Japan, South Africa, Brazil (Smith, 1996: xv), and China. In Australia, another term for gentrification is "trendification." The term "gentrification" has received a makeover, being removed from many policy and planning discourses, together with its class and displacement problems. It has been replaced with terms such as "renaissance," "regeneration," and "revitalization," which direct attention away from the politically sensitive nature of gentrification processes (Mathews, 2010: 662).

Music Downtown Eastside. Klisala Harrison, Oxford University Press (2020). © Oxford University Press.
DOI: 10.1093/oso/9780197535066.001.0001.

A play on the word "gentry," "gentrification" was coined by sociologist Ruth Glass in 1964 (Glass, 1964: xvii). Examples were first noted on a significant scale in North American and European cities in the 1970s (Ley, 1986: 521). Although this chapter focuses on center-city redevelopment, gentrification is a suburban and rural phenomenon as well, occurring in different ways (Lees, Bang, and López-Morales, 2015) in the global South, East, and North.

Gentrification pressures can best be understood as part of economic and political processes of development and displacement, occurring on a global scale (Harrison, 2020; Ley, 1986). Gentrification happens within a global context of restructuring and broad economic trends, especially the rise of nonlocal sources of development financing and widespread deregulation of financial markets. This impacts city development in the areas of finance and property investment (Mitchell, 1996: 483). A boom of urban development in Vancouver started in the 1990s, resulting in a rapid inflow of capital and large-scale urban development projects funded by nonlocal sources. In addition to rapid rise in rents and mammoth price and tax increases for homeowners, this had impacts of "ongoing construction of high-rise luxury residential buildings and retail space, gentrification in the areas surrounding these developments, increasing homelessness, and the loss of single-resident occupancy (SRO) hotels, inhabited by many of the poorest members of the downtown" (Mitchell, 1996: 487). This kind of development has been affecting the Downtown Eastside more and more intensely. Upscale building development is set to only increase. At the same time, homelessness is on the rise (Swanson, Mugabo, and Chan, 2017).

Gentrification displaces urban poor. As economic and political forces push urban poor out from the Downtown Eastside's SRO hotels and social housing units, the popular music programs specifically for them are closing. As I showed in Table 3.3, 4 out of 10 music therapy programs or jams using popular music that I studied in the Downtown Eastside closed by 2019. These were all participatory music programs in which anyone off the street could take part. Defunding of social programs for urban poor is both a symptom of and contributor to deepening gentrification since the poor aren't afforded social space.

As gentrification encroaches, today's dwindling music programs are accessed by the homeless and street-involved as well as by now-displaced poor who continue to frequent the Downtown Eastside. The rough street scene, an attraction for some, has not disappeared despite gentrification, with the nearby Port of Vancouver providing seemingly unstoppable access to illicit drugs arriving on foreign container ships.

If and as urban poor are displaced, this threatens their right to the city, particularly the part of the city that they chose to be part of, the Downtown Eastside.

Lefebvre conceptualized the right to the city as "a superior form of rights" encompassing the "right to freedom, to individualization in socialization, to habitat and to inhabit" (Lefebvre, 1996: 173). Recent urban rights activism maps Lefebvre's ideas from his 1968 book *Le droit à la ville* (The right to the city) onto specific human rights (many enshrined in United Nations [UN] treaties since the 1970s). The right to the city thus refers to the collection of human rights that people living in cities can experience.

Urban planning scholar Peter Marcuse explains that the right to the city calls for a bundle of human rights to be enjoyed by all people living in urban environments, especially urban poor:

> The homeless person in Los Angeles has not won the right to the city when he is allowed to sleep on a park bench in the center of the city. Much more is involved, as the concept refers to a set of rights, not individualistic rights. An intuitively analogous concept might be that of citizenship: citizenship involves a set of rights, and the claim to citizenship is not a claim to the right to vote, or to protection of the law, or to a right of entry, but to a status that provides all of these rights as a right to the single status of citizenship. (Marcuse, 2012: 35)

The right to the city concept originated as a call for "the necessities to a decent life," especially for people deprived of those (Marcuse, 2012: 34). Within this, the phrase has always advocated for meeting basic needs like "access to shelter, food, clean water, health, and education" (Schmid, 2012: 43). As Lefebvre wrote, the "*right to the city* legitimates the refusal to allow oneself to be removed from urban reality by a discriminatory and segregative organization" (Lefebvre, 1996: 195; italics in original). In that the right to the city refers to people's capabilities to remake themselves through "creating a qualitatively different kind of urban sociality" (Harvey, 2003: 939; Lefebvre, 1996), the concept centrally involves self-determination. By contrast, gentrification's displacement of urban poor extinguishes their capability to self-determine where they live. The right to the city, as David Harvey writes, necessitates a "vigorous anti-capitalist movement that focuses on the transformation of daily urban life as its goal" (Harvey, 2013: xvi). Inequities produced by capitalism continue to reign when the right to the city is not upheld.

At the same time as gentrification displaces the poor and results in the closure of music programs designed for them, economic opportunities open up particularly for professional performing artists working or wanting to work in a socioeconomically depressed urban neighborhood. The new funds especially nurture the development of presentational performance skills and thus, arts professionalization in the locale. This has been the trend in the Downtown Eastside, as it is in many city neighborhoods during gentrification. Following new funding opportunities relevant to the Downtown Eastside area, professional artists established new organizations aimed at developing musical skills of the poor, for example, music academies working with disadvantaged youth, such as the Sarah McLachlan School of Music and Saint James Music Academy. Organizations that continued to exist since before gentrification typically increased their revenues as well. Table 3.2 showed that the annual revenues of 9 out of 10 organizations offering participatory and presentational music-making increased for the most recent five years.[1] During gentrification, for about half of these organizations, revenue increased as did dollar amounts spent on charitable activities, such as donating space for music-making. As a result, established performing arts companies could focus their work on artistic capability development in the neighborhood.

In interviews that I conducted with organizers, administrators, professional artists, and local musicians, I heard only about positive effects of participating in initiatives that developed performing arts skills, particularly through the music theater productions in which I performed violin, and arranged for my university students to volunteer as cast and crew. Yet on the Internet in private blogs, I read extremely critical comments about professionals exploiting the poor for their own artistic and career benefits. Bloggers critiqued instances when the upper crust of the poor, not the indigent, artistically performed and represented the poorest of the poor. They also wrote that arts administrators and professionals as well as the upper crust of the poor gained the most financially from the performances, for example, through employment and artist fees. The implication is that the indigent, who were often represented artistically in public performances of music theater, did not benefit as much (NowPublic, 2006; Reliable Sources, 2006). Indeed, one music director told me that instead of the indigent, he found it easiest to work with the working poor, persistently unemployed, and dependent poor who rely on income support (Torjman, 1998: 22–23) as well as with arts professionals. I will share how some local theater companies worked with and overcame such challenges in creative ways. They prioritized paying artists in training, including urban poor, as well as professional artists[2] who took key roles in the performances, which I will

---

[1] After controlling for inflation rates using the Bank of Canada's online inflation calculator, the following organizations increased revenue, by the Canadian dollar amount provided in parentheses: First United Church ($938,452 in 2017 dollars), PHS ($9,428,551 in 2018 dollars), Saint James Music Academy ($266,932 in 2018 dollars), Sarah McLachlan School of Music ($458,697 in 2018 dollars), and Vancouver Moving Theatre ($341,066 in 2018 dollars). The Carnegie Community Centre's revenue grew more modestly, by $72,626 (in 2017 dollars).

[2] When I took part in music theater productions in the mid-2000s, participants—for example, chorus members, actors, and band members—were paid $20 CAD per rehearsal or performance. A rehearsal or performance could be several hours, but a workshop could extend all day. Professionals

describe. Some of the urban poor participants went on to professional careers in the arts[3] after developing skills and performing in local projects (Harrison, 2013b).

Gentrified neighborhoods often become arts districts, and arts districts resulting from gentrification end up offering professional arts. As ethnomusicologist Jeff Todd Titon comments, "professionalization . . . is encouraged when cultural tourism is the goal, and professionalization quickly becomes commercialization" (Fenn and Titon, 2003: 129). The oft-cited example of the gentrification of Manhattan's Lower East Side as a cultural mecca, as geographer Neil Smith wrote, "attracted tourists, consumers, gallery gazers, art patrons, potential immigrants— all fueling gentrification" (Smith, 1996: 19). Other examples of gentrified, professional arts areas are many and worldwide including Beijing's Dashanzi Arts District (called 798), Shanghai's Suzhou Creek, London's East End, and residential landscapes of Rio de Janeiro, as well as many inner or center cities in the United States and Canada.

Academics have extensively explored entanglements of artists with gentrification but have neglected the role of the poor in presentational arts, capability development, and their relationships to the right to the city, my focus here. Reflecting on New York's Lower East Side, art historian Rosalyn Deutsche and journalist Cara Gendel Ryan (1984) theorized three moments of gentrification: first, an influx of artists from elsewhere into a gentrifying area; second, contingent upon the success of the first, the movement of the middle socioeconomic class into the area and the sharp rise of rental prices; and third, the aestheticization of the poor in the arts, after which the poor move out of the field of vision: "As a process of dispersing a 'useless' class, gentrification is aided and abetted by an 'artistic' process whereby poverty and homelessness are served up for aesthetic pleasure" (Deutsche and Ryan, 1984: 111). Perspectives that cast artists as easing gentrification received a vast boost from the subsequent and related creative economy and creative class theses. Proponents, especially economist Richard Florida, theorized that a creative economy of local artists has an innate ability to attract

---

are paid at the discretion of the organizers, ranging from minimum wage to industry-standard fees. Emerging artists receive honorariums (email communication, Savannah Walling, July 22, 2016).

[3] Nevertheless, reported income levels of performing musicians are toward the bottom of a national income hierarchy for professional artists in Canada as well as for employment specifically in the arts. A company specializing in social science research of the Canadian arts sector, Hill Strategies Research, notes that in 2001, musicians and singers in Canada had average earnings of $16,090 CAD—which was below Canada's low-income cut-off ($18,400 CAD) for a single person living in a community of 500,000 or more. Conductors, composers, and arrangers reported an average income of $27,381, and producers, directors, and related occupational workers (in music and other arts), an income of $43,111 (Hill Strategies Research, 2013). Working as a musician was found to be the second-worst-paying job in the arts in Canada, the worst being dancing.

affluent class members who enjoy success in nonartistic arenas due to their "creative" skills, and thus, form a creative class. During gentrification, the creative class buy redeveloped properties like condos. As a formerly socioeconomically depressed neighborhood transforms into an arts district, and features works by many actual artists, the creative class consumes local arts. Local arts and artists pique the interest of the creative class to spend time and money in the neighborhood, which boosts local business more generally (Florida, 2002; Grodach, 2013). By contrast, many recent studies interpret resistance to gentrification in the artistic expressions that emerge during such processes of urban redevelopment. The interpretations separate out what artists do from "destructive" economic and social forces of gentrification, but again, tend not to focus on the indigent (see Donish, 2013; Loughran, 2008, 2009; Somdahl-Sands, 2008; Szöke, 2015; Vona, 2015; Wang, 2016; Yu, 2017). When gentrification succeeds, artists typically must move out of a neighborhood because it becomes too expensive for them to live there (see Young, 2014).

In the following, I will document and examine the presentational music performances in the Downtown Eastside during its intensifying gentrification, focusing particularly on the history of music theater in the Downtown Eastside. What has been the role of urban poor, and particularly popular musicians active in the jams and music therapy sessions, in those presentational performances? Which human rights included in the right to the city have the performances supported for urban poor? I also consider which kinds of urban poor have benefited.

Professional performing artists started getting involved, through music theater, with urban poor of the Downtown Eastside in the late 1990s. Numerous popular music theater performances developed out of activism that sought to destigmatize the neighborhood and build opportunities and political voice for and with residents. The music theater initiatives began, their organizers said, as ethical acts that professional performing artists undertook through a sense of social responsibility and justice (e.g., interviews with Savannah Walling, December 18, 2003, October 16, 2012, October 19, 2016, November 4, 2016; interview with Donna Wong Juliani, January 25, 2005).

Jim Green, an anthropologist who positioned himself as an anti-poverty activist,[4] instigated the local music-drama productions by approaching Donna Wong Juliani, director of Vancouver's micro-opera company Opera Breve. He asked Opera Breve to give concerts in an opera performance series at Four Corners Bank, located kitty-corner to the Carnegie Community Centre. Wong Juliani recalled

---

[4] An organizer for the Downtown Eastside Residents Association, Green worked toward improving housing conditions of the poor and eradicating homelessness through developing social housing.

that Green said to her, "I am [also] president of a bank in the Downtown Eastside and my people that I am thinking of are my clients, the clients of the bank who would never [miss] an opportunity to experience opera really; even though I serve on the Vancouver Opera board, the two worlds are so far apart in terms of accessibility. Do you suppose you could come and do some of your opera in my bank?" (interview with Donna Wong Juliani, January 25, 2005). Green and Wong Juliani observed much local interest in combining music and drama during a following Singing Bank series that featured seven evenings of opera over two years (1999–2000). Wong Juliani remembers:

> He called me up in September. We did an October Halloween show, themed it around "spooky stuff," and then we did a Christmas show. And it was standing room only. People [from the Downtown Eastside, and often urban poor] lined up around the block to get in to see. It was free, okay, and it was only publicized around that neighborhood (we didn't want the rest of the city rushing down to see something they could pay for and see in the usual venues). And it was absolutely magical from all quarters. (interview with Donna Wong Juliani, January 25, 2005)

The bank series attracted national attention in Canada, including a visit from the governor general's consort at the time—philosopher, novelist, and essayist John Ralston Saul.

Jim Green then asked the Juliani family if staging an opera featuring Downtown Eastside locals could be possible. It turned out not to be, practically speaking, because locals were not trained in opera. Popular song and music were achievable outcomes though. (Other organizations later took up opera initiatives with urban poor, especially Vancouver Opera, the Carnegie Community Centre, and the Kettle Society.)

By 2002, Savage God theater company, directed by Canadian theater icon John Juliani (Donna Wong Juliani's husband; 1940–2003), staged a cabaret written and performed by Downtown Eastside locals as a Valentine's Day greeting to the neighborhood, addressing the overarching title *I Love the Downtown Eastside*. The show comprised 49 short performances that told about what performers loved and didn't love about their neighborhood, through popular songs, other music, movement, poems, sketches, stand-up comedy, read prose, and testimonials. Some of the show's creators and performers were among the poorest of the poor. Others included residents, most of whom could be categorized as working poor, persistently unemployed and dependent poor, and two children of artists working in the neighborhood. Wong Juliani recalled:

> The room was packed with audience, and I think everybody, myself included, were all nervous wrecks about just getting through the show, right. But it was. It took off. It really, really took off. It was an extraordinary presentation. And then at the very last beat of the show the entire audience got up on its feet and were clapping and cheering and whistling and just like, if I had stood at the door and slipped a toonie [\$2 CAD coin] to everybody and said, "Listen, when the show is over, would you please stand up and applaud? Please, just give them back some positive feedback," it wouldn't have been nearly as effective. But there it was, absolutely spontaneous and the reaction to the show itself and to what the audience had been moved to experience. Because it was very moving. People told their life story, not long, very shortened versions, but told about themselves and sang about themselves and some of them sang their own songs that they had composed and created. (interview with Donna Wong Juliani, January 25, 2005)

Downtown Eastsiders responded to the performance of local story with local music astoundingly positively—an altogether different response compared to the censorship of original songs by local singer-songwriters within popular music jams.

By 2002–2003, other Downtown Eastside organizations including Vancouver Moving Theatre (or VMT), Theatre in the Raw, and the Carnegie Community Centre, among others, started organizing many other presentational music performances and events. VMT took the lead in producing the highest number of musical shows. Music theater productions—plays filled with popular music in their majority—included *In the Heart of a City: The Downtown Eastside Community Play* (2003), *Through the People's Voice: One-Act Plays* (2004), *Condemned—The Carnegie Opera* (2006), *We're All in This Together: The Shadows Project—Addiction and Recovery* (2007), *The Returning Journey* (2007), *A Downtown Eastside Romeo and Juliet* (2008), *Bruce—The Musical* (2008), and two music theater showcases (2009 and 2011). *Storyweaving: Weaving First Nations Memories from the Past into the Future* (2012) and *Weaving Reconciliation* (2017–2018) addressed Indigenous Canadian topics. VMT produced all of the aforementioned performances except *Condemned* and *Bruce*. Downtown Eastside urban poor with musical and theatrical talent could audition to perform in all of these shows. Downtown Eastside artists including singer-songwriters were invited to perform at myriad other events, too, for example, the Heart of the City Festival, produced annually by VMT since 2004.

VMT's executive producer Terry Hunter said that VMT, in creating these events, responded to locals, especially urban poor, expressing a need for further skills and education in the performing arts including music and theater: "After the community play, we had a conversation with the community play participants and they were very clear about what they wanted next. They wanted ongoing and sustainable arts activities in this community and they wanted [involved] stories to reflect the concerns of this community and they wanted training to perform those stories themselves" (email communication with Terry Hunter, October 29, 2019). VMT, as a long-time performing arts company based in the Downtown Eastside, had the skills to act on this drive. VMT's main goal, executive director Savannah Walling said, then became to "help contribute in ways that are going to nourish and seed, and generate lasting ripples" (interview with Savannah Walling, October 19, 2016). Performance projects that facilitated skill development for the indigent took support from certain music programs in aid organizations. Stephanie Swenson, reflecting on her music therapy practice using popular songs at The 44, said that she coached participants who felt they needed music tutoring beyond what the projects offered, to prepare them for specific performances:

> A client might be involved in a play, or performance in another setting in the [Downtown Eastside] and would ask me to teach them the guitar part or to write a song for the play or to teach them a singing part so they could be successful and prepared for their performance. These lessons helped people develop skills to perform at the Heart of the City Festival, at Carnegie performances, and for [the] Women Rock program. (email from Stephanie Swenson, October 16, 2019)

Music lessons for urban poor, as aid, informed these participants' capabilities to participate in music theater productions and other opportunities in the performing arts locally.

Whereas urban poor first took a prominent role as creators and performers of *I Love the Downtown Eastside*, the first entire show dedicated to protesting the challenges gentrification poses to right to the city was *Condemned*, produced by the Carnegie Community Centre. Six community writers, as they called themselves, some indigent and all urban poor, wrote the play text and song lyrics for *Condemned*, with mentorship from writer Joan Skogan and composer, conductor, and dramaturge Ramona Luengen. The writers were Grant Chauncey, James Elmore, Patrick Foley, Leith Harris, Jason Logan, and Mike Richter. The show combined local writers and singers with professional directors. Earle Peach directed the music; Susanna

Uchatius directed workshop performances in 2006, and John Cooper directed final performances in 2007. *Condemned* featured a professional band. The employed musicians had nonmusic jobs in the Downtown Eastside and/or lived elsewhere yet wanted to be involved. Fourteen singer-actors, with limited formal music training, sang the songs. The blogs critiqued the singers as not being indigent and mostly living outside the neighborhood (NowPublic, 2006; Reliable Sources, 2006).

As with most of the music theater productions in the Downtown Eastside, the poorest of the poor formed the writing team that scripted the song lyrics and dialogue. With professional guidance and mentorship, urban poor wrote what the amateur singer-actors received training to perform. These representations unfolded within a setting, typical for professional theater, of a producer/manager, director, codirector, play officer running the play office, designer, musical director, stage manager, lighting person, assistant to the director, assistant designer, and assistant stage managers. The theater professionals curated how the scripts were realized.

Through writing lyrics and dialogue, local urban poor explicitly and publicly rejected gentrification and its human rights threats. *Condemned* tells the story of Joe, who finds himself homeless. The apartment building where he lives is condemned for razing and redevelopment. Anna, a survival sex worker, comforts him, only to find herself in the same housing situation. Yet a researcher videotapes evidence that a real estate agent and a developer have fabricated a story about a crystal methamphetamine lab existing in Joe's building, in order to justify condemning it. Although activists protest and organize to take court action, bulldozers are already destroying Joe's home. One of the actor-singers, Bharbara Gudmundson, commented:

> It brings to the forefront what it is that's actually going on. People [outside the neighborhood] know what's going on, but they don't see it, they don't feel the trauma. They see the little bits and pieces when the violence happens. (CBC Arts, 2008)

The writers based *Condemned* on a true story, local poet Sandy Cameron wrote: "On September 15, 2005, members of the Vancouver Police and the Vancouver Fire Departments raided the Pender Hotel without a warrant, allegedly in search of a crystal meth lab" (Cameron, 2007). Urban poor penned lyrics of strident protest as gentrification pushed them and their neighbors out of the neighborhood. The producer of a 2008 remount, Mel Lehan, said, "The [2010 Winter] Olympics are bringing demolition, development speculation and people are being forced out onto the street" (Cameron, 2007). Gentrification remained a relevant issue during show remounts.

The lyrics of *Condemned* identify housing as a human right. The song "Rise Up People," for example, asks people to join a fight that insists that having "a home is a fundamental right" (Walling, Hunter, and Greenaway, 2015: 65). Article 25 of the Universal Declaration of Human Rights (UDHR) recognizes that everyone "has the right to a standard of living adequate for the health and well-being of himself and of his family, including food, clothing, housing and medical care and necessary social services." The legally enforceable UN International Covenant on Economic, Social and Cultural Rights (ICESCR) similarly recognizes "the right of everyone to an adequate standard of living for himself and his family, including adequate food, clothing and housing" (art. 11.1). These are among the many human rights implied by the right to the city.

Condemned thus took a human rights stance against gentrification, particularly the razing of run-down buildings to make way for redevelopment. It promoted the right to the city, and especially the human right of housing. The premiere's program—paralleling the performance—contained gentrification-related information. It spread news about four SRO hotels where urban poor had lived and that had been closed, potentially illegally. Sandy Cameron wrote a history of Downtown Eastside hotels, highlighting the substandard living conditions in SRO hotel rooms. He added, about the poorest of the poor, "If they should lose their rooms, the most marginalized people in our society will end up on the street, in shelters, in jails, in hospitals, or in the morgue" (Carnegie Community Centre, 2006). The program encouraged audience members to take specific political actions against SRO closures and a lack of low-income housing in Vancouver including writing a letter to the prime minister, premier, or mayor (letter drop-off was organized at the Carnegie Community Centre).

Condemned features two songs with melody, harmony, and lyrics by Mike Richter (Photo 8.1), who identifies as urban poor after taking a voluntary vow of poverty. The rest of the music was composed by professional Earle Peach. While Peach had earlier facilitated the Carnegie's music program, Richter has been singing and performing guitar for many years in popular music jams of the Carnegie Community Centre and other Downtown Eastside organizations.

Richter's songs, "Nitty Gritty City" and "Jimmy the Binner," formed the opening and closing numbers of *Condemned*. "Nitty Gritty City," Richter said,

> was built on a bass riff that Stan Hudac had worked out on piano. He liked to use that bass riff when he played [Glenn Miller's] "In the Mood." So, with his permission, I took that same riff, and then I just built different chords off that. It's his underlying rhythmic feel that's under all that, and I kind of

PHOTO 8.1. Downtown Eastside singer, songwriter, and guitarist Mike Richter.
Photo by Loni Taylor, 2009.

built the whole thing, musically around that. The bridge is different, but the
guts of the song really comes from that riff. (interview with Mike Richter,
November 6, 2016)

Stan Hudac (1948–2017) shared his virtuosic jazz piano skills around the neighborhood wherever there was a piano. He became lovingly called the Piano Man.
Richter noted that "the words had come separately" to him (he was one of the
community writers penning the libretto), but in line with Hudac, he tried to accompany them with "jazzy kinds of chord sounds" (interview with Mike Richter,
November 6, 2016). Richter honored Hudac though incorporating his riff into
"Nitty Gritty City," which Richter described as a "technical piece" since it is difficult to sing well (interview with Mike Richter, November 6, 2016), containing
angular melodies with many intervallic leaps and jumps.

Another music theater production featuring lyrics and musical sounds of the
poor is the popular music shadow play *We're All in This Together: The Shadows
Project—Addiction and Recovery*, produced by VMT (developed starting 2005,
with final performances in 2007). Like *Condemned*, *We're All in This Together* is an

example of urban poor taking a huge role in writing a music theater script. People with poverty backgrounds penned most of the song lyrics as well as the dialogue. A writing team of 10 wrote the play's 12 scenes, in a collaborative process devised and overseen by director James Fagan Tait with lead writers Rosemary Georgeson and Savannah Walling. Each writer was matched up with one scene that was theirs to develop in year 1, and then in year 2, the writers participated in a writers' retreat on Galiano Island led by Indigenous dramaturg and playwright Marie Clements; the team fleshed out the show into 18 scenes.

We're All in This Together tells about three generations of two families from different social backgrounds struggling with addiction:

A child from an inner-city family dreamed of a dragon's irresistible treasure. His young mother struggled to survive and live sober in this world; his lost aunt to climb back to health; his grandmother coped with ancestral memories of dislocation. In an interweaving sub-story, an average family from the suburbs reminded us how life's pleasures can grow into habits that take over and run people's lives, while three people employed in the illegal—and legal—global pharmaceutical business, argued over their success in profiting off human misery. (Walling et al., 2015: 79)

Drug and alcohol addiction were in focus. VMT conducted 1,000 surveys, interviews, and conversations about addiction; it found these types of addiction to be foremost in the minds of Downtown Eastsiders and their artistic collaborators. The play also referenced other kinds of addiction, like to food, gaming, shopping, raging, and work.

Together with song and dialogue, shadow puppetry told the story about people living in urban poverty and the suburbs. Silhouettes on a white screen indexed diverse ethnicities that struggle with addiction through stencils (shadow puppets) that were made using Chinese woodblock printing techniques, evoked German expressionism, and influenced by Chinese and Pacific Northwest Coast First Nations myth. Georgeson, who belongs to the Coast Salish and Dene Indigenous groups, made the story a personal one rooted in her family's ties to local land going back to the time when it was trees and clam beds. She included her "family's history in the Downtown Eastside and how it has affected them over the generations and seeing the effects of a once-thriving area go downhill so rapidly" (Vancouver Moving Theatre, 2007: 81). She added that of her "seven years clean and sober," she has "celebrated four of them here on the Downtown Eastside" (Vancouver Moving Theatre, 2007: 15).

PHOTOS 8.2 AND 8.3. The band, shadow puppetry, and chorus of *We're All in This Together: The Shadows Project—Addiction and Recovery*.
Photos by Ken Tabata, 2007.

The song lyrics by urban poor again carried the plot together with sparse dialogue that they also wrote. The play's Indigenous protagonist, Katie, sang and spoke her struggles with loneliness, and drug and alcohol addiction when becoming home-less in the Downtown Eastside. Show lyrics all dealt with the "dragon" of addiction (Photos 8.2 and 8.3), and were sung by a chorus and soloists. "Red Poppies," with lyrics by Leith Harris, for instance, tells about growing poppies to manufacture heroin. "You Are Not Alone," a song with lyrics by Wendy Chew, addressed the loneliness potentially fueling addiction, while offering comfort to people who feel sad and lonely.

Like with the other music theater productions, a professional team developed the capabilities of amateur writers and singer-actors to create a rich production. Different professional directors guided each year of a two-year development process for *We're All in This Together*, James Fagan Tait in year 1 and Kim Collier in year 2. There were different professional musical directors each year, Joelysa Pankanea in year 1 and Ya-wen Wang in year 2. Pankanea, a Vancouver composer working in theater and film, created the musical score.

The artistic capability development undertaken through this and earlier music theater projects resulted in a heightened level of artistic professionalization. The singers sounded more professional; I enjoyed hearing participants in popular music jams and music therapy sessions succeeding with vocal solos in front of audiences of several hundred people. The accompanying visuals were complex and lush. Shadow puppetry behind the singing chorus illustrated the lyrics of poppies growing in a field far away—indicated by a globe and a peasant working in a field. An intricate poppy shadow accompanied the lyrics "Red poppies as far as the eye can see." Previously all shadows were black and white, but when the chorus sang "A hand squeezes juice from a poppy," the entire screen and poppy image turned red. As lyrics described a world of forgetfulness, pain relief, escape, and dreams, the shadow of a live female dancer moving in circles was superimposed on the red poppy image and swirling, bright-white light projections. As the lyrics described "a world of death," the shadow of a live male dancer appeared, grasping a vein in his arm, his head reaching skyward while the slide changed to an image of dead faces in black, white, and purple.

Some music theater productions, like *We're All in This Together*, included the instrumental sounds of local popular music jams and music therapy sessions. The band that accompanied *We're All in This Together* featured popular musicians who took part in music jams at the Health Contact Centre and Carnegie Community Centre.

The band consisted of Mike Richter on electric bass guitar, keyboard, and voice, and Dean Obrol (1954–2009) on electric guitar. Richter pointed out Obrol's impressive lead guitar playing: "Dean was playing all the nice fancy stuff on guitar. He inspired a lot of us around [the Carnegie Community Centre], a lot of the guitar players" (interview with Mike Richter, November 6, 2016). Several other musicians besides musical director Ya-wen Wang performed keyboard, accordion, taiko, and percussion as well as recorder, acoustic guitar, dulcimer, and violin. Some were urban poor of the Downtown Eastside. The sonic texture heard in popular music jams—dominated by guitar, voice, and drums—came to the fore of the show's sound because the other instruments featured only sporadically.

Participants who had postsecondary education or an arts career already before finding themselves in poverty circumstances took leadership roles in music theater more often than those who did not (see interview with Priscillia Tait, December 12, 2003; email from Priscillia Tait, August 23, 2016). Mike Richter, for example, had had music lessons as a child, then became a professional engineer after earning a BSc degree from McGill University. Others, such as Dalannah Gail Bowen, went on to develop as an artist after a career break. Bowen is one of VMT's "success stories" (Photo 8.4; see Harrison, 2013b, and Hombrebueno, Cheung, and Lee, 2009, for other success stories). She described her life before participating in the Downtown Eastside community play as dire:

> In 2003, I was living the life of a crack addict. I was couch surfing in places that I never in my wildest dreams thought I would be in and I can honestly say that it was the lowest point in my life. Every day my sole purpose was to feed my addiction. The recognition that I was deeply in trouble came when I no longer only did the drugs in the evening but morning, noon and night. . . . [I]t

PHOTO 8.4. Dalannah Gail Bowen.
Photo by Dee Lippingwell, submitted in 2016.

became my whole reason to exist. . . . After thirty-six years of making music, I was no longer singing very much. I did the occasional gig but nothing big. It was like my lifeline was cut off. (Walling et al., 2015: 90)

A talented blues singer with a passionate and textured voice, Bowen found the encouragement in community arts to recover from addiction and restart her music career—even take it to an international and award-winning level. By 2006, she played a role in an award-winning production of *Urinetown: The Musical* at the Downtown Eastside's Firehall Arts Centre. She wrote a one-woman show and her first musical about her "living through hell" in one and a half years in the Downtown Eastside—*The Returning Journey*, produced by the Firehall Arts Centre in 2007. That same year, at age 62, she recorded her first blues album, *Momma's Got the Blues*. It received airplay in Canada and in far-away Poland, France, and Argentina. The record placed among the top 50 blues albums in North America in the 2008 International Songwriting Awards. Bowen, among select other participants in the music theater productions, ended up working professionally in the arts,[5] including in, and beyond, what became a rapidly developing arts industry and district in the Downtown Eastside. Skill development through music theater supported these participants' economic rights, particularly their human right to work (ICESCR, art. 6.1), as artists.

Sometimes an individual director decided to foreground and include artists with more cultural capital, such as Bowen or Richter, who had honed his performance skills to a professional level independently. Bourdieu's notion of cultural capital refers to the capability to decode culture as a form of coded knowledge that is often status and education derived (Bourdieu, 1984 [1979]: 70; Bourdieu, 1993: 7, 270). A musical director for one production said that including street-involved people was not a priority because a rehearsal schedule would not adjust to them. It was "too irregular for them to really fit in because a lot of them, just, they hit the street and then they're gone, right. So, there'd be people that would come for one or two rehearsals and then they'd disappear" (in Harrison,

---

[5] Additionally, together with Owen Owen Owen, Bowen became the first BC blues artist to place in the International Blues Challenge in Memphis. In 2015, she was honored as a Master Blues Artist in the Blues Hall of Fame in the United States. African Canadian and Cherokee, she also performed with Snowy Owl Drummers, a group of Indigenous singers and hand drummers from the Cherokee, Cree, Squamish, Lakota, and Anishnabe nations. Furthermore, Bowen founded the Downtown Eastside Centre for the Arts, a grassroots community arts organization that has provided an accessible and welcoming environment for creative engagement, creative exploration, and creative expression in the Downtown Eastside community. Working from the belief that art is a healing tool, the Downtown Eastside Centre for the Arts has created opportunities to effect personal change by providing guided art practice in a safe and supportive setting.

2008: 191). In low-threshold or other service organizations, music programs had rigid weekly schedules for every activity including music, which people attended, on time, each week. These amateur musicians were seen not to fit in sonically too. One guitarist, which the musical director described as "hammered all the time," was mocked for wanting "to play Santana and the Beatles" like in the popular music jams and music therapy sessions, and refusing "to tune his guitar to A440. He wanted it, you know, like at 325 or something" (in Harrison, 2008: 181). Additional reasons for exclusion had to do with struggles faced by the poor for daily survival and immense time that the struggle consumes. Many urban poor could not participate regularly because they needed to stand in a line-up for free food and to secure a place to sleep for the night. In all, the poorest of the poor were less likely or were not invited to participate in all of the rehearsals and skill training required to take part in a music theater production, whereas the working poor and poor dependent on income support (Torjman, 1998: 22–23) with more stable living circumstances were more likely to participate.

VMT, in particular, worked productively with this challenge through extensive facilitation of the group writing of song lyrics and music theater narratives in ways that could include people experiencing stresses of poverty. VMT provided free food, payment for participants, and child care when needed. VMT also built into productions extensive community consultation processes so that even people in the most precarious living circumstances could have their voices and stories heard. Other poverty-related obstacles to participation, like no housing, proved too great for any performing arts project to resolve.

At the same time, the music theater initiatives I have described welcomed anyone who considered themselves a member of the Downtown Eastside community, including newcomers who moved into the neighborhood during gentrification and those who self-identified with the neighborhood (e.g., due to work, a family member, or a history there). While many people with poverty backgrounds benefited as participants in the arts initiatives, many who did not experience poverty in any way did too. To some extent, the artistic productions served, during gentrification, as means for people of different socioeconomic backgrounds to interact toward common goals of skill building and presentational performance, while also—through artistic representations and involvement of people with poverty backgrounds—resisting erasure of urban poor and their right to the city. Savannah Walling argued that "one of the most important things that we've been doing has been to try to work in a way that we continue to remind the community members themselves and people outside the community and the media that this is a community that has value and worth. Because if there's not that reminder or if there's not that perception, then it is really, really easy to wipe it out or disappear it" (interview with Savannah Walling, October 19, 2016).

At the same time, the music theater productions contributed to the development of an arts district in the Downtown Eastside, which often is an outcome of gentrification. The new arts district also included diverse events in which local artists—including singer-songwriters and other emerging musicians from the neighborhood—could perform. Performing artists and arts companies organizing music theater developed these. One example was the 2011 Downtown Eastside Artists in the Street Program, which "supported local artists with training, promotion and employment at local events . . . across Vancouver" (Walling et al., 2015: 140). Additional examples were leadership training programs in community-engaged arts; Breaking into the Biz Forum weekends of information sharing, discussion, and skill building (2004–2008); Arts for All Institutes, held in the Downtown Eastside on a continuing basis (e.g., in 2009, 2010, 2013, 2014, and 2016); and national symposiums such as one exploring new styles of collaborative community play building and interdisciplinary creation titled New Directions: The Fourth National Canadian Community Play Symposium (2008), TRACKS: Seventh Canadian Community Play and Art Symposium (2015), and a six-day national symposium bringing together community-engaged Indigenous and settler/immigrant artists, thinkers, and educators who collaborate to create art with, for, and about communities (2015).

In addition to the annual, 100- to 150-event Heart of the City Festival, VMT coproduced various smaller festivals, like The Spirit Rising Festival (2011), Carnegie 30th Anniversary Celebration (2010), Eastside Stories: The People. The Voices (2009), and the Japantown Multicultural Neighbourhood Celebration (2009). Still other events in which local performers had opportunities to practice their performance skills combined storytelling with music and dance, for instance, at East End Blues and All That Jazz (2006/2009/2011), Bread and Salt: A Tribute to the East End's Historic Ukrainian Community (2013), and The Big House: A Community Gathering and Cultural Feast (2015).

Within this arts district, performing arts leaders worked hard to open up life possibilities for their participants, including urban poor. All of VMT's music theater projects, for instance, have substantially built skills and capabilities in performing arts creation and performance. These intensive efforts have promoted education, and the right to education (ICESCR, art. 13.1; Convention on the Elimination of All Forms of Discrimination against Women [CEDAW], art. 10) for all involved including urban poor, immensely. For the community play *In the Heart of a City*—which chronicled the Downtown Eastside's history and involved about 500 people—VMT offered 43 preproduction, skill-building and art-making workshops in puppet making, choreography, acting, popular theater, theater sports, theater games, singing, (Indigenous Canadian) Métis dancing, hand drumming, flag making, banner creation, and mural making. During nine weeks of rehearsals, the professional artistic team provided guidance in singing, music ensemble performance, acting techniques, stage managing, choreography, shadow puppetry, set building, theater lighting, and costume and prop creation. To give another of very many examples, over two years, VMT organized numerous workshops to build local capabilities in forum theater, shadow theater, writing, collage, and digital media training toward the final performances of *We're All in This Together: The Shadows Project—Addictions and Recovery*. Workshops included a writers' retreat, forums and panels, public presentations for gathering audience feedback, and mentoring during rehearsals and for performances. Larry Reed, director of San Francisco's ShadowLight Productions, gave workshops on how to create modern projected shadow theater, which is three-dimensional compared to historical forms in which two-dimensional puppets were pressed against a shadow screen while an oil lamp or light bulb produced the shadows.

In conclusion, gentrification erases the human rights and capabilities developed through music programs for urban poor that close, sometimes together with aid organizations hosting them. At the same time, new opportunities open up for performing arts that are presentational and prioritize professionalism.

Since the late 1990s, during the gentrification of the Downtown Eastside, many new music theater productions have emerged, together with other arts events. Within a setting of professional music theater elements (direction, staging and props, lighting, costuming, musical accompaniment, and production), people with poverty backgrounds have appeared as singers and actors, performing lyrics and dialogue that they have created themselves, with professional mentorship. Operating from the perspective of social responsibility and justice, the music theater productions starred the indigent as lyricists and script writers, and, as performers, other people experiencing poverty (especially the working poor, persistently unemployed and dependent poor). Additional people with a connection to the neighborhood, including newcomers and the creative class, also had roles in the productions, which arts professionals curated overall. One singer-songwriter who has taken a vow of poverty, Mike Richter, contributed his own songs. Usually, professional music directors composed the score. While these productions promoted the cultural right to "participate in the cultural life of the community, to enjoy the arts" (UDHR, art. 27.1) for all participants, they created new cultural life in the Downtown Eastside. This new cultural life defined a fledgling arts district, which according to the urban redevelopment literature facilitates the final stages of gentrification.

The urban poor participants, for their part, developed and exercised their capabilities to write song lyrics and perform music theater. Doing so promoted their human rights to freedom of expression and freedom indispensable for creative activity. The skill development exercised participants' human right to education and promoted their right to work not only in the arts, but a range of jobs that require, for instance, excellent groupwork and ability to follow direction. These are some of the same human capabilities and rights promoted through music tutoring at aid organizations.

A gap exists between which kinds of participants these two types of initiatives typically included. Undertaking presentational performance is generally a less accessible activity than participatory performance. It thrives most when participants already experience psychological and emotional health and well-being, which intertwines with prosocial behaviors including good communication. Music therapy at aid organizations sought to develop the human right to health. People may not be in full psychological health, and therefore are unable to fully exercise the right, if they experience trauma, mental health issues or backgrounds of addiction. People living in poverty typically experience a broad range of other social deprivations as well, including low cultural capital (ability to decode culture, linked to higher education and status) due to low education and low status. Sometimes music theater projects gave urban poor with more cultural capital more opportunities than urban poor with less cultural capital. There were locals who might want to participate in presentational performances, but experienced such severe deprivations of their human rights to health or housing, for example, that they could not. Capability inequality thus manifested in performance roles and lack thereof.

Specific arts organizers worked to bridge the gap between presentational performances featuring people with more capabilities and cultural capital, and participatory performances being accessed by people experiencing less, plus human rights deprivations. VMT provided a variety of resources and services, such as food, payment for participants and child care, so that more artists really struggling with poverty issues could participate. Thanks to concerted efforts, skill development through music theater could enhance some of the human rights included in the right to the city, for and with some of the poorest of the poor. This could not avert the likelihood that gentrification will displace more of the poor from the Downtown Eastside together with their right to the city. Even local arts that protested this, by existing, contributed to an arts district that arguably fueled gentrification.

III

Conclusions

9

THE POWER TO DO SOMETHING

IN *MUSIC DOWNTOWN Eastside*, I have analyzed the dynamic relationships between music, human rights, and the development of human capability or the
"power to do something" (Sen, 2009: 19). Bearing in mind that social deprivations
of human rights and capabilities in part define poverty, I explored whether and
how (popular) music practices can enhance human rights and related capabilities
of the poorest of the poor, such as homeless and street-involved people—a.k.a.
the indigent—who feel that music is a "thing" that can never be taken away from
them. I described urban poor exercising and developing their capabilities within
formally organized music-making at nonprofit organizations such as community centers, health centers, and churches of Downtown Eastside Vancouver.
I documented popular music facilitators and music therapists actively promoting
the poor's capabilities of life management, self-expression, grieving, creating a
safe space, positive parent–child interactions, and connecting socially and with
their own feelings.

I considered music-making as a social site where human rights, intertwined
with capabilities, are promoted and/or negated. This perspective grounded my
mapping of how human rights circulate in musical moments, and what this means

Music Downtown Eastside. Klisala Harrison, Oxford University Press (2020). © Oxford University Press.
DOI: 10.1093/oso/9780197535066.001.0001.

for the specific social deprivations of rights and capabilities important in current definitions of poverty.

Capabilities enable human rights. If one has more capabilities, one enjoys more human rights more fully. Many capabilities but not all come with socioeconomic wealth. Therefore, a socioeconomically privileged person enjoys more human rights in comparison to a person who lives in poverty. For example, money can buy an education in music which develops capabilities. Music education activates the human right to education, in turn contributing to the right to work using the skills it builds (musical or other). Enjoying human rights begets the enjoyment of more human rights, as well.

For musical and cultural practitioners, capabilities are usefully understood as targets for development that, in turn, strengthen human rights. My defining capabilities in this practical way extends Amartya Sen's perspective that capabilities concern "the responsibilities and obligations of societies and of other people generally to help the deprived, which can be important for both public provisions within states and for the general pursuit of human rights" (Sen, 2009: 238). Music, arts and culture practitioners can enhance specific capabilities that, in turn, promote human rights in a given population. In Downtown Eastside Vancouver, where music facilitators and therapists work with the poorest of the poor who by and large struggle with non-musical problems of poverty, the capabilities developed are for the most part non-musical yet nurtured through music-making.

Human rights motivate ideas, approaches and policies implemented through music and culture. In urban poverty settings, I showed how ideas from the health equity movement take support from the right to health; how the right to self-determination motivates the social work method of noninterference; and how advocates of the harm reduction approach assert that it enables a variety of human rights for addicted people. I used health equity ideas, the noninterference method, and harm reduction as (analytical) units for cross-case analysis at different music sessions across the Downtown Eastside in which I studied human rights promotion, negation and conflict. The music session facilitators and music therapists chose which capabilities and human rights to develop among the poor.

Various music therapists and facilitators in Downtown Eastside organizations react against autonomy erosion that urban poor experience by rebuilding, via music, their capability to exercise autonomy and thereby strengthen their right to health. Lack of autonomy, or sense of control over one's life circumstances, increases morbidity and mortality rates. According to the public health literature, this is one reason that the poor die younger than the more affluent, and that health problems proliferate in poverty. The health equity movement argues that autonomy is necessary for the flourishing of the right to health.

At the same time, some other activities of the very same organizations may be experienced as the opposite. Aid organizations in the Downtown Eastside monitor the behavior of indigent poor accessing their support and services toward their very survival. Organizations do this to maintain order and security, but for the poor, their sense of autonomy can feel eroded. Well-intentioned and activist projects of music in poverty rarely shift socially broader contexts of inequality that erode human rights; they work within them.

I detailed how, at The 44, group music therapy prioritized autonomy. The music therapist and her clients together made a songbook of words and chords of songs that the participants liked to hear and excelled at performing. The songbook increased participants' control (and autonomy) over the music that they chose to play and also gave them self-confidence in their performance capabilities. At The 44, the music therapist also left social space for the participants to discuss the song selections. The participants themselves (autonomously) chose to talk about and grieve individuals who had died, particularly former members of their music therapy group. Each of the songbook's songs represented an individual who liked the song or performed it well, yet many former participants had died. Downtown Eastside organizations usually do not pay for celebrations of life for the many urban poor who die there. Therefore, this presented an invaluable opportunity to grieve. At The 44, via music, the poor autonomously exercised self-care of their grieving processes and mental health. However, the music therapy process did not change any organizational structure that dissolved autonomy of the participants in the first place.

While most often directed at non-musical capabilities, all local music initiatives—according to the aims, missions, and mandates of aid organizations—*also* sought to support "the right freely to participate in the cultural life of the community, to enjoy the arts" (UDHR, art. 27.1). In practice though, while some participants, especially men performing song covers, freely participated, others like women and songwriters of all genders felt excluded from popular music jams and music therapy. Some women argued that barriers to their participation stemmed from systemic inequities in Canadian society, when men treat women as inferior and women of low socioeconomic status cannot access music education. Songs created by local songwriters, but that few locals knew, did not fit a dominant value of the popular music scene—inclusivity. With everybody's participation in singing and, as possible, instrumental performance being highly valued, songwriters who attempted to perform their own songs were discouraged from doing so with sonic harassment. People who censored original songs by making overwhelmingly loud noises, and performing hit songs instead, promoted their own their human rights to freely participate in the cultural life of the community as well as to freedom of expression and freedom indispensable for creative activity. The censorship discouraged songwriters from exercising these same human rights in the same musical moments. It also discouraged the musical capabilities involved in writing and performing original songs. It suppressed human rights engaged by original songs' lyrics and sounds, which in the Downtown Eastside included freedom of religion, Indigenous cultural rights, and civil and political rights, such as the right to freedom of thought and conscience.

Thus, I documented various human rights of different people conflicting in musical and cultural moments. In cases of rights conflicts, which often engage social inequities and socioeconomic hierarchies, defining who belongs to a community or to a social group may resist or reinforce those inequities and hierarchies. This makes the roles of any evaluator of human rights promotion or violation, and any intervenor in human rights in cultural contexts, extremely political. Participants at the community level are firmly embedded in these politics, as well.

The number of human rights circulating in single musical moments, and the kinds of capabilities that develop the rights, can be many. Considering both music facilitators and participants, I studied if and how various kinds of human rights—especially the right to health, women's rights, and the right to self-determination—are respected, strengthened, weakened, threatened, or violated in the popular music jams and therapy sessions. I also documented when the enhancement or limiting of capabilities subsequently enables or blocks rights. At Sheway, I documented how multiple human rights were exercised and strengthened in single musical moments that emerged from a harm reduction approach. The music therapist used music to model the capability to undertake healthy parenting for mothers with addiction backgrounds interacting with their babies. The development of this capability enacted the human right of provision of assistance to parents regarding performance of childrearing. At the same time, through singing and performing songs, and enhancing their capabilities to do so, the mothers strengthened their right to (music) education. Writing song lyrics about how the women access Sheway's services furthermore supported the mothers' human right to access of medical services and attention in case of illness and, when those services addressed their addictions, the right to prevention, treatment, and control of diseases, for example, illnesses communicated by the sharing of drug paraphernalia. The music therapist used song lyrics to teach the mothers how to take care of their health and well-being by using Sheway's services. When singing songs, the women also exercised their right to freedom of expression. The mothers maintained a safe and non-violent social space when musicking, and in so doing, protected their human right to security.

When it comes to human rights promotion and implementation, I emphasized that there exists a lack of always-simple causal relationships between human rights intentions and cultural outcomes. With Women Rock, I observed that human rights actually promoted within artistic practices may not be precisely the same rights as those drawn attention to in discourses or observations motivating those actions, with the same intensity, for the same reasons or for the same people. Any of these elements may differ at different points in time. Whereas the organizers set out to support the human right to education and additional women's rights, their work impacted participants' lives in a perhaps deeper way than initially envisioned. It addressed their felt and often painful experiences of systemic inequities regarding those rights.

I found that different musical and cultural formats may direct human rights impacts differently—affecting different human rights or different people. Rights-strengthening aims of protests, for example, most frequently aim at people beyond a protest setting, but the rights exercised in the protest itself are those of the protesters. For example, the Downtown Eastside's Women's Memorial March and its music aimed at supporting the right to life and health of women at risk of murder and disappearance. In the March, protesters exercised their own civil and political rights through singing, particularly their rights to freedom of thought, to hold opinions without interference, and to freedom of expression. By contrast, when Women Rock organizers of a musical event aligned their value of promoting human rights with what they hoped to accomplish through music and also conscientiously saw the rights implementation through, the rights intentions and outcomes aligned better—but not entirely (yielding some unexpected yet welcomed results). Human rights intentionality matters, but people tend not to think of musical and cultural formats or genres in human rights terms. Musical formats and genres have consequences for rights trajectories. As well, any causal relationships between human rights intentions, and outcomes in music and culture, may be complex and changeable; various actors can revise them over time.

I find it important, particularly regarding marginalized people, to look beyond what is immediately obvious in any attempts to promote human rights and capabilities, to the less often heard and seen. This includes internal and subjective human struggles, which human rights scholarship typically ignores. Struggles toward exercising human rights can be highly personal. I received permission to share the stories of Lori and Stewart Wilson, songwriters who told in their lyrics about struggling toward better mental health after suffering traumas of life on the street. With some kinds of human rights, like the rights to freedom of thought, to hold opinions, or to freedom of expression—barring censorship—it is up to individuals like the Wilsons to exercise those rights. These are civil and political rights, but they emerge from a person and may well involve the person struggling internally to be able to get to the point of expressing them. For various participants in music-making, severe trauma—whether that was living on the street as a child or suffering a debilitating accident—had blocked their capabilities to be able to opine, express themselves and even interact with others. Music therapy was claimed to help, but statements by some musicians implied that they needed much more support for healing and developing these capabilities. For songwriters in the Downtown Eastside whose songs peers excluded from the popular music jams and music therapy sessions, making their own music despite exclusion took a lot of internal persistence. For people who experience marginalization and even feel broken inside due to poverty and systemic inequities, having the capability to struggle internally is extremely important. Nurturing capabilities inside oneself, one's mind, and one's body is at the heart of how human rights can be promoted through music.

I documented the darker side of human rights implementation, as well, namely times when cultural practitioners claim to be implementing rights but violate them. In the broad project of analyzing human rights implementation through culture, it is important to watch for those approaches and policies that more frequently result in human rights violations. Although well intentioned, noninterference (never interfering with the behavior of a client as it occurs) sometimes resulted in community participants threatening and violating human rights, while workers took no responsibility. I witnessed, during popular music sessions, violations of the right to health, the right to life, and the right to security of the person and protection against violence or bodily harm. Participants' self-determination of their music-making processes also suffered from a trade-off dynamic that exists in some music therapy programs. Participants expressed a keen desire to develop their music performance capabilities through music education. They might trade this off for improving their musical skills within music therapy that had a music education component, because that was all they could access for free.

Human rights are the responsibility of us all, even though depending on our social deprivation or privilege, we may have varying capabilities to exercise them. Individuals have the power to influence whether capabilities and, consequently, human rights are promoted, strengthened, threatened, violated, or respected in cultural moments. It is no secret that regular citizens as well as nonstate actors like nongovernmental organizations are the main promoters of human rights globally, ideally in collaboration with nation-states (Donders and Vleugel 2014, Helbig 2009, León 2009).

However, it behooves us to heed critiques of human rights if we seek to promote them, for example, human rights being criticized as utopian political myths. In closing, I would like to encourage further thinking on the politics of human rights activism, including that concerning music, the arts and culture. Political aspects of human rights in arts and culture deserve further attention within broader social spheres in addition to at local levels.

Throughout this book, I approached human rights, after Sen, as strong ethical pronouncements about what should be done (Sen, 2009: 257), and not utopian political myths. When interpreted as ethical pronouncements, rights can be promoted through developing capabilities in musical practices. Subsequently, the implementation success of human rights (and related capabilities) can be evaluated, which has powerful implications for human rights activism and the law everywhere. However, I also showed how, when it comes to Downtown Eastside people who experience poverty, the implementation of human rights and related capabilities goes unmonitored when arts practitioners and organizations claim to promote them through music. Whether this leaves human rights, as religion scholar Jenna Reinbold puts it, in the realm of "political mythmaking, a genre of narrative designed to channel and thereby to quell social anxiety and to orient select groups toward desirable beliefs and practices" (Reinbold, 2011: 147), or not, is open to interpretation unless a detailed analysis is undertaken. Drawing on my study, which details socio-cultural processes by which human rights are promoted via developing capabilities, more comprehensive methodological approaches for evaluating human rights (and related capability development) can be created (for example, mixed-method and quantitative research approaches). One can also ask whether without rights-related monitoring, and particularly when it comes to the most socially deprived people in society, when do policies, methods and approaches aimed at promoting human rights run the risk of not doing so through music and culture? My study, in finding a minority of practitioners violating human rights when approaches they use claim to promote them, opens the question of what are the circumstances in which the musical and cultural implementation of human rights turns out to be utopian (extending Reinbold, 2011) including "mere words on paper" (Nussbaum, 2011: 65). I also describe, practically, how developing capabilities and corresponding human rights happens through music in and as culture, and therefore how the implementation of human rights can be analyzed in their cultural contexts. I offer a way of avoiding human rights being political myths and words on paper.

There is also the question of whether specific human rights may be utopian without a change in the world, national, and local political orders. Certain human rights are concepts left open to the inequities of capitalism that produce urban poverty in the first place. Such inequities refract within the economics of music programs for urban poor's human rights and capabilities in Downtown Eastside Vancouver. Whereas music facilitators with no formal music qualification received very little compensation, music therapists were well paid and some administrators could earn over $100,000 CAD annually. Funds from a combination of governments, donations, gifts from other charities, and sponsors enabled those financial differences. I argued that the urban redevelopment process of gentrification intensifies this financial dynamic, as more money becomes available to nonprofit organizations located in a neighborhood being redeveloped for middle and upper class uses. I documented Downtown Eastside music programs in aid organizations, which intended to support the poor's human rights and capability development, increasingly closing over 20 years. Gentrification, which happens in the contexts of restructuring and broad economic trends, ultimately displaces the poor, silencing their local culture and music.

Human rights, as political concepts, have been developed through international treaty processes by nations that are overwhelmingly capitalist. Human rights and the concomitant capabilities that are exercised most under capitalism may well take front seat compared to others in contexts aligned with economic development. Strengthening, for instance, the human rights to education and work (through providing capabilities via education that enhance work possibilities) can be understood to feed into capitalist systems of socioeconomic inequality and inequity in which people with more education and better jobs enjoy more socioeconomic benefits and those without have fewer. Activism like offering skills training in the arts to urban poor, which exercises the human right to education, has been undertaken through popular music theater projects and Women Rock in Vancouver's Downtown Eastside. These develop capabilities such as to perform well, communicate well, excel in groupwork and project self-confidence that are useful for employment.

I think we should pay more attention to whether capabilities that enable human rights promote socioeconomic inequality when viewed in a broader social context. In popular music theater of the Downtown Eastside, the encouragement of human rights, like the rights to education and work, via skill-building in performing arts and music, with people experiencing poverty, became an interclass endeavor—a sharing of capability by people already working in the arts with those who did not. Here inequality existed in broader Canadian society, but not between different socioeconomic classes engaged in the neighborhood musically. The sharing of skills by those who had them, with those who lacked them could be viewed as perpetuating systemic inequality because those skills can be put to use in capitalist settings, such as at paid presentational performances in the gentrified arts district that the Downtown Eastside was becoming. Nevertheless, promoting human rights and capabilities, for and with urban poor, was usually perceived by Downtown Eastsiders I interviewed, including the poor, as hugely positive. No one wants to suffer due to being socially and economically marginalized; in some select cases, capability development efforts of music, particularly the music theater initiatives and Women Rock, lifted people out of poverty.

Other human rights, and the capabilities that make them possible, do not need to be implicated in particularly capitalist structures of inequality and inequity, or are implicated less directly, such as the rights to health, security of the person, freedom of thought, and freedom of expression. Of the variety of musical initiatives arranged for urban poor in the Downtown Eastside, service organizations focused most on these kinds of rights.

The gross human rights violations that permeate poverty contexts impelled me to insist that the poorest members of society should enjoy the same rights and capabilities as the most privileged also in musical moments. To this end, institutions and musical practitioners can act much, much more on human rights and capabilities that have important implications for the everyday survival of marginalized people and improvement of their quality of life. Popular music, being easy to access for almost all of us, is one potent means of strengthening the rights and related capabilities of the poorest members of our societies. Nevertheless, probable corruptions in specific human rights as concepts—occurring, for example, when well-intentioned people promote the rights to work and education through music, but systemically, this entrenches socioeconomic inequality—speaks for a need for further consideration. I encourage more thinking about what different kinds of human rights actually do with inequality, and, in light of this, which kinds of actions citizens want to take at the macrosocial levels of government, law and society, as well as in local music and culture.

References

Aboriginal Healing Foundation. (2000). *Annual Report 2000*. Ottawa, Ontario: Aboriginal Healing Foundation. http://www.ahf.ca/downloads/annual-report-2000.pdf (accessed November 3, 2019).

Allen, Jeff, and Steven Farber. (2019). "Sizing Up Transport Poverty: A National Scale Accounting of Low-Income Households Suffering from Inaccessibility in Canada, and What to Do about It." *Transport Policy* 74: 214–223.

Araújo, Samuel. (2006a). "A violência como conceito na pesquisa musical; Reflexões sobre uma experiência dialógica na Maré, Rio de Janeiro" [Violence as a concept in musical research: Reflections on a dialogic experience in Maré, Rio de Janeiro]. *TRANS: Revista transcultural de música/Transcultural music review*. https://www.redalyc.org/pdf/822/82201007.pdf.

Araújo, Samuel. (2006b). "Conflict and Violence as Theoretical Tools in Present-Day Ethnomusicology: Notes on a Dialogic Ethnography of Sound Practices in Rio de Janeiro." *Ethnomusicology* 50(2): 287–313.

Araújo, Samuel. (2008). "From Neutrality to Praxis: The Shifting Politics of Ethnomusicology in the Contemporary World." *Muzikološki zbornik/Musicological Annual* XLIV(1): 13–30.

Araújo, Samuel. (2009). "Los paisajes sonoros de las favelas" [The soundscapes of the favelas]. In *Ciudadanias en escena; performance y derechos culturales en Colombia* [Citizens on Stage: Performance and Cultural Rights in Colombia], edited by Paolo Vignolo, pp. 232–237. Bogotá: Universidad Nacional de Colombia, Facultad de Ciencias Humanas.

Araújo, Samuel. (2010). "Sound Praxis: Music, Politics, and Violence in Brazil." In *Music and Conflict*, edited by John Morgan O'Connell and Salwa El-Shawan Castelo-Branco, pp. 217–231. Urbana, Chicago, and Springfield: University of Illinois Press.

Araújo, Samuel, and Vincenzo Cambria. (2013). "Sound Praxis, Poverty, and Social Participation: Perspectives from a Collaborative Study in Rio de Janeiro." *Yearbook for Traditional Music* 45: 28–42.

Baker, Geoffrey. (2016). "Editorial Introduction: El Sistema in Critical Perspective." *Action, Criticism, and Theory for Music Education* 15(1): 10–32.

Baker, Geoffrey. (2017). *El Sistema: Orchestrating Venezuela's Youth.* Oxford: Oxford University Press.

Baltazar, Margarida, Daniel Västfjäll, Erkin Asutay, Lina Koppel, and Suvi Saarikallio. (2019). "Is It Me or the Music? Stress Reduction and the Role of Regulation Strategies and Music." *Music & Science* 2: 1–16.

Barr, Nicholas. (2012). *Economics of the Welfare State* (5th ed.). Oxford: Oxford University Press.

Barz, Gregory F., and Timothy J. Cooley. (2008). *Shadows in the Field: New Perspectives for Fieldwork in Ethnomusicology* (2nd ed.). New York: Oxford University Press.

Bates, Vincent C. (2016). "Foreword: How Can Music Educators Address Poverty and Inequality?" *Action, Criticism & Theory for Music Education* 15(1): 1–9.

bc211. (2018). "First United Church Harm Reduction Services." Service Description and Info. http://redbookonline.bc211.ca/service/44426969_44426969/first_united_church_harm_reduction_services (accessed August 26, 2019).

Benford, Robert D., and David A. Snow. (2000). "Framing Processes and Social Movements: An Overview and Assessment." *Annual Review of Sociology* 26: 611–639.

Bennett, Andy, and Richard A. Peterson, eds. (2004). *Music Scenes: Local, Translocal and Virtual.* Nashville: Vanderbilt University Press.

BigFoot, Dolores Subia, and Beverly W. Funderburk. (2011). "Honoring Children, Making Relatives: The Cultural Translation of Parent-Child Interaction Therapy for American Indian and Alaska Native Families." *Journal of Psychoactive Drugs* 43(4): 309–318.

Bishop, Jack. (2004). "Who Are the Pirates? The Politics of Piracy, Poverty, and Greed in a Globalized Music Market." *Popular Music and Society* 27(1): 101–106.

Booth, Charles. (1892). *Pauperism and the Endowment of Old Age.* London: Macmillan.

Borchert, Gustavo. (2012). *Sistema Scotland: A Critical Inquiry into the Implementation of the El Sistema Model in Raploch.* MMus thesis, University of Glasgow.

Bourdieu, Pierre. (1977). "Symbolic Power." *Annales* 32: 405–411.

Bourdieu, Pierre. (1984 [1979]). *Distinction: A Social Critique of the Judgement of Taste.* New York: Routledge & Kegan Paul.

Bourdieu, Pierre. (1993). *The Field of Cultural Production: Essays on Art and Literature.* Oxford: Polity Press.

Braveman, Paula, and Sofia Gruskin. (2003). "Defining Equity in Health." *Journal of Epidemiology and Community Health* 57(4): 254–258.

Bruhn, Herbert. (2000). *Musiktherapie: Geschichte, Theorie, Methoden* [*Music Therapy: History, Theory, Methods*]. Göttingen, Germany: Hogrefe.

Buergenthal, Thomas. (1997). "The Normative and Institutional Evolution of International Human Rights." *Human Rights Quarterly* 19: 703–723.

Burak, Cop, and Doğan Eymirlioğlu. (2005). "The Right of Self-Determination in International Law towards the 40th Anniversary of the Adoption of ICCPR and ICESCR." *PERCEPTIONS: Journal of International Affairs* 10(4): 115–146.

Cambria, Vincenzo. (2012). *Music and Violence in Rio de Janeiro: A Participatory Study in Urban Ethnomusicology.* PhD dissertation, Wesleyan University.

Cameron, Sandy. (2007). "Condemned." *Carnegie Newsletter*. July 1. https://issuu.com/carnegienewsletter/docs/july_1__2007__carnegie_newsletter (accessed November 5, 2019).

Carnegie Community Centre. (2006). *Condemned—The Carnegie Opera*. Show program. Vancouver: Carnegie Community Centre Association.

Carnegie Community Centre. (2014). "Carnegie Community Centre: Barring Guidelines." http://www.carnegie.vcn.bc.ca/aug_114_page2/carnegie-community-centre--barring-guidelines (accessed May 11, 2017 [link broken]).

Caswell, Glenys. (2011–2012). "Beyond Words: Some Uses of Music in the Funeral Setting." *OMEGA-Journal of Death and Dying* 64(4): 319–334.

Cavalierri, Walter, and Diane Riley. (2012). "Harm Reduction in Canada: The Many Faces of Regression." In *Harm Reduction in Substance Use and High-Risk Behaviour: International Policy and Practice*, edited by Richard Pates and Diane Riley, pp. 382–394. London: Wiley-Blackwell.

CBC Arts. (2008). "Downtown Eastside Residents Bring Homelessness to Opera Stage." CBC News: Entertainment. February 5. http://www.cbc.ca/news/entertainment/downtown-eastside-residents-bring-homelessness-to-opera-stage-1.745849 (accessed November 3, 2019).

City of Vancouver. (2001). "Administrative Report." CC File No. 4161. http://council.vancouver.ca/010731/a16.htm (accessed August 26, 2019).

City of Vancouver. (2005). "Housing Plan for the Downtown Eastside." http://vancouver.ca/files/cov/housing-plan-for-the-downtowneastside-2005.pdf (accessed April 11, 2013 [link broken]).

City of Vancouver. (2006). "2005-06 Downtown Eastside Community Monitoring Report." Vancouver: City of Vancouver. https://sunnvancouver.files.wordpress.com/2011/05/2006dtesplanning.pdf (accessed November 3, 2019).

City of Vancouver. (2012). "Evelyne Saller Centre." http://vancouver.ca/commsvcs/nonmarketoperations/esaller.htm (accessed June 10, 2012 [link broken]).

City of Vancouver. (2013). "Downtown Eastside: Local Area Profile 2013." Vancouver: City of Vancouver. https://vancouver.ca/files/cov/profile-dtes-local-area-2013.pdf (accessed August 19, 2019).

City of Vancouver. (2019a). "Carnegie Community Centre." http://vancouver.ca/commsvcs/carnegiecentre/ (accessed June 10, 2012 [link broken]).

City of Vancouver. (2019b). "Evelyne Saller Centre." http://vancouver.ca/commsvcs/nonmarketoperations/esaller.htm (accessed June 7, 2019 [link broken]).

City of Vancouver. (2019c). "Legacy Open Data Catalogue." https://data.vancouver.ca/datacatalogue/employeeRemunerationExpensesOver75k.htm (accessed June 24, 2019).

Comaroff, Jean, and John L. Comaroff. (2012). "Theory from the South: Or, How Euro-America Is Evolving toward Africa." *Anthropological Forum* 22(2): 113–131.

Cowan, Jane K. (2006). "Culture and Rights after 'Culture and Rights.'" *American Anthropologist* 108(1): 9–24.

Cowan, Jane K., Marie-Bénédicte Dembour, and Richard A. Wilson, eds. (2001). *Cultural and Rights: Anthropological Perspectives*. Cambridge: Cambridge University Press.

Crowe, Barbara. (2004). *Music and Soul Making: Toward a New Theory of Music Therapy*. Lanham, MD: Scarecrow Press.

CSDH. (2008). "Closing the Gap in a Generation: Health Equity through Action on the Social Determinants of Health." Commission on Social Determinants of Health. Final Report. Geneva: World Health Organization. http://apps.who.int/iris/bitstream/10665/43943/1/9789241563703_eng.pdf (accessed August 19, 2019).

Culbert, Lori. (2006). "Ode to the Missing but Not Forgotten." *Vancouver Sun*, June 5, 2006. CBCA Fulltext Reference.

CUPE Local 15. (n.d.). "City of Vancouver." News & Events. http://www.cupe15.org/workplace/city-vancouver (accessed August 13, 2019).

Davidson, Jane W., and Sandra Garrido, eds. (2016). *Music and Mourning*. Oxon, UK, and New York: Routledge.

Daykin, Norma. (2012). "Developing Social Models for Research and Practice in Music, Arts, and Health: A Case Study of Research in a Mental Health Setting." In *Music, Health, & Wellbeing*, edited by Raymond A. R. MacDonald, Gunter Kreutz, and Laura Mitchell, pp. 65–75. Oxford: Oxford University Press.

Deci, Edward L., and Ryan, Richard M. (1985). *Intrinsic Motivation and Self-Determination in Human Behavior*. New York: Plenum Press.

Dennis, Michael J., and David P. Stewart. (2004). "Justiciability of Economic, Social and Cultural Rights: Should There Be an International Complaints Mechanism to Adjudicate the Rights to Food, Water, Housing, and Health?" *American Journal of International Law* 98: 462–515.

DeNora, Tia. (2003). *Rethinking Adorno: Rethinking Music Sociology*. Cambridge: Cambridge University Press.

Deutsche, Rosalyn, and Cara Gendel Ryan. (1984). "The Fine Art of Gentrification." *October* 31: 91–111.

Dingle, Genevieve A., Christopher Brander, Julie Ballantyne, and Felicity A. Baker. (2013). "'To be Heard': The Social and Mental Health Benefits of Choir Singing for Disadvantaged Adults." *Psychology of Music* 41(4): 405–421.

Dirksen, Rebecca. (2013). "Surviving Material Poverty by Employing Cultural Wealth: Putting Music in the Service of Community in Haiti." *Yearbook for Traditional Music* 45: 43–57.

Donders, Yvonne. (2010). "Do Cultural Diversity and Human Rights Make a Good Match?" *International Social Science Journal* 61(199): 15–35.

Donders, Yvonne M. (2012). "Cultural Rights in the Convention on the Diversity of Cultural Expressions: Included or Ignored?" In *The UNESCO Convention on the Diversity of Cultural Expressions: A Tale of Fragmentation of International Law?*, edited by Toshiyuki Kono and Steven Van Uytsel, pp. 165–182. International Law Series. Cambridge, Antwerp, and Portland: Intersentia.

Donders, Yvonne, and Vincent Vleugel. (2014). "The Receptor Approach: A New Human Rights Kid on the Block or Old Wine in New Bags? A Commentary on Professor Zwart's Article in HRQ." *Human Rights Quarterly* 36(3): 653–662.

Donish, Cassandra Joy. (2013). *Geographies of Art and Urban Change: Contesting Gentrification Through Aesthetic Encounters in San Francisco's Mission District*. MA thesis, University of Oregon.

Downtown Eastside Women's Centre. (2014–2015). *2014–15 Annual Report*. Vancouver: Downtown Eastside Women's Centre. http://dewc.ca/wp-content/uploads/2012/12/2015-new-version-Annual-Report.pdf (accessed June 8, 2019).

Durkheim, Emile. (1951 [1897]). *Suicide*, edited by George Simpson, translated by J. A. Spaulding and G. Simpson. Repr. New York: Free Press.

Elliot, Richard, Joanne Csete, Evan Wood, and Thomas Kerr. (2005). "Harm Reduction, HIV/AIDS and the Human Rights Challenge to Global Drug Control Policy." *Health and Human Rights* 8(2): 105–138.

Ellison, Mary. (1985). "Consciousness of Poverty in Black Music." *Popular Music and Society* 10(2): 17–46.

Evans, Paul, and Mark Y. Liu. (2019). "Psychological Needs and Motivational Outcomes in a High School Orchestra Program." *Journal of Research in Music Education* 67(1): 83–105.

Ezard, Nadine. (2001). "Public Health, Human Rights and the Harm Reduction Paradigm: From Risk Reduction to Vulnerability Reduction." *International Journal of Drug Policy* 12(3): 207–219.

Fachner, Jörg. (2006). "Music and Drug-Induced Altered States of Consciousness." In *Music and Altered States: Consciousness, Transcendence, Therapy and Addictions*, edited by David Aldridge and Jörg Fachner, pp. 82–96. London and Philadelphia: Jessica Kingsley Publishers.

Farmer, Paul. (2005). *Pathologies of Power: Health, Human Rights, and the New War on the Poor*. Berkeley and Los Angeles: University of California Press.

Feb 14th Annual Women's Memorial March. (2019). "Their Spirits Live Within Us." Other Cities. Vancouver. https://womensmemorialmarch.wordpress.com/national/ (accessed November 3, 2019).

Fenn, John, and Jeff Todd Titon. (2003). "A Conversation with Jeff Todd Titon." *Folklore Forum* 34(1–2): 119–131.

Fiol, Stefan Patrick. (2008). *Constructing Regionalism: Discourses of Spirituality and Cultural Poverty in the Popular Music of Uttarakhand, North India*. PhD dissertation, University of Illinois at Urbana-Champaign.

Fiol, Stefan. (2013). "Of Lack and Loss: Assessing Cultural and Musical Poverty in Uttarakhand." *Yearbook for Traditional Music* 45: 83–96.

First United. (2014). "2014 Annual Report." https://firstunited.ca/blog/annual-report/ (accessed June 18, 2019).

First United. (2017). "First United." https://firstunited.ca (accessed June 7, 2019).

Florida, Richard. (2002). *The Rise of the Creative Class . . . and How It Is Transforming Work, Leisure, Community & Everyday Life*. New York: Basic Books.

Fraser, James C., and Edward L. Kick. (2007). "The Role of Public, Private, Non-Profit and Community Sectors in Shaping Mixed-Income Housing Outcomes in the US." *Urban Studies* 44(12): 2357–2377.

Garrido, Sandra, and Waldo F. Garrido. (2016). "The Psychological Function of Music in Mourning Rituals: Examples from Three Continents." In *Music and Mourning*, edited by Jane W. Davidson and Sandra Garido, pp. 55–68. Oxon, UK, and New York: Routledge.

Geertz, Clifford. (1973). *The Interpretation of Cultures*. New York: Basic Books.

Ghetti, Claire M. (2004). "Incorporating Music Therapy into the Harm Reduction Approach to Managing Substance Use Problems." *Music Therapy Perspectives* 22(2): 84–90.

Glass, Ruth. (1964). "Introduction: Aspects of Change." In *London: Aspects of Change*, edited by Centre for Urban Studies, pp. xiii–xxiii, xxiv–xxvi, xxx–xxxvi. London: MacGibbon and Kee.

Goodale, Mark. (2009). "Introduction: Human Rights and Anthropology." In *Human Rights: An Anthropological Reader*, edited by Mark Goodale, pp. 1–19. Chichester, UK: Wiley-Blackwell.

Gorski, Paul. (2008). "The Myth of the Culture of Poverty." *Educational Leadership* 65(7): 32–36.

Government of Canada. (2016). "What Is the Difference between a Registered Charity and a Non-Profit Organization?" https://www.canada.ca/en/revenue-agency/services/charities-giving/giving-charity-information-donors/about-registered-charities/what-difference-between-a-registered-charity-a-non-profit-organization.html (accessed August 12, 2019).

Government of Canada. (2019a). *CONSTITUTION ACT, 1982*. https://laws-lois.justice.gc.ca/eng/const/page-15.html (accessed November 27, 2019).

Government of Canada. (2019b). "How to Get Information about a Charity." Charities. https://www.canada.ca/en/revenue-agency/services/charities-giving/charities/information-about-a-charity.html (accessed October 24, 2019).

Government of Canada. (2019c). "Harm Reduction Fund." https://www.canada.ca/en/public-health/services/funding-opportunities/harm-reduction-fund.html (accessed September 2, 2019).

Grodach, Carl. (2013). "Cultural Economy Planning in Creative Cities: Discourse and Practice." *International Journal of Urban and Regional Research* 37(5): 1747–1765.

Haig-Brown, Celia. (1988). *Resistance and Renewal: Surviving the Indian Residential School.* Vancouver: Arsenal Pulp Press.

Hancock, Michelle. (2000). "Hopes and Dreams in the Downtown Eastside." *Shared Vision: Improving Quality of Life*: 20–25.

Harris, Rachel. (2004). *Singing the Village: Music, Memory and Ritual among the Sibe of Xinjiang.* Oxford: Oxford University Press.

Harrison, Klisala. (2008). *Heart of the City: Music of Community Change in Vancouver, Canada's Downtown Eastside.* PhD dissertation, York University.

Harrison, Klisala. (2009). "'Singing My Spirit of Identity': Aboriginal Music for Well-Being in a Canadian Inner City." *MUSICultures* 36: 1–21.

Harrison, Klisala, ed. (2013a). "Music and Poverty Special Issue." *Yearbook for Traditional Music* 45: xi, 1–96.

Harrison, Klisala. (2013b). "Music, Health, and Socio-Economic Status: A Perspective on Urban Poverty in Canada." *Yearbook for Traditional Music* 45: 58–73.

Harrison, Klisala. (2013c). "The Relationship of Poverty to Music." *Yearbook for Traditional Music* 45: 1–12.

Harrison, Klisala. (2015). "Evaluating Values in Applied Ethnomusicology." In *The Oxford Handbook of Applied Ethnomusicology*, edited by Svanibor Pettan and Jeff Todd Titon, pp. 93–108. New York: Oxford University Press.

Harrison, Klisala. (2016). "Why Applied Ethnomusicology?" *COLLeGIUM: Studies across Disciplines in the Humanities and Social Sciences* 21: 1–21. https://helda.helsinki.fi/bitstream/handle/10138/167843/Collegium%20Vol%2021%20Introduction.pdf?sequence=1.

Harrison, Klisala. (2018). "Community Arts, Employment and Poverty: Exploring the Roles of Musical Participation and Professionalisation in Health Equity." In *Music, Health and Wellbeing: Exploring Music for Health Equity and Social Justice*, edited by Naomi Sunderland, Natalie Lewandowski, Dan Bendrups, and Brydie-Leigh Bartleet, pp. 177–199. London: Springer.

Harrison, Klisala. (2019). "The Social Potential of Music for Addiction Recovery." *Music and Science* 2: 1–16, May 31, 2019. https://journals.sagepub.com/doi/full/10.1177/2059204319842058.

Harrison, Klisala. (2020). "Musical Economics of Urban Poverty: City Redevelopment and Gentrification in the Financing, Organization and Interpretation of Music." In *The Oxford Handbook of Economic Ethnomusicology*, edited by Anna Morcom and Timothy Taylor. New York: Oxford University Press. DOI: 10.1093/oxfordhb/9780190859633.013.25.

Harrison, Klisala, Kristina Jacobsen, and Naomi Sunderland. (2019). "New Skies Above: Sense-Bound and Place-Based Songwriting as a Trauma Response for Refugees and Asylum Seekers." *Applied Arts & Health* 10(2): 147–167.

Harrison, Klisala, Elizabeth Mackinlay, and Svanibor Pettan, eds. (2010). *Applied Ethnomusicology: Historical and Contemporary Approaches*. Newcastle upon Tyne: Cambridge Scholars Publishing.

Harvey, David. (2003). "The Right to the City." *International Journal of Urban and Regional Research* 27(4): 939–941.

Harvey, David. (2013). *Rebel Cities: From the Right to the City to the Urban Revolution*. London: Verso.

Hatcher, Jeff. (2004). *I Am Your Son: Therapeutic Songwriting with a Man Living with Complex Trauma*. Master's thesis, Simon Fraser University.

Hathaway, Andrew D. (2001). "Shortcomings of Harm Reduction: Toward a Morally Invested Drug Reform Strategy." *International Journal of Drug Policy* 12(2): 125–137.

Hathaway, Andrew D., and Kirk I. Tousaw. (2008). "Harm Reduction Headway and Continuing Resistance: Insights from Safe Injection in the City of Vancouver." *International Journal of Drug Policy* 19: 11–16.

Heiderscheit, Annie. (2009). "Songs, Music and Sobriety: An Overview of Music Therapy in Substance Abuse." In *The Use of the Creative Therapies with Chemical Dependency Issues*, edited by Stephanie L. Brooke, pp. 136–161. Springfield, IL: Charles C Thomas Publisher.

Helbig, Adriana. (2009). "Representation and Intracultural Dynamics: Romani Musicians and Cultural Rights Discourse in Ukraine." In *Music and Cultural Rights*, edited by Andrew N. Weintraub and Bell Yung, pp. 169–186. Chicago and Urbana: University of Illinois Press.

Hendricks, C. Bret. (2001). *A Study of the Use of Music Therapy Techniques in a Group for the Treatment of Adolescent Depression*. PhD dissertation, Texas Tech University.

Hepburn, James G. (2000). *A Book of Scattered Leaves: Poetry of Poverty in Broadside Ballads of Nineteenth-Century England. I: Study and Anthology*. Lewisburg, PA: Bucknell University Press.

Hickey, Maud. (2018). "'We All Come Together to Learn about Music': A Qualitative Analysis of a 5-Year Music Program in a Juvenile Detention Facility." *International Journal of Offender Therapy and Comparative Criminology* 62(13): 4046–4066.

Hill Strategies Research. (2013). "A Statistical Profile of Artists in Canada." Statistical Insights on the Arts. http://hillstrategies.com/content/statistical-profile-artists-canada (accessed May 3, 2013).

Hombrebueno, Mark, KaGeen Cheung, and Miranda Lee, with written contributions by Gord McCullough. (2009). "Moments of Beauty/Moments of Grace: Building Community in the Downtown Eastside." http://vancouvermovingtheatre.com/wp-content/uploads/2014/05/DTES-Music-Theatre-Showcase-ILLUSTRATED-ESSAY-final-by-UBC-students.pdf (accessed December 13, 2017).

HRI. (2009). "Harm Reduction and Human Rights: The Global Response to Drug-Related HIV Epidemics." Harm Reduction International. https://www.hri.global/files/2010/06/01/GlobalResponseDrugRelatedHIV(2).pdf (accessed August 26, 2019).

HRI. (2017). "Why Human Rights?" http://www.ihra.net/advocacy-human-rights (accessed May 19, 2017 [link broken]).

Impey, Angela. (2002). "Culture, Conservation and Community Reconstruction: Explorations in Advocacy Ethnomusicology and Participatory Action Research in Northern Kwazulu Natal." *Yearbook for Traditional Music* 34: 9–24.

Instruments of Change. (2012a). "Women Rock!" Our Projects. http://instrumentsofchange.org/projects.html (accessed November 1, 2019).

Instruments of Change. (2012b). "Women Rock! Interviews, May 2012." Gallery/Media. https://instrumentsofchange.org (accessed June 7, 2019 [link broken]).

IFRC. (2019). "Drug Use Prevention, Treatment, and Care: Harm Reduction Works." International Federation of the Red Cross and Red Crescent Societies. https://www.ifrc.org/en/what-we-do/health/harm-reduction/ (accessed August 26, 2019).

Istvanffy, Jay, ed. (1977, 2012). "Your Welfare Rights: A Guide to BC Employment and Assistance." Legal Services Society, BC. http://www.lss.bc.ca/resources/pdfs/pubs/Your-Welfare-Rights-eng.pdf (accessed May 22, 2017 [link broken]).

Jawad, Rania. (2013). *Theatre Encounters: A Politics of Performance in Palestine*. PhD dissertation, New York University.

Jensen, Bent. (1999). "Music Therapy with Psychiatric In-Patients: A Case Study with a Young Schizophrenic Man." In *Clinical Applications of Music Therapy in Psychiatry*, edited by Tony Wigram and Jos De Backer, pp. 44–60. London and Philadelphia: Jessica Kingsley Publishers.

Jones, Steve. (1995). "Covering Cobain: Narrative Patterns in Journalism and Rock Criticism." *Popular Music & Society* 19(2): 103–118.

Kalir, Barak. (2019). "Repressive Compassion: Deportation Caseworkers Furnishing an Emotional Comfort Zone in Encounters with Illegalized Migrants." *PoLAR: Political and Legal Anthropology Review* 42(1): 68–83.

Kallio, Alexis Anja, and Heidi Westerlund. (2016). "The Ethics of Survival: Teaching the Traditional Arts to Disadvantaged Children in Post-Conflict Cambodia." *International Journal of Music Education* 34(1): 90–103.

Kartomi, Margaret J. (2012). *Musical Journeys in Sumatra*. Urbana: University of Illinois Press.

Kassam, Ashifa. (2017). "Canada Eases Steps to Open Supervised Drug Injection Sites amid Opioid Crisis." *The Guardian*, May 21, 2017. https://www.theguardian.com/world/2017/may/21/canada-opioid-crisis-supervised-drug-injection-sites.

Keane, Helen. (2003). "Critiques of Harm Reduction, Morality and the Promise of Human Rights." *International Journal of Drug Policy* 14: 227–232.

The Kettle Society. (2019). "Who We Are." The Kettle Society. Strength through mental health. https://www.thekettle.ca (accessed June 7, 2019).

Kim, Jinah. (2017). "Effects of Community-Based Group Music Therapy for Children Exposed to Ongoing Child Maltreatment & Poverty in South Korea: A Block Randomized Controlled Trial." *Arts in Psychotherapy* 54: 69–77.

Kingfisher, Catherine. (2007). "Discursive Constructions of Homelessness in a Small City in the Canadian Prairies: Notes on Destructuration, Individualization, and the Production of (Raced and Gendered) Unmarked Categories." *American Ethnologist* 34(1): 91–107.

Koelsch, Stefan, and Thomas Stegemann. (2012). "The Brain and Positive Biological Effects in Healthy and Clinical Populations." In *Music, Health & Wellbeing*, edited by Raymond MacDonald, Gunter Kreutz, and Laura Mitchell, pp. 436–456. Oxford: Oxford University Press.

Küpers, Elisa, Marijn van Dijk, Gary McPherson, and Paul van Geert. (2014). "A Dynamic Model That Links Skill Acquisition with Self-Determination in Instrumental Music Lessons." *Musicae Scientiae* 18(1): 17–34.

Lee, Juyoung, Jane W. Davidson, and Katrina S. McFerran. (2016). "Registered Music Therapists' Motivations and Perceptions of the Impact of Their Practices on the Well-Being of Clients and Themselves." *Australian Journal of Music Therapy* 27: 27–43.

Lees, Loretta, Hyun Bang Shin, and Ernesto López-Morales, eds. (2015). *Global Gentrifications: Uneven Development and Displacement*. Bristol: Policy Press.

Lefebvre, Henri. (1968). *Le droit à la ville [The right to the city]*. Paris: Anthropos.

Lefebvre, Henri. (1996 [1967]). *Writings on Cities: Henri Lefebvre*, translated and edited by Eleonore Kofman and Elizabeth Lebas. Malden, MA; Oxford, UK; and Victoria, Australia: Blackwell Publishing.

León, Javier F. (2009). "National Patrimony and Cultural Policy: The Case of the Afroperuvian *Cajón*." In *Music and Cultural Rights*, edited by Andrew N. Weintraub and Bell Yung, pp. 110–139. Chicago and Urbana: University of Illinois Press.

Ley, David. (1986). "Alternative Explanations for Inner-City Gentrification: A Canadian Assessment." *Annals of the Association of American Geographers* 76(4): 521–535.

Loughran, Maureen. (2008). "'But What If They Call the Police?' Applied Ethnomusicology and Urban Activism in the United States." *Muzikološki zbornik/Musicological Annual* 44(1): 51–67.

Loughran, Maureen. (2009). *Community Powered Resistance: Radio, Music Scenes and Musical Activism in Washington, D.C.* PhD dissertation, Brown University.

Mabughi, Nyiwul, and Tarek Selim. (2006). "Poverty as Social Deprivation: A Survey." *Review of Social Economy* 68(2): 181–204.

MacDonald, Raymond, Gunter Kreutz, and Laura Mitchell, eds. (2012). *Music, Health, and Wellbeing*. Oxford: Oxford University Press.

MacPherson, Donald. (2001). *A Framework for Action: A Four-Pillar Approach to Drug Problems in Vancouver*. Vancouver: City of Vancouver. https://www.researchgate.net/publication/242480594_A_Four-Pillar_Approach_to_Drug_Problems_in_Vancouver.

Marcuse, Peter. (2012). "Whose Right(s) to What City?" In *Cities for People, Not for Profit: Critical Urban Theory and the Right to the City*, edited by Neil Brenner, Peter Marcuse, and Margit Mayer, pp. 24–41. London and New York: Routledge.

Marlatt, G. Alan, Mary E. Larimer, and Katie Witkiewitz. (2012). *Harm Reduction: Pragmatic Strategies for Managing High-Risk Behaviours* (2nd ed.). New York: Guilford Press.

Marwell, Nicole P. (2009). *Bargaining for Brooklyn: Community Organizations in the Entrepreneurial City*. Chicago and London: University of Chicago Press.

Mathews, Vanessa. (2010). "Aestheticizing Space: Art, Gentrification and the City." *Geography Compass* 4(6): 660–675.

McCorquodale, Robert. (1994). "Self-Determination: A Human Rights Approach." *International & Comparative Law Quarterly* 43(4): 857–885.

McKnight, John L., and John P. Kretzmann. (1996). *Mapping Community Capacity*. Evanston, IL: Institute for Policy Research, Northwestern University.

Media Advisory. (2005). *Women's Memorial March*. Pamphlet. Vancouver: Women's Memorial March Organizing Committee.

Mendus, Susan. (1995). "Human Rights in Political Theory." *Political Studies* 43(4): 10–24.

Merry, Sally Engle. (1997). "Legal Pluralism and Transnational Culture: The Ka Ho'okolokolonui Kanaka Maoli Tribunal, Hawai'i, 1993." In *Human Rights, Culture and Context*, edited by Richard A. Wilson, pp. 28–48. London and Sterling, VA: Pluto Press.

Merry, Sally Engle. (2003). "Human Rights Law and the Demonization of Culture (and Anthropology along the Way)." *Polar: Political and Legal Anthropology Review* 26(1): 55–77.

Merry, Sally Engle. (2006). "Transnational Human Rights and Local Activism: Mapping the Middle." *American Anthropologist* 108(1): 38–51.

Merry, Sally Engle. (2011). "Measuring the World: Indicators, Human Rights, and Global Governance." *Current Anthropology* 52(3): S83–S95.

Messer, Ellen. (1993). "Anthropology and Human Rights." *Annual Review of Anthropology* 22(1): 221–249.

Miguel, Ana Flávia. (2016). *Skopeologias: músicas e saberes sensíveis na construção partilhada do conhecimento* [*Skopeologies: Music and Sensitive Knowledge in the Shared Construction of Knowledge*]. PhD dissertation, University of Aveiro.

Miller, Jonas G., Sarah Kahle, and Paul D. Hastings. 2015. "Roots and Benefits of Costly Giving: Children who are Altruistic have Greater Autonomic Flexibility and Less Family Wealth." *Psychological Science* 26(7): 1038–1045.

Milloy, John S. (1999). *A National Crime: The Canadian Government and the Residential School System, 1879 to 1986.* Winnipeg: University of Manitoba Press.

Mitchell, Katharyne. (1996). "Visions of Vancouver: Ideology, Democracy, and the Future of Urban Development." *Urban Geography* 17(6): 478–501.

Mitlin, Diana, and David Satterthwaite. (2007). "Strategies for Grassroots Control of International Aid." *Environment and Urbanization* 19(2): 483–500.

Moisala, Pirkko. (1991). Antropologinen Musiikintutkimus [The Anthropology of Music]. In *Kansanmusiikin Tutkimus: Metodologian Opas* [*Folk Music Research: A Methodological Guide*], edited by Pirkko Moisala, pp. 105–137. Helsinki: Vapt-Kustannus.

Moisala, Pirkko. (2013). "'Nobody Should Be Forced to Make a Living by Begging': Social Exclusion and Cultural Rights of Gāine/Gandharva Musicians of Nepal." *Yearbook for Traditional Music* 45: 13–27.

Moisala, Pirkko, Milla Tiainen, Taru Leppänen, and Hannah Väätäinen. (2014). "Noticing Musical Becomings: Deleuzian and Guattarian Approaches to Ethnographic Studies of Musicking." *Current Musicology* 98: 7–29.

Moore, Robin D. (2017). *College Music Curricula for a New Century.* New York: Oxford University Press.

Nagel, Jessica, and Michael J. Silverman. (2017). "Experiences and Perspectives of Music Therapists Providing Services to Families Experiencing Poverty: A Qualitative Investigation." *Voices: A World Forum for Music Therapy* 17(2). https://voices.no/index.php/voices/article/view/2345.

Native Women's Association of Canada. (2015). "Canadian Human Rights Act." https://www.nwac.ca/policy-areas/human-rights-in-canada/canadian-human-rights-act/ (accessed December 15, 2015 [link broken]).

Newsome, Jennifer K. (2008). "From Researched to Centrestage: A Case Study." *Muzikološki zbornik/Musicological Annual* 44(1): 31–50.

Nikleva, Stephen, prod., and Earle Peach, mast. (2000). *These Are the Faces: Carnegie Centre CD Project.* Vancouver: Carnegie Community Centre Association. CD.

Nordstrom, Carolyn. 1995. War on the Front Lines. In *Fieldwork under Fire: Contemporary Studies of Violence and Survival*, ed. Carolyn Nordstrom and Antonius C. G. M. Robben, 128-53. Berkeley, Los Angeles and London: University of California Press.

Norfield, Jennie, and Sanna Nordin-Bates. (2012). "How Community Dance Leads to Positive Outcomes: A Self-Determination Theory Perspective." *Journal of Applied Arts & Health* 2(3): 257–272.

Norris, Patricia. (2000). "Clinical Work on the New Frontier Using Elements of the Map." *Bridges* 11(4): 4–5.

Novac, Sylvia, Joyce Brown, and Carmen Bourbonnais. (1996). *A Room of Her Own: A Literature Review on Women and Homelessness.* Ottawa, Ontario: Canadian Housing Information Centre.

NowPublic. (2006). "CBC Duped about Downtown Eastside Homeless." http://www.nowpublic.com/cbc_duped_about_downtown_eastside_homeless#comments (accessed November 3, 2019 [link broken]).

Nussbaum, Martha C. (1997–1998). "Capabilities and Human Rights." *Fordham Law Review* 66: 273–300.

Nussbaum, Martha C. (2011). *Creating Capabilities: The Human Development Approach.* Cambridge, MA, and London: The Belknap Press of Harvard University Press.

Ochoa Gautier, Ana María. (2003). *Entre los Deseos y los Derechos: Un Ensayo Crítico sobre Políticas Culturales [Between Desires and Rights: A Critical Essay on Cultural Policies].* Bogotá, Colombia: Ministerio de cultura.

Oenning da Silva, Rita de Cácia. (2006). "Reversing the Rite: Music, Dance, and Rites of Passage among Street Children and Youth in Recife, Brazil." *World of Music* 48(1): 83–97.

OHCHR. (1996–2019a). "Convention on the Elimination of All Forms of Discrimination Against Women." Office of the High Commissioner, United Nations Human Rights. https://www.ohchr.org/en/ProfessionalInterest/pages/cedaw.aspx (accessed October 23, 2019).

OHCHR. (1996–2019b). "Convention on the Rights of the Child." Office of the High Commissioner, United Nations Human Rights. https://www.ohchr.org/en/professionalinterest/pages/crc.aspx (accessed October 23, 2019).

OHCHR. (1996–2019c). "International Covenant on Civil and Political Rights." Office of the High Commissioner, United Nations Human Rights. https://www.ohchr.org/en/professionalinterest/pages/ccpr.aspx (accessed October 23, 2019).

OHCHR. (1996–2019d). "International Covenant on Economic, Social and Cultural Rights." Office of the High Commissioner, United Nations Human Rights. https://www.ohchr.org/en/professionalinterest/pages/cescr.aspx (accessed October 23, 2019).

OHCHR. (1996–2019e). "International Convention on the Elimination of All Forms of Racial Discrimination." Office of the High Commissioner, United Nations Human Rights. https://www.ohchr.org/en/professionalinterest/pages/cerd.aspx (accessed October 24, 2019).

Organization of American States (OAS). (2014). *Report of the Inter-American Commission on Human Rights on Missing and Murdered Indigenous Women in British Columbia.* Inter-American Commission on Human Rights. https://ccrweb.ca/en/oas-iachr-report-2014-missing-murdered-indigenous-women-girls-bc (accessed July 22, 2020).

Padilla, David J. (1993). "The Inter-American Commission on Human Rights of the Organization of American States: A Case Study." *American University Journal of International Law and Policy* 9: 95–115.

Peddie, Ian, ed. (2011a). *Popular Music and Human Rights*, Vol. I: British and American Music, Ashgate Popular and Folk Music Series. Surrey, UK: Ashgate.

Peddie, Ian, ed. (2011b). *Popular Music and Human Rights*, Vol. II: World Music, Ashgate Popular and Folk Music Series. Surrey, UK: Ashgate.

Pettan, Svanibor, and Jeff Todd Titon, eds. (2015). *The Oxford Handbook of Applied Ethnomusicology.* Oxford and New York: Oxford University Press.

PHS. (2019). "Mission Statement." PHS Community Services Society. https://www.phs.ca/mission-statement/ (accessed June 9, 2019).

Piff, Paul K., Daniel M. Stancato, Stéphane Côté, Rodolfo Mendoza-Denton, and Dacher Keltner. 2012. "Higher Social Class Predicts Increased Unethical Behavior." *Proceedings of the National Academy of Sciences of the United States of America* 109(11): 4086–4091.

Pogge, Thomas. (2002). *World Poverty and Human Rights: Cosmopolitan Responsibilities and Reforms.* Cambridge, UK, and Malden, MA: Polity Press.

Pogge, Thomas. (2005). "World Poverty and Human Rights." *Ethics & International Affairs* 19(1): 1–7.

Positive Outlook. (2005). *The Circle of Song*. Vancouver: Vancouver Native Health Society. CD.

Price, David, and Lee Barron. (1999). "Developing Independence: The Experience of the Lawnmowers Theatre Company." *Disability & Society* 14(6): 819–829.

Prince, Raymond. (1982). "Shamans and Endorphins: Hypothesis for a Synthesis." *Ethos* 10(4): 299–302.

Ramos, Silvia, and Ana María Ochoa. (2009). "Music and Human Rights: The AfroReggae Cultural Group and the Youth from the *Favelas* as Responses to Violence in Brazil." In *Music and Cultural Rights*, edited by Andrew N. Weintraub and Bell Yung, pp. 219–240. Chicago and Urbana: University of Illinois Press.

Reinbold, Jenna. (2011). "Political Myth and the Sacred Center of Human Rights: The Universal Declaration and the Narrative of 'Inherent Human Dignity.'" *Human Rights Review* 12(2): 147–171.

Reliable Sources. (2006). "CBC Duped about Downtown Eastside Homeless." *Downtown Eastside Enquirer*. November 3. http://downtowneastsideenquirer.blogspot.com/2006/11/cbc-duped-about-downtown-eastside.html (accessed November 3, 2019).

Rice, Timothy. (1987). "Toward the Remodeling of Ethnomusicology." *Ethnomusicology* 31(3): 469–488.

Ritter, Jonathan. (2011). "Chocolate, Coconut, and Honey: Race, Music, and the Politics of Hybridity in the Ecuadorian Black Pacific." *Popular Music and Society* 34(5): 571–592.

Robertson, James. (2000). "An Educational Model for Music Therapy: The Case for a Continuum." *British Journal of Music Therapy* 14(1): 41–46.

Rock 'n' Roll Camp for Girls. (2012). "Our Mission 'n' History." Portland, OR. http://www.girlsrockcamp.org/about/our-mission-history/ (accessed November 3, 2019).

ROCK101. (2019). "About." https://www.facebook.com/pg/Rock101Van/about/?ref=page_internal (accessed June 7, 2019).

Rowntree, B. Seebohm. (1901). *Poverty: A Study of Town Life*. London: Macmillan and Co.

Rustad, Robin A., Jacob E. Small, David A. Jobes, Martin A. Safer, and Rebecca J. Peterson. (2003). "The Impact of Rock Videos and Music with Suicidal Content on Thoughts and Attitudes about Suicide." *Suicide and Life-Threatening Behavior* 33(2): 120–131.

Ruud, Even. (2012). "The New Health Musicians." In *Music, Health, & Wellbeing*, edited by Raymond A. R. MacDonald, Gunter Kreutz, and Laura Mitchell, pp. 87–96. Oxford: Oxford University Press.

Sandler, Felicia. (2009). "In Search of a Cross-Cultural Legal Framework: Indigenous Musics as a Worldwide Commodity." In *Music and Cultural Rights*, edited by Andrew N. Weintraub and Bell Yung, pp. 241–271. Chicago and Urbana: University of Illinois Press.

Sarah McLachlan School of Music. (n.d.). "About Our School." https://www.sarahschoolofmusic.com/aboutourschool (accessed July 4, 2019).

Sardo, Susana. (2018). "Shared Research Practices on and about Music: Towards Decolonising Decolonial Ethnomusicology." In *Making Music, Making Society*, edited by Josep Martí and Sara Revilla, pp. 217–238. Newcastle upon Tyne, UK: Cambridge Scholars Publishing.

Scarantino, Barbara Anne. (1987). *Music Power*. New York: Dodd, Mead & Co.

Schmid, Christian. (2012). "Henri Lefebvre, the Right to the City, and the New Metropolitan Mainstream." In *Cities for People, Not for Profit: Critical Urban Theory and the Right to the City*, edited by Neil Brenner, Peter Marcuse, and Margit Mayer, translated by Christopher Findlay, pp. 42–62. London and New York: Routledge.

Schön, Donald A., Bishwapriya Sanyal, and William J. Mitchell, eds. (1999). *High Technology and Low-income Communities: Prospects for the Positive Use of Advanced Information Technology*. Cambridge, MA: MIT Press.

Schulkind, Matthew D., Laura Kate Hennis, and David C. Rubin. (1999). "Music, Emotion, and Autobiographical Memory: They're Playing Your Song." *Memory & Cognition* 27(6): 948–955.

Schwartz, Jessica A. (2012). "A 'Voice to Sing': Rongelapese Musical Activism and the Production of Nuclear Knowledge." *Music & Politics* 6(1): 1–21.

Sebire, Simon J., Joanna M. Kesten, Mark J. Edwards, Thomas May, Kathryn Banfield, Keeley Tomkinson, Peter S. Blair, Emma L. Bird, Jane E. Powell, and Russell Jago. (2016). "Using Self-Determination Theory to Promote Adolescent Girls' Physical Activity: Exploring the Theoretical Fidelity of the Bristol Girls Dance Project." *Psychology of Sport and Exercise* 24: 100–110.

Seeger, Anthony. (2010). "The Suya and the White Man: Forty-Five Years of Musical Diplomacy in Brazil." In *Music and Conflict*, edited by John Morgan O'Connell and Salwa el-Shawan Castelo-Branco, pp. 109–125. Urbana: University of Illinois Press.

Seery, Emma, and Ana Caistor Arendar. (2014). *Even It Up: Time to End Extreme Inequality*. Oxfam. https://www.oxfamamerica.org/static/media/files/even-it-up-inequality-oxfam. pdf (accessed March 8, 2019).

Sen, Amartya. (1985). *Commodities and Capabilities*. Amsterdam: North-Holland.

Sen, Amartya. (1987). "The Standard of Living." In *The Standard of Living*, edited by Geoffrey Hawthorn, pp. 20–38. Cambridge: Cambridge University Press.

Sen, Amartya. (1999). *Development as Freedom*. New York: Random House.

Sen, Amartya. (2009). *The Idea of Justice*. London: Penguin Books.

Shafir, Gershon, and Alison Brysk. (2006). "The Globalization of Rights: From Citizenship to Human Rights." *Citizenship Studies* 10(3): 275–287.

Shanks, Barry. (1988). "Transgressing the Boundaries of a Rock 'n' Roll Community." Paper delivered at the First Joint Conference of IASPM-Canada and IASPM-USA, Yale University, October 1, 1988.

Shaw, Carolyn M. (2003). "Limits to Hegemonic Influence in the Organization of American States." *Latin American Politics and Society* 45(3): 59–92.

Shaw, Carolyn M. (2004). *Cooperation, Conflict, and Consensus in the Organization of American States*. New York: Palgrave Macmillan.

Sheway. (2019a). "About Sheway: Program Overview." http://sheway.vcn.bc.ca/about-sheway/ program-overview/ (accessed August 26, 2019 [link broken]).

Sheway. (2019b). "Sheway: A Community Program for Women and Children." http://sheway. vcn.bc.ca/files/2012/05/sheway_brochure.pdf (accessed June 8, 2019 [link broken].

Silva, Alexandre Dias. (2011). *A Maré no ritmo das ONGs: Uma análise sobre o papel das oficinas musicais de Organizações Não-Governamentais no bairro Maré/Rio de Janeiro* [*Maré in the Rhythm of the NGOs: An Analysis on the Role of the Musical Workshops of Non-Governmental Organizations in the Neighborhood Maré/Rio de Janeiro*]. MA thesis, Universidade Federal do Rio de Janeiro.

Silverman, Phyllis R., and Dennis Klass. (1996). "Introduction: What's the Problem." In *Continuing Bonds: New Understandings of Grief*, edited by Dennis Klass, Phyllis R. Silverman, and Steven Nickman, pp. 3–27. Washington, DC: Taylor & Francis.

Silvers, Michael B. (2018). *Voices of Drought: The Politics of Music and Environment in Northeastern Brazil*. Urbana: University of Illinois Press.

SJMA. (n.d.). "About Us." Saint James Music Academy. https://sjma.ca/about-us/ (accessed July 4, 2019).

Slater, Tom. (2012). "Missing Marcuse: On Gentrification and Displacement." In *Cities for People, Not for Profit: Critical Urban Theory and the Right to the City*, edited by Neil Brenner, Peter Marcuse, and Margit Mayer, pp. 171–196. London and New York: Routledge.

Slotta, James. (2017). "Can the Subaltern Listen? Self-Determination and the Provisioning of Expertise in Papua New Guinea." *American Ethnologist* 44(2): 328–340.

Small, Christopher. (1998). *Musicking: The Meanings of Performing and Listening.* Middletown, CT: Wesleyan University Press.

Smith, Jeffrey G. (2007). "Creating a 'Circle of Song' within Canada's Poorest Postal Code/ Créer un cercle de chansons au sein du code postal le plus pauvre du Canada." *Canadian Journal of Music Therapy* 13(2): 103–114.

Smith, Neil. (1996). *The New Urban Frontier: Gentrification and the Revanchist City.* London and New York: Routledge.

Somdahl-Sands, Katrinka. (2008). "Citizenship, Civic Memory and Urban Performance: Mission Wall Dances." *Space and Polity* 12(3): 329–352.

Speed, Shannon. (2006). "At the Crossroads of Human Rights and Anthropology: Toward a Critically Engaged Activist Research." *American Anthropologist* 108(1): 66–76.

Stack, Steven, David Lester, and Jonathan S. Rosenberg. (2012). "Music and Suicidality: A Quantitative Review and Extension." *Suicide and Life-Threatening Behavior* 42(6): 654–671.

Stammers, Neil. (1993). "Human Rights and Power." *Political Studies* 41(1): 70–82.

Statistics Canada. (2015). "Table 4: Market Basket Measure Thresholds for Reference Family of Two Adults and Two Children, by MBM Region." Tables and figure. https://www150.statcan.gc.ca/n1/pub/75f0002m/2011002/tbl/tbl04-eng.htm (accessed March 6, 2019).

Statistics Canada. (2019). "Low Income Cut-Offs (LICOs) before and after Tax by Community Size and Family Size, in Current Dollars." Add/Remove data. https://www150.statcan.gc.ca/t1/tbl1/en/cv.action?pid=1110024101#timeframe (accessed March 6, 2019).

Stellar, Jennifer E., Vida M. Manzo, Michael W. Kraus, and Dacher Keltner. (2012). "Class and Compassion: Socioeconomic Factors Predict Responses to Suffering." *Emotion* 12(3): 449–459.

Stoicescu, Claudia, ed. (2012). *The Global State of Harm Reduction: Towards an Integrated Response.* London: Harm Reduction International.

Straw, Will. (1991). "Systems of Articulation, Logics of Change: Communities and Scenes in Popular Music." *Cultural Studies* 5(3): 368–388.

Swanson, Jean, Lama Mugabo, and King-Mon Chan. (2017). *Crisis: Rents and the Rate of Change in the Downtown Eastside. Carnegie Community Action Project's 2017 Hotel Survey & Housing Report.* Vancouver: Carnegie Centre. http://www.carnegieaction.org/wp-content/uploads/2018/03/CCAP-2017-Hotel-Report-1.pdf (accessed June 27, 2019).

Szöke, Teréz. (2015). *Investigating the Geographies of Community-Based Public Art and Gentrification in Downtown Eastside, Vancouver.* MA thesis, University of Guelph.

Tan, Soi Beng. (2008). "Activism in Southeast Asian Ethnomusicology: Empowering Youths to Revitalize Traditions and Bridge Cultural Barriers." *Muzikološki zbornik/Musicological Annual* 44(1): 69–83.

Taylor, Paul, ed. (2003). *The Heart of the Community: The Best of the Carnegie Newsletter.* Vancouver: New Star Books.

Titon, Jeff Todd. (1992). "Music, the Public Interest, and the Practice of Ethnomusicology." *Ethnomusicology* 36(3): 315–322.

Titon, Jeff Todd. (2013). "Music and the US War on Poverty: Some Reflections." *Yearbook for Traditional Music* 45: 74–82.

Torjman, Sherri. (1998). *Community-Based Poverty Reduction.* Ottawa, Ontario: Caledon Institute of Social Policy.

Townsend, Peter. (1979). *Poverty in the United Kingdom: A Survey of Household Resources and Standards of Living.* Harmondsworth: Penguin.

Tracks, Jimm G. Good. (1973). "Native American Non-Interference." *Social Work* 18(6): 30–34.

Turino, Thomas. (2008). *Music as Social Life: The Politics of Participation*. Chicago: University of Chicago Press.

United Nations. (n.d.-a) "United Nations Declaration on the Rights of Indigenous Peoples." Department of Economic and Social Affairs. Indigenous Peoples. https://www.un.org/development/desa/indigenouspeoples/declaration-on-the-rights-of-indigenous-peoples.html (accessed November 6, 2019).

United Nations. (n.d.-b) "Convention on the Rights of Persons with Disabilities." Department of Economic and Social Affairs. Disability. https://www.un.org/development/desa/disabilities/convention-on-the-rights-of-persons-with-disabilities/convention-on-the-rights-of-persons-with-disabilities-2.html (accessed October 24, 2019).

Vancouver Coastal Health. (2012). "Health Contact Centre." http://www.vch.ca/about_us/news/media_contacts/fact_sheets/services_in_the_downtown_eastside (accessed June 10, 2012 [link broken]).

Vancouver Heritage Foundation Places That Matter Community History Resource. (2016–2019). "Gathering Place Community Centre." https://www.vancouverheritagefoundation.org/place-that-matters/gathering-place-community-centre/ (accessed June 7, 2019).

Vancouver Moving Theatre. (2007). *The Shadows Project; Addition and Recovery; We're All in This Together: A Contemporary Fable from the Downtown Eastside*. Program booklet. Vancouver: Vancouver Moving Theatre.

Vancouver Moving Theatre. (2019). "Vancouver Moving Theatre." http://vancouvermovingtheatre.com (accessed July 4, 2019).

Vancouver Native Health Society. (2003). *Annual Report 2003*. Vancouver: Vancouver Native Health Society.

Vancouver Native Health Society. (2006). "Annual Report 2006." http://www.vnhs.net/images/downloads/annual-reports/vnhs-annual-report-2006.pdf (accessed July 4, 2019).

Varga, Sándor. (2013). "Zenészfogadás az erdélyi Mezôségen" [Recruiting Musicians in the Transylvanian Plain]. In *Jubileumi kötet a Zenetudományi Intézet 40 éves fennállása alkalmából* [*Jubilee Volume for the 40th Anniversary of the Zenetudományi Intézet*], edited by Gábor Kiss, Gabriella Gilányi, Gergely Loch, Zsuzsa Czagány, and Ágnes Papp, pp. 251–287. *Zenetudományi dolgozatok*.

Vona, Viktoria. (2015). *The Role of Art and Artists in Contesting Gentrification in London and New York City*. PhD dissertation, Kings College London.

Wald, Gabriela. (2017). "Orquestas juveniles con fines de inclusión social: De identidades, subjetividades y transformación social" [Youth Orchestras as Social Inclusion Projects: Identities, Subjectivities, and Social Transformation]. *Revista foro de educación musical, artes y pedagogía/Magazine Forum of Music Education, Arts and Pedagogy* 2(2): 59–81.

Walling, Savannah, Terry Hunter, and John Endo Greenaway, eds. (2015). *From the Heart of a City: Community-Engaged Theatre and Music Productions from Vancouver's Downtown Eastside: 2002–2013*. Vancouver: Vancouver Moving Theatre.

Wang, Wan-Jung. (2016). "Applied Theatre and Cultural Memory in East and Southeast Asia." In *Critical Perspectives on Applied Theatre*, edited by Jenny Hughes and Helen Nicholson, pp. 61–81. Cambridge: Cambridge University Press.

Wax, Rosalie H., and Robert K. Thomas. (1961). "Anglo Intervention vs. Native Noninterference." *Phylon* 22: 53–56.

Weintraub, Andrew N. (2009). "Introduction." In *Music and Cultural Rights*, edited by Andrew N. Weintraub and Bell Yung, pp. 1–18. Chicago and Urbana: University of Illinois Press.

Weintraub, Andrew N., and Bell Yung, eds. (2009). *Music and Cultural Rights*. Chicago and Urbana: University of Illinois Press.

West, Therese, and Gail Ironson. (2008). "Effects of Music on Human Health and Wellness: Physiological Measurements and Research Design." In *The Oxford Handbook of Medical Ethnomusicology*, edited by Benjamin D. Koen with Jaqueline Lloyd, Gregory Barz, and Karen Brummel-Smith, pp. 410–443. New York: Oxford University Press.

Whitburn, Joel. (1994). *Joel Whitburn's Top Country Singles, 1944–1993*. Menomonee Falls, WI: Record Research.

Whitburn, Joel. (2003). *Joel Whitburn's Top Pop Singles, 1955–2002*. Menomonee Falls, WI: Record Research.

Whitburn, Joel. (2004). *Joel Whitburn's Top R&B/Hip-Hop Singles, 1942–2004*. Menomonee Falls, WI: Record Research.

Whitburn, Joel. (2005). *Joel Whitburn's Top Country Songs, 1944 to 2005*. Menomonee Falls, WI: Record Research.

Whittaker, Laryssa K. (2014). *Beyond "Mzansi Golden Economy": Inequality, Wellbeing, and the Political Economy of Music as Youth Development in South Africa*. PhD dissertation, Royal Holloway, University of London.

WHO. (2019). "Who We Are: Constitution." World Health Organization. https://www.who.int/about/who-we-are/constitution (accessed August 16, 2019).

Wiesand, Andreas Joh., Kalliopi Chainoglou, and Anna Sledzińska-Simon, with Yvonne Donders. (2016). *Culture and Human Rights: The Wroclaw Commentaries*. Berlin/Boston, Cologne, and Wroclaw: Walter de Gruyter GmbH, ARCult Media GmbH, and City of Wroclaw.

Wilkinson, Richard. (2000). *Mind the Gap: Hierarchies, Health and Human Evolution*. New Haven, CT, and London: Yale University Press.

Wise, Stephanie. (2009). "Extending a Hand: Open Studio Art Therapy in a Harm Reduction Center." In *The Use of the Creative Therapies with Chemical Dependency Issues*, edited by Stephanie L. Brooke, pp. 37–50. Springfield, IL: Charles C. Thomas Publisher.

WISH Drop-In Centre Society, Vancouver Youth Choir, and Atira Women's Resource Society. (2019). "Free Concert & Singalong for Women of the DTES." https://www.facebook.com/events/408795286562544/ (accessed June 8, 2019).

Wodak, Alex. (1998). "Health, HIV Infection, Human Rights, and Injecting Drug Use." *Health and Human Rights* 2(4): 24–41.

Women's March. (2019). Washington, DC. Twitter. https://twitter.com/womensmarch/status/1086731359677231104?lang=en (accessed November 3, 2019).

Wood, Diane. (2004). "Spirituality." *Carnegie Newsletter*. August 15. http://carnegie.vcn.bc.ca/index.pl/august_15_2004 (accessed November 3, 2019 [link broken]).

Yılmaz, Ferruh. (2011). "The Politics of the Danish Cartoon Affair: Hegemonic Intervention by the Extreme Right." *Communication Studies* 62(1): 5–22.

Young, Allison. (2014). *Street Art, Public City: Law, Crime and the Urban Imagination*. Oxon, UK, and New York: Routledge.

Yu, Betty. (2017). "Chinatown Art Brigade: Resisting Gentrification through the Power of Art, Culture and Stories." *Visual Inquiry: Learning & Teaching Art* 6(2): 173–178.

Yupsanis, Athanasios. (2010). "The Concept and Categories of Cultural Rights in International Law—Their Broad Sense and the Relevant Clauses of the International Human Rights Treaties." *Syracuse Journal of International Law & Commerce* 37(2): 208–266.

Index

Note: Tables, figures and footnotes are indicated by *t*, *f* and n following the page number